NOVEL SHAKESPEARES

The Shakespeare and Company Bookshop in Paris.
(*Photo Julie Sanders*)

NOVEL SHAKESPEARES

Twentieth-century women novelists and appropriation

Julie Sanders

Manchester University Press

Manchester and New York

distributed exclusively in the USA by Palgrave

The right of Julie Sanders to be identified as the author of this work
has been asserted by her in accordance with the Copyright, Designs
and Patents Act 1988.

Published by Manchester University Press
Oxford Road, Manchester M13 9NR, UK
and Room 400, 175 Fifth Avenue, New York,
NY 10010, USA

Distributed exclusively in the USA by
Palgrave, 175 Fifth Avenue, New York,
NY 10010, USA

Distributed exclusively in Canada by
UBC Press, University of British Columbia, 2029 West Mall,
Vancouver, BC, Canada V6T 1Z2

British Library Cataloguing-in-Publication Data
A catalogue record for this book is available from the British Library

Library of Congress Cataloging-in-Publication Data applied for

ISBN 0 7190 5815 5 *hardback*
      0 7190 5816 3 *paperback*

First published 2001

10 09 08 07 06 05 04 03 02 01   10 9 8 7 6 5 4 3 2 1

Designed and typeset by Illuminati, Grosmont

Printed in Great Britain
by Bell & Bain Limited, Glasgow

To Mike, Lynn, and the twins

I don't suppose this is how he imagined his readers.
If he imagined them at all.
KATE ATKINSON, *Human Croquet*

Contents

Acknowledgements

The initial inspiration for this book came from a course I have taught at Keele University for the past few years on Shakespearean appropriation in the twentieth century. My thanks are due, therefore, to all the students who have discussed, argued about, and often opened my eyes to, topics explored here. Special thanks to Jonathan Adams, Linda Andrews, Melissa Barham, Philip McCullough, Karen Richards, James Richardson and Carrie Thomas.

Any book about Shakespearean appropriation owes a special debt to two scholars, Marianne Novy and Kate Chedgzoy. I have not yet met Marianne Novy, but the debt is palpable. I am lucky enough to count Kate as one of my greatest friends, and she has contributed to this book in countless ways, not least reading chapters for me at the most inconvenient of times for her.

Others, too, have offered comments and suggestions on sections of this book. Huge thanks, therefore, to my colleagues at Keele: David Amigoni, James McLaverty and Helen Stoddart; and to the department as a whole for supporting this project in numerous ways, both practical and intellectual. Thanks, too, to Ian Bell, Fred Botting, Richard Godden, Ann Hughes, Di Paton, Roger Pooley, Sarah Poynting and Anthea Trodd for articles and advice. As usual, Jonathan Bate and Richard Dutton have been more inspirational than I can say. Gaynor Macfarlane sourced books and was, as always, there for me. Two critics whose work features heavily in specific chapters on Iris Murdoch and Angela Carter died during the final stages of *Novel Shakespeares*. The lucid critical voices of

Malcolm Bradbury and Lorna Sage provide their own best memorial in these pages.

The librarians at Keele, the University Library in Cambridge, the British Library in London and the State Library in Albany, NY offered practical assistance, frequently in the face of my incompetence. Special thanks to Catherine Trippett at Random House for advice (and encouragement) over what she herself described as the 'minefield' of permissions. At Manchester University Press, Matthew Frost and Deirdre Boleyn have lived through much of this project. I am thankful for their enthusiasm and support.

This book circles around the topos of family, and it is fitting that I should acknowledge my own here. The dedication is to my Stateside family: my dad, Lynn, Jaclyn and Aston. They frequently allow their house to be turned upside down so I can get in some New England research and R&R, and I am deeply grateful and, it goes without saying, full of love for them. On this side of the Atlantic, Kay (my mum), my brother Neil and his partner Liese know how much they mean to me. Finally, and as ever, there is the man who plants the garden, grows the food and does everything I believe in with such commitment and grace. To my husband (my oh my…) John Higham, my love, always.

Unless otherwise noted, all Shakespearean references are to *The Norton Shakespeare*. Excerpts from Barbara Trapido's *Juggling* (Harmondsworth, Penguin, 1995), Copyright © Barbara Trapido 1994, reproduced by permission of Penguin Books Ltd and Felicity Bryan. Extracts from *Wise Children* Copyright © Angela Carter 1991 and *Black Venus* Copyright © Angela Carter 1985, reproduced by permission of the Estate of Angela Carter c/o Rogers, Coleridge & White Ltd, 20 Powis Mews, London W11 1JN. Extracts from *Human Croquet* by Kate Atkinson (London, Doubleday, 1997), © Kate Atkinson, 1997, by permission of Transworld Publishers, all rights reserved. Quotations from *King of Shadows* by Susan Cooper, © Susan Cooper 1999, published by Bodley Head, reprinted by kind permission of The Random House Group Ltd and Susan Cooper. Excerpts from *A Fairly Honourable Defeat* (Harmondsworth, Penguin, 1970), *The Sea, The Sea* (Harmondsworth, Penguin, 1978) and *The Black Prince* (Harmondsworth, Penguin, 1973) by Iris Murdoch, first published by Chatto & Windus, reprinted by permission of The Random House Group Ltd and Ed Victor Ltd. Quotations from *Indigo* by Marina Warner, Copyright © Marina Warner 1992, published by Chatto & Windus, used by permission of The Random House Group Ltd and PFD on behalf of Marina Warner. Excerpts from *Bombay Ice* by Leslie Forbes ©Leslie Forbes 1998, published by Phoenix House, reprinted by permission of the Orion Publishing Group. Excerpts from *The Women of Brewster Place* (New York, Penguin, 1983) © Gloria Naylor 1980, 1982, used by permission of Viking Penguin, a division of Penguin Putnam Inc. Those from *Linden Hills* (New York, Penguin, 1986), © Gloria Naylor 1985, used by permission of Viking Penguin, a division of Penguin Putnam Inc. and Sterling Lord Literistic Inc. Quotations from *The Men of Brewster Place* © Gloria Naylor 1998, used by kind permission of Hyperion, NY. Extracts from *Mama Day* Copyright © Gloria Naylor 1988 and *Bailey's Cafe* Copyright © Gloria Naylor 1992, by permission of Sterling Lord Literistic Inc. Extracts from *A Thousand Acres* by Jane Smiley (London, Flamingo, 1992) © Jane Smiley 1991, reprinted by permission of HarperCollins Publishers Ltd and Abner Stein. Excerpts from *A Walking Fire* by Valerie Miner (Albany, NY, SUNY Press, 1994), © Valerie Miner 1994, by kind permission of SUNY Press. Extracts from *Sweet Desserts* by Lucy Ellmann (London, Virago Press, 1998), © Lucy Ellmann 1988, used by permission of Little Brown and Company. Excerpts from *Cat's Eye* by Margaret Atwood (London, Virago Press, 1990), Copyright © O.W. Toad Limited 1988, by permission of Bloomsbury Publishing Plc. Quotations from *A Natural Curiosity* by Margaret Drabble (Copyright © Margaret Drabble 1989) and *The Gates of Ivory* by Margaret Drabble (Copyright © Margaret Drabble 1991) by permission of PFD on behalf of Margaret Drabble.

Every best effort has been made to trace the copyright holders, but if any have been inadvertently overlooked the publishers will be pleased to make the necessary arrangements at the first opportunity.

'Mere sparks and clandestine glories': Women writers, Shakespeare and appropriation

> Tout texte se construit comme mosaïque de citations, tout texte est absorption et transformation d'un autre texte.
>
> Julia Kristeva, *Semiotike*

Intertextuality is an essential condition of modern literature. Roland Barthes famously declared that 'any text is an intertext', engaged as written materials are in an ongoing process of absorbing and transforming the materials of preceding and contemporaneous cultures.[1] Perhaps unsurprisingly, the particular set of intertexts provided by the dominant, enduring, transhistorical and cross-cultural signifier of 'Shakespeare' and his work has provoked considerable intellectual interest. Cultural appropriations of Shakespeare are fast becoming a genre in their own right. Numerous books have emerged that seek to anthologise or establish separate canons of 'adaptations of Shakespeare', across a range of genres and media.[2] Complementary literary critical studies increasingly focus on related questions about the cultural capital of 'the Bard'.[3] Nevertheless, the terms in which this area of interest is articulated – adaptation, appropriation, reworking, revision – remain a site of contestation and debate.

For Daniel Fischlin and Mark Fortier, editors of a recent collection of plays which, in their account, 'adapt' or provide 'spinoffs' from Shakespearean drama, the word 'appropriation' is potentially pejorative in its connotations: 'This word suggests a hostile take-over, a seizure of authority over the original' (2000: 3). While they acknowledge that conscious takeovers or aggressive campaigns of this nature might appeal to 'contemporary sensibilities steeped in a politicized understanding of culture' (3), Fischlin and Fortier eschew the phrase in their own anthology, preferring the less negative 'adaptation'. One of their cited grounds for this rejection of the terms of appropriation is that the procedure can 'take place without altering the original itself – a sonnet quoted in full on a Valentine's card, for instance' (3). Admittedly, in this example the text of the sonnet is not altered, but the statement suppresses the fact that the understanding of it, and the reading that might be produced of it, is automatically affected by its new context. The Valentine's Day associations, the poem's presence as part of an artefact designed as a social gesture or gift and as part of the contemporary culture of commodification, all hold relevance for the way in which Shakespeare and the sonnet are being appropriated. Particular contexts – historical, social, political, and even critical – will prove crucial to the readings of Shakespearean appropriations offered in this study.

In a more positive engagement with the phrase, Christy Desmet and Robert Sawyer have recently described acts of appropriation as 'creative and critical practice' (1999: 8). Their deployment of the term allows for a more productive dynamic than Fischlin and Fortier's antagonistic interpretation. While Desmet and Sawyer are undoubtedly interested in textual appropriations which are 'talking back to Shakespeare' (11), their more multivalent understanding of the term allows for celebratory as well as contestatory engagement, for conservative as well as radical harnessing of the Shakespearean intertexts. Other critics appear to empathise with this position. For Kate Chedgzoy, appropriation frequently entails a questioning or critique of the original textual authority (1995: 2); whereas for Marianne Novy, who focuses on a specifically feminine (and frequently feminist) enterprise, appropriations shade into the self-authenticating process of 're-vision' (1993).[4]

In dictionary definitions, while 'appropriation' can mean to annex or arrogate, to impound or seize, there are alternative interpretations which involve a less hostile sense or usage, a greater sense of setting something apart from its original purpose, of making things pertinent or 'appropriate' to a new or different set of structures, personal, political or cultural. As its title suggests, *Novel Shakespeares* is particularly interested in how contemporary women novelists engage in this parallel process of textual takeover and adaptation – the rendering apposite or appropriate, as it were, of Shakespearean drama in a new context.

The gendered as well as generic focus of this book demands more detailed explanation. One of the driving questions behind this study was whether appropriation in a specific generic context, in this case that of the novel, could be read in gendered terms. Are particular politics at stake in women revising Shakespeare in the form of prose narrative? If so, are those politics expressed in specific patterns of narrative strategy and approach that might be traced across a series of appropriations by such writers? The study is, then, in part a search for genuine relations and kinship between authors and texts, at the levels of both content and form, in addition to the surface or sometimes subtextual Shakespearean connection.

In seeking to identify kinships in this way, however, the project is not a futile attempt at homogenisation. In establishing the context of each of the novels discussed here, in terms of both their relation- ship to Shakespeare and the historico-critical moment in which they were produced, I wish to stress the individual aesthetics of each author, while also identifying links and intersections. The recognition of the omnipresence of intertextuality does not diminish the creative process understood to be at play in these novels.

The focus on narrative is a product of the gendered emphasis of this study. Women's poetry, plays, short stories, and filmmaking have all referred to and adapted Shakespeare in some measure, but by far the largest contingent of female appropriators are to be found in the realm of prose narrative, not least in the current era. A central question to be posed, therefore, was why exactly the shift from the dramatic to the narrative form was being effected. What impact did that generic transition have on the treatment, and the implicit rewriting, of the Shakespearean intertext or intertexts? The multiplication of Shakespearean – and other – textual presences in these novels is, of course, simply a further indication of the polysemic aspect of the appropriation dynamic.

The choice of Shakespeare raises undoubted questions of canon formation and women writers' associations with what Fischlin and Fortier have aptly described as the 'broadly accepted group of works that is a consensual (though not uncontested) site of

foregrounded study within the academy' (2000: 6). By adapting
Shakespeare, women writers self-consciously range themselves
either within or alongside the academy in an often tense, occasionally directly resistant, relationship. By opting for an alternative
genre to that of their male-authored dramatic precursors, they
assert the innovative and creative aspect of their work.

   Shakespeare is, of course, an obvious choice in seeking to debate
the canon, since his corpus of works stands so clearly positioned in
the hierarchy of value within it. Authors who allude to or quote
Shakespeare have the greatest chance of their reading audience
both registering the allusion and being able to see a writer's critical
movement beyond the mere act of quotation or recitation. Writing
of Virginia Woolf's *Between the Acts* (1941), Gillian Beer observed:
'Woolf undoes the canon. Fragments from famous works wind in
and out of people's consciousness, half-remembered, often mis-
remembered, valued nonetheless. In memory, they are shards
scattered or shared among a community' (Woolf, 1992: xix). *Between
the Acts* famously deploys central phrases from Shakespeare's *Troilus
and Cressida* – 'orts, scraps, and fragments' – as a form of refrain
throughout its theatrically self-referential sequences: 'The lines ...
are persistently referred to, re-arranged, and riffled through the
text' (Woolf, 1992: xix). Shakespeare's sceptical and scabrous play
about the Trojan War and attendant societal collapse serves as an
apposite analogue in the novel to the Second World War, which
makes its own impact on Woolf's fictional village community in the
shape of aeroplanes flying overhead, and that community's anxieties
about impending fragmentation. But *Troilus and Cressida* is not the
only Shakespearean text alluded to in the course of the book: *King
Lear*, the sonnets, *Macbeth* and *The Tempest* all 'play their parts',
according to Beer (Woolf, 1992: xix). 'The book', she says 'is not
so much studded with quotation and allusion as combed through:
sometimes mere sparks of reference remain, sometimes clandestine
glories' (Woolf, 1992: xix).

   In many ways, this book concerns itself with 'clandestine glories'
of this kind. Woolf is one of a host of twentieth-century women
writers who have alluded to, appropriated, and often revised Shakespeare in their work (Novy, 1990).[5] *Novel Shakespeares* concentrates on late-twentieth-century examples of such writers, partly
out of a desire to conduct a historicist analysis of a series of novels

produced across a clearly defined time period. Nevertheless, as will emerge in the course of the chapters that follow, the patterns of adaptation, purpose and strategy differ sometimes according to temporal context, but often according to national, ethnic or religious identities, and to the educative and institutional structures in which an individual author was raised or consciously situates (or situated) herself.

Particular plays occur and recur in the appropriations studied here with greater frequency than others. The special pertinence to women writers of plays such as *King Lear* or *The Tempest*, with their obvious themes of fathers and daughters and patriarchal rule, is therefore explored. In a related vein, the heightened relevance of romantic comedies, with their witty exploration of the pressures of heterosexual marital structures on same-sex friendships, and the societal pressures of gender expectations – most vividly realised in the cross-dressing scenes of a number of these playtexts – will be considered in detail. Elsewhere, however, it is interrelationships conducted at a linguistic, metaphorical and structural level that form the basis of the comparisons carried out between novels by women which appropriate Shakespeare. This introductory chapter will outline these relationships and recurring themes, which will then be explored in the context of both critical analysis and detailed close reading in the relevant chapters.

'A moment of precarious, brilliant symmetry'; or, an outline of the argument

Chapter 1 concentrates on Barbara Trapido's 1994 novel *Juggling*, a vibrant example of a work which appropriates a whole range of Shakespearean texts and topics. In the process of a narrative which charts the growth to self-knowledge of Christina Angeletti, a journey which includes revelations about parentage, sexuality and intellectual power, the tropes and structures of Shakespearean drama are deployed as shaping intertexts. The romantic comedies *A Midsummer Night's Dream*, *Twelfth Night*, and *As You Like It*, among others, inform *Juggling*'s identifiable themes and leitmotivs: providing templates for the novel's investment in overweening patriarchs, carefully plotted escapes into alternative worlds and family structures, twins and twinnings, and the battle of the sexes. These plays also provide structural paradigms for Trapido's careful narrative ordering of events. Elsewhere, the late plays' themes of lost children and familial reconciliation can be identified. In Trapido's case, the influence of Structuralist criticism of Shakespeare proves tangible in her text of five acts and an epilogue. In one self-conscious gesture, *Juggling*'s female protagonist produces her own essay on the topic of Shakespeare and genre as part of a university course: this text-within-a-text can – and does, of course – serve as a manual for Trapido's intricate novel.

Angela Carter's *Wise Children* (1992), a postmodern tapestry of parody, pastiche, intertextual allusion and deconstruction, is the focus of Chapter 2. In her text, Carter plays in an erudite and self-conscious way with the binaries of Shakespearean tragedy and comedy. She focuses on two linked theatrical families: the 'legitimate' tragedians (and Shakespeareans) the Hazards, and the music-hall twins Dora and Nora Chance. In the process, she creates a complex web of allusion to Shakespeare that attacks the sanctifying processes of bardolatry and the seizure of Shakespeare by high culture, while celebrating the popular cultural origins of his work and his plays' continued redefinitions (and, as a result, relevance) in the living media of performance, film and culture. As with Trapido, Carter's structural processes are of interest: both the self-conscious festive structuring of her narrative and her deployment of an 'unreliable narrator'. The latter is a figure or rhetorical strategy which emerges in several of the novels studied here. The special relevance of this technique for appropriations which seek to offer alternative points of view on canonical texts will therefore be explored in detail.

Both Trapido and Carter concern themselves with the convention of happy endings, for which Shakespearean comedy, with its marriages, dances and last-minute resolutions, provides such a pertinent example. Kate Atkinson, whose *Human Croquet* (1997) is the focus of Chapter 3, is also interested in the extent to which the achievement of closure is merely a temporal trick or illusion. The topic of time – one to which Shakespeare returned on numerous occasions throughout his career – provides a further linking category between the women writers being discussed. If Shakespearean drama undergoes metamorphosis into narrative (and it is no coincidence that Atkinson shares Shakespeare's interest in this Ovidian theme), then narrative itself is under scrutiny in many of these texts. A linear, teleological history is being resisted in a majority of these novels. *Wise Children* moves in and out of present and past moments in a deliberately non-chronological order; *Human Croquet* goes even further by making time-travel a central topos. This is explored in more detail in Chapter 4, which compares *Human Croquet* to other time-travelling novels by women: Susan Cooper's children's book *King of Shadows* (1999), which recounts in ingenious ways a 1599 Globe production of *A Midsummer Night's Dream*; and Erica Jong's *Serenissima* (1987) which, as its name suggests, has *The Merchant of Venice* as a chief intertext. A linking fact between all three appropriations is that time travel initiates a direct encounter not only with the Shakespearean text but with the dramatist himself.

Human Croquet, whose primary intertexts are once again the romantic comedies, is narrated by sixteen-year-old Isobel Fairfax. Her narrative voice is, however, refracted at various points through that of the adult Isobel. She is, tellingly, a writer of historical fiction – which not only casts doubt on the verity or authenticity of the sixteen-year-old Isobel's claims, but makes evident to the reader the novel's heightened awareness of the constructs of history and time.

Isobel is yet another example of the 'unreliable narrator', as are Bradley Pearson and Charles Arrowby in Iris Murdoch's *The Black Prince* (1973) and *The Sea, The Sea* (1978) respectively. Chapter 5 considers Murdoch's career-long engagement with the Shakespearean model, examining the metatheatrical elements of her novels as well as the specific narrative encounters she made with plays from *Hamlet* (in *The Black Prince*), and *A Midsummer Night's Dream* and *Othello* (in *A Fairly Honourable Defeat* (1970)) to *The Tempest* (in *The Sea, The Sea*). Murdoch's authorial interests in Platonic philosophy and surrealist theatre, as well as the moral value she accorded Shakespeare, are all seen to impact upon her complex and ambiguous acts of appropriation and allusion. Postmodern consciousness of form is also a particular aspect of her work, evidenced by the alternative endings provided by the multiple 'Postscripts by *Dramatis Personae*' appended to *The Black Prince*, and the shifting narratorial style and stance of Arrowby (an equivocal Prospero figure) in *The Sea, The Sea*.

The Tempest is one of the plays most commonly appropriated by women novelists. Connected concerns about voicing the silenced or oppressed female characters of the play (the onstage Miranda, but also the offstage absent presences of Claribel, Sycorax and Miranda's unnamed mother) clearly link such writers' textual ruminations – from Marina Warner's *Indigo* (1992) to Michelle Cliff's *No Telephone to Heaven* (1987). But the different points of interest and investment found in this play by these writers is of equal importance when we are exploring their texts. While Murdoch's interest in *The Tempest*'s themes of art and magic can be more fruitfully read alongside other 1970s appropriations of the play such as John Fowles's enigmatic *The Magus* (revised in 1977), Marina Warner's *Indigo* (the focus of Chapter 6) is seen to be the product of a 1980s critical interest in postcolonial readings of Shakespeare's island drama. Warner's novel replaces a linear understanding of history and time with a cyclical and mythical one. A written text with a striking interest in the value of oral culture and the folk tradition of storytelling, *Indigo* is a feminist and politicised re-vision of the 1611 play. Significantly, the novel voices *The Tempest*'s infamous 'absent presence', the witch Sycorax, as a Liamuigan wise-woman in the seventeenth century. In the course of the narrative, Sycorax adopts Dulé (Caliban) and Ariel, who is re-created as female. This reclamatory version of the Shakespearean play's prehistory is juxtaposed throughout, and at times overlaps, with the life-story of Miranda Everard in the modern day. Miranda is struggling with her own family links to the island of Liamuiga, and to a confused postcolonial cultural inheritance that has parallels with Warner's own autobiography.

Chapter 7 provides a further postcolonial take on *The Tempest*, but this time figured through the generic conventions and strategies of film and detective fiction. Leslie Forbes's *Bombay Ice* (1998) is set in the sub-Jacobean world of the Bollywood film industry in modern-day India. The novel's own version of the unreliable narrator, Ros Benegal, goes to Mumbai in an effort to solve a family mystery, finding herself embroiled as a result in a world of serial killers and high-powered corruption. Forbes's multilayered text – which is interested in topics as diverse as film genres, chaos theory, gender and performance, Münchhausen's syndrome, and ancient myth – makes cultural capital of many of the themes and images of Shakespeare's play and, like a number of the novels considered here, resists a clear sense of terminus or closure. Why women writers in particular question the efficacy of closure will be considered in the course of various chapters.

Both Warner and Forbes write from a white woman's perspective, for all that Warner's personal history is bound up with the postcolonial guilt which stamps itself on the pages of *Indigo*. 'Race' and ethnicity are crucial points of reference in any study of cultural appropriations. Gloria Naylor's *Mama Day* (1988), explored in Chapter 8, offers the opportunity to consider an African-American vantage point on Shakespeare's late play, which has itself been frequently associated with the history of the Americas and the New World in the early modern period. Like Warner, Naylor decentres Prospero from her narrative re-vision, centralising instead the character and voice of the conjure-woman Miranda Day, who provides the magical heart of the novel's Willow Springs island community. A number of recent critical accounts of Naylor have stressed her antagonism to the politics of her source-play, but this chapter attempts to nuance understandings of her canon by examining her ongoing ruminations upon Shakespeare as a figure of potential cultural empowerment in ostensibly black American communities. Deployments of Shakespeare, and specific plays, including *Dream* and *The Tempest*, in all five of her published novels are interrogated and interpreted to this end.

If *The Tempest* is a recurring presence in the canon of women novelists' appropriations of Shakespeare – due not least to its depiction of a lone father-ruler – *King Lear* is another popular reference point, for similar reasons. Chapters 9 and 10 look at a number of works which directly appropriate *Lear*: some in an allusive capacity; some which invoke the play in the form of a more sustained understanding of plot and structure. Jane Smiley's *A Thousand Acres* (1992) (discussed in Chapter 9) displaces Shakespeare's drama into the 1970s American Midwest. Smiley's defiant decision to rewrite *Lear*, providing the vilified older sisters, Goneril and Regan, with both motive and sympathy, is investigated, as is her use of a first-person female narrator in assigning this revised point of view. Smiley's own political and social contexts are seen to influence the land-based events of this novel. That seminal document of the environmental movement, Rachel Carson's *Silent Spring*, and the attendant ecological concerns it sparked, feed into this novel's dominant themes of pesticides, poisons and the dangers of corporate capitalism for our relationship to the natural world as well as each other.

A Thousand Acres is one of several of the focus texts in *Novel Shakespeares* (for example, *Wise Children*, *Juggling*, and *Indigo*) that consider the dysfunctional aspects of the late-twentieth-century family. This is regularly achieved via the filtering medium of Shakespeare's own multivalent dramatic depictions of familial relationships and fissures. Valerie Miner's *A Walking Fire* (1994), explored in Chapter 10, is concerned with family breakdown, using its narrative rewrite of *Lear* to read this in highly politicised terms. In this novel, Cora (a Cordelia analogue) is an opponent of the Vietnam War who has been in hiding in Canada for many years. She returns to her homestead in Oregon only when she learns that her estranged father is dying. The plot trajectory which ensues engages with domestic issues such as the potential violence of sibling rivalry within the context of wider national and international events – not least the rise of aggressive right-wing politics in the USA during the 1980s.

A dying father and an emotionally distanced daughter also open up the space for Lucy Ellmann's narrator in *Sweet Desserts* (1988), to invoke the Lear–Cordelia paradigm. Ellmann's text, with its strategic models based in collage techniques rather than linear narrative, provides further example of the innovative way in which all the women novelists studied here attend to the intricacies of genre as well as Shakespeare. Margaret Atwood's *Cat's Eye* (1990), the final novel considered in this context, concerns itself with the attendant dangers of artistic models and precedents. This novel's narrator, Elaine, is an artist who is attempting to come to terms with the psychological fallout of intense childhood bullying. That the source of her emotional and physical haunting is a character called Cordelia is an indication that Atwood's is no straightforward adaptation of *Lear*. Instead, the author interrogates the dangers inherent in trying to live up to expectations formed by our cultural inheritance – be it in the shape of being named for a 'good' Shakespearean daughter, or in terms of her native Canada's efforts to extricate itself from its British colonial past. Atwood is one of many novelists here whose cultural identity shapes her reading of Shakespeare as much as her gender.

The conclusion to this book attempts to consider some of the related patterns and concerns identified among this diverse community of women writers. Why certain plays seem more ripe for female appropriation than others is examined. Women writers' interest in the marginal (and the connected effort of marginalising the central via skewed or displaced readings of texts such as *Hamlet*) is explored via a range of contexts from Margaret Drabble's London middle-class world to the South African township politics of Nadine Gordimer or the assertive Jamaican counter-politics of Michelle Cliff's writing. There is a procedure at work in this conclusion of opening out the canon of women's appropriations rather than offering any fixed or finite assessment. In this respect, *Novel Shakespeares* emulates the structural openness of its subject texts in the formulations of its own arguments.

There is an additional question to be asked before this introduction draws to its own arbitrary close: why might Shakespeare or early modern drama as a whole be particularly suited to such narrative transformations by contemporary women writers? Marguerite Alexander has suggested that there are certain affinities between early modern drama and postmodern fiction. Both are highly self-conscious of their own artifice: if Shakespeare, Middleton, Ford and others used metatheatre to draw attention to the conventions of their own acts of creativity, so the modern novel frequently deploys metafictional devices such as the unreliable first-person narrator. Alexander compares Jacobean drama and postmodern fiction as 'often morally ambiguous', and dealing with 'relative values rather than absolutes' (1990: 19). A linking theme in all the chapters in this study is the refusal and positive deconstruction of moral and literary absolutes by these women writers. Gender, sexuality, politics and genre are all implicated in this process, but the family remains a particular focus for the invocation of those 'relative values' identified by Alexander. As Kate McLuskie has suggested: 'An important part of the feminist project is to insist that the alternative to the patriarchal family and heterosexual love is not chaos but the possibility of new forms of social organization and affective relationships' (1985: 106). It is the view of *Novel Shakespeares* that the 'new forms' advocated by the women writers considered here extend beyond notions of the family, and into narrative form and genre as well. Shakespeare and early modern drama are expert facilitators; the very familiarity of these intertexts enables processes of deconstruction and innovation that carry us into new, entirely modern contexts and structures. It is important to note that for Trapido, Carter, Atkinson and others, Shakespeare is not the sole intertext and that, at many points in their combative and complicated narratives, they are as much in dialogue and debate with themselves and each other as with his plays.

Of course, this book would be – to steal a phrase from Henry James – a much baggier monster if it were to attempt to deal with women writers who use Shakespeare and his playtexts and poetry in a purely allusive or embedded manner (those 'shards' cited by Beer). This volume focuses on those novels and writers which carry out a sustained engagement with Shakespeare – either via the medium of a particular play, or via a wider implication of the cultural valency of the 'Bard' and his texts. Equally, there is a 'brother' volume to be written on the male equivalents to the appropriations studied. That book would encounter writers as diverse as Alan Isler, John Edgar Wideman, Niall Dundee, Salman Rushdie, Caryl Phillips and John Updike, and might seek to identify whether parallel gender-based (if only partial) kinships could be established among that male writing community.[6] Several of these male-authored texts are mentioned and cross-referenced in *Novel Shakespeares*, but a fully developed account of their particular strategies cannot be offered. That, then, is for another time.

What will be clear from a reading of this book, though, is that in appropriating Shakespeare or a specific Shakespearean text, these women writers are often engaging with the critical and historical reception of the playwright and his work as much as with subjective interpretation. Literary criticism has shaped all of these writers' responses to the texts they cite, in particular those schools of criticism that emerge out of political subject positions such as feminism (along with its attendant qualifiers of gender, race and class) and postcolonialism. Writers are products of particular times and moments in the history of Shakespeare studies. *Indigo* and *Bombay Ice* could not have been written without postcolonial theory; *Wise Children* acknowledges a debt to Bakhtin in its carnivalesque pastiches. Modernism – in particular the writings of T. S. Eliot and Virginia Woolf – has had a particular influence, as has

Structuralist criticism, on Trapido's *Juggling*. Particular kinds of 'Shakespeare' are being invoked, deployed and occasionally questioned by these novels, as much as any fixed notion of an original text. Women writers frequently 'talk back' to Shakespeare, to use Atwood's phrase, questioning the silence or marginalisation of female characters, according voices or rewriting endings, and even providing explanatory prequels to events.[7] The act of engagement is rarely passive; Shakespeare is not invoked simply as an authenticating male canonical presence in these works but, rather, as a topos to be explored, dissected and reconfigured as much as any other.

In her account of Woolf's 'limber sentences', Gillian Beer has spoken of the 'ritual repetitions' which shape the way we use language (Woolf, 1992: xxi). Shakespeare is an intrinsic part of those rituals, although his appearance (sometimes literal) in the texts considered here also proves Beer's point that 'though things are said many times they never mean quite the same' (Woolf, 1992: xxi). The Shakespeare of this book is a labile, ever-changing creature; his texts and ideas are as subject to metamorphosis and transformation as the characters, sentences and structures inside them.

Notes

1 See Barthes (1981: 39). For a recent discussion of intertextuality, see Allen (2000).

2 See, for example, Fischlin and Fortier (2000); Clark (1997); and Davies and Wells (1995).

3 See Chedgzoy (1995); Marsden (1991); Bristol (1996); and Novy (1993, 1995).

4 Novy's source for this suggestive use of the term is Adrienne Rich's 'When We Dead Awaken: Writing as Re-Vision' (1979).

5 For a full investigation of the meanings of 'appropriation', see Marsden (1991: 1) and Fischlin and Fortier (2000).

6 See Isler, *The Prince of West End Avenue* (1994); Wideman, *Philadelphia Fire* (1995 (1990)); Dundee, *Natterjack* (1996); Rushdie, *The Moor's Last Sigh* (1995); Phillips, *The Nature of Blood* (1997); and Updike, *Gertrude and Claudius* (2000).

7 I am thinking of Atwood's short story 'Gertrude talks back', where she re-imagines the closet scene with a feisty Gertrude chiding her son, and ultimately confessing to murder (1993a).

ONE

'Not quite Shakespeare': Barbara Trapido's *Juggling*, intertextuality and keeping off the grass

Barbara Trapido's novels offer readers a panoply of absent parents, lost children, nunneries, twins and forceful patriarchs. A basic connection with some general Shakespearean themes therefore seems clear in her work, although Trapido, like the Bard himself, is frequently working with cultural archetypes, as often as not derived from myth and folklore as from specific Shakespeare plays. Although he is a dominant reference point, Shakespeare is not the sole object of Trapido's intertextuality; her writing weaves a complex web of allusions that engages with Yeats, Schubert, Woolf, T. S. Eliot, Donne, Ovid, Mozart and Modigliani, alongside more obviously populist artists such as writers of children's fiction.

A critic must ask what the significance might be of deploying intertexts from different genres and historical periods in a modern novel. Trapido seems to be engaged upon a pattern of inter-textualities which deliberately refuses to conform to literary hierarchies of status – Miffy the Rabbit and Mr Toad exist without apology alongside Shakespeare – but which also, in its undemarcated melding of modernism with classicism, refuses to adhere to teleological literary histories. As this book progresses, we will see that Trapido is not alone in deploying Shakespeare's continued literary relevance as a means of deconstructing other linear models of history and specifically textual histories. She extends this enthusiasm for blurring boundaries to her own *œuvre*, weaving a warp and weft of cross-reference across her novels, where characters frequently reappear at different stages in their lives, intersect and interact.[1]

For obvious reasons, this chapter will concentrate on Trapido's specific engagement with Shakespeare in her narratives – a tendency which is most explicit and certainly most sustained, in her novel *Juggling*, first published in 1994. In doing so, however, it will make clear that her intertextuality extends to non-fictional writing about Shakespeare, in particular literary criticism, as well as plays, poetry and novels. T. S. Eliot's essays on Shakespearean drama are directly referred to in *Juggling*, and elsewhere traces of influence from Woolf to Bakhtin can be identified. Trapido is not unusual, as we shall see, in appropriating Shakespeare via the filtering medium of twentieth-century criticism. Particular schools of thought such as feminism, psychoanalysis, and Structuralism bear most sway, although the interest in textualities of history ascribed to Trapido above might also be identified as having obvious sympathies with the New Historicist project.[2]

Juggling has an important intertext within Trapido's own canon; its events and characters follow on from those detailed in *Temples of Delight* (1990). A central peg of events in *Juggling* is the protagonist Christina Angeletti's discovery of the truth about her unstable parentage. Knowing her sister Pam to be adopted, Christina is forced to entertain the notion that her 'father', Joe, is not her biological parent. In essence, the novel constitutes Christina's complicated search for a sure and certain identity, not least through romantic attachment, and Trapido structures this through a series of allusions to, and parallels with, the plotlines of Shakespeare's romantic comedies.

Pam and Joe were characters in *Temples of Delight*. In that novel, readers pursued the fortunes of Alice Pilling (Christina's mother) from the days of an all-girls school and intense female friendships, through failed relationships with both Roland Dent and Matthew Riley (who resurfaces in the fifth act of *Juggling* as Christina's biological father) and the death of Jem McCrail, as well as the complicated set of circumstances by which Alice finds herself adopting Jem's baby daughter Pamina. Pamina (Pam) is named after a character in Mozart's *The Magic Flute*, itself a pertinent intertext in *Temples*. In the closing moments of the narrative, Alice discovers that the validity of her adoption is questionable, since Giovanni (Joe) Angeletti, Jem's Italo-American publisher, has forged letters from his dying client. That he then seduces and marries the now-pregnant Alice allows him to become Pam's father and the 'father' of Alice's unborn child, despite personal infertility. These questionable actions serve to establish Joe as a dubious patriarch, which proves crucial to events in *Juggling*.

Trapido finds a series of paradigms for the adopted children and patriarchs of her novel in the characters of Shakespearean comedy. At the beginning of *Juggling*, Christina is aware of Pam's complicated origins, but not of her own. It is telling that she thinks in literary (and Shakespearean) terms when she is imagining her parents' union:

> Christina knew that, on first meeting, her parents had detested each other and had fought and quarrelled terribly – over the baby and everything else. For her, all reference to this phase of their acquaintance had got bound up with Joe's bedtime readings of *A Midsummer Night's Dream* from Lamb's *Tales from Shakespeare*. She knew that the fairy king and queen had fought and quarrelled bitterly over the beautiful dark boy and that the king had put a spell in Titania's eyes. And she knew that afterwards they had lain in a fairy bower in a dream that was always midsummer. (Trapido, 1995 (1994): 9)

The function of this intertextual moment is multilayered. Christina, by confusing the 'fairy story' of her parents' coming-together with Shakespeare's *A Midsummer Night's Dream*, also aligns the argumentative Joe and Alice with that play's quarrelling fairy monarchs, Oberon and Titania. Oberon's embodiment of patriarchal control (the enforced degradation of Titania with an ass being a central moment of the play) taints Joe by association. In the playtext, the Indian Boy is the cause of Oberon and Titania's falling-out. Oberon is jealous of the gynocentric world Titania ascribes the child:

> The fairyland buys not the child of me.
> His mother was a vot'ress of my order,
> And in the spicèd Indian air by night
> Full often hath she gossiped by my side,
> And sat with me on Neptune's yellow sands,
> Marking th'embarkèd traders on the flood,
> ...
> But she, being mortal, of that boy did die;
> And for her sake do I rear up her boy;
> And for her sake I will not part with him.
> (2.1.122–7, 35–7)

At first glance, the adoption of the dead mother's baby by her closest female companion offers a direct parallel to Alice's decision to take care of Pam. What Christina cannot yet know is that the story also has a personal application.

In this manner Trapido draws Shakespeare, and in particular the framework of Shakespearean comedy, into the narrative of *Juggling* from very early on. But it is important to note that even here, Shakespeare is not received pure or 'straight'. The six-year-old Christina invokes *Dream* via Charles and Mary Lamb's nineteenth-century bowdlerised versions for children.[3] Her version of the *Dream* is as yet devoid of its genuine undercurrents of sexual anxiety, fertility, and eroticism.[4] A recurring trope of Trapido's novel is that experience is read in terms of children's literature: from *Peter Pan* and the lost boys, through Lewis Carroll's *Alice* books, to such populist characters as Miffy the Rabbit. Shakespeare, Beatrix Potter and Kenneth Grahame's *The Wind in the Willows* enter the cultural narrative with the same ease of reference. Trapido seems almost to reduce the status of the Shakespearean text by this act of juxtaposition. However, there is also a sense in which the disparity of the conjunctions tutors us as readers to search for darker, deeper subtexts than a surface child-like reading might offer.

In exploring the 'postmodern' fictions of the late twentieth century, we are frequently required to read 'intertextually', to consider texts as narratives that have 'absorbed and transformed other texts and discourses' (Amigoni, 2000: 18).[5] In the sixteenth and seventeenth centuries, Shakespeare had been engaged in comparable acts of absorption and transformation. This fact alone makes his texts ripe for intertextual invocations and deployment in postmodern literature of this kind, but their specific cultural valency is an additional factor. As texts, Shakespeare's plays are well known, at least as archetypes or plot structures, to the general reading public. They are texts on which we all have – frequently differing – opinions and stances, as well as ones that inform our quotidian practice and language. Trapido's novels recognise this.[6] There are allusions to Shakespeare – some casual, some sustained – in all her works, but in *Juggling* there is something more at play: something that suggests that Shakespearean comedy as a genre has particular things to say to the female experience.

'You've got to respect your father's wishes'

Juggling pursues Christina Angeletti through various stages of her growth into adulthood and self-knowledge. The opening scene takes place in a museum:

> When Christina was six, she went with her father to a museum. They stood for many minutes before a frieze depicting the Battle of the Greeks and the Amazons. The Greeks were all men and the Amazons were all women but Christina got it wrong. Since she had only recently learnt how to read, she thought that Amazon said 'Amazin'. It was perfectly obvious to her that the men were all amazing. The lines of their ranked bodies, veering just slightly from the perpendicular, made an impressive dense rhythm, something like tall, italic handwriting. The women were all lying on the ground. Their faces passive, their bodies displaying too much rounded curve for any such angular geometry, they lay listing elegantly from the horizontal in defeat. (1995: 3)

The geometry of this sequence has resonance for understandings of gender-based relationships throughout the novel. The easy equation that appears to be established between masculinity and the perpendicular (embodied by the Greek warriors Christina so admires in the museum frieze) and femininity and the horizontal (and, by extension, the submissive: this is epitomised here by the defeated Amazons) is, in truth, consistently challenged by the social observations of both the novel and its central character. Christina's initial interpretation of the battle of the sexes will be assertively rewritten, much as Shakespeare is, by Trapido's narrative.

A clue for attentive readers lies in the chapter heading: 'Pam, Christina and the Nearly Father. Intersecting Circles'. As a geometrical figure, the circle challenges the certainties of straight lines, alerting us to the fact that neither Greek nor Amazon achieves a certainty of subject position in the frieze. *Juggling*'s structure offers a series of intersecting circles rather than a neat linear trajectory. Its closing words, a pun on Christina's honeymoon encounter with Roland (a maths teacher) in a guesthouse with suitably crooked floors, are telling: 'I think ... that I had better lie down and close my eyes and think of Venn diagrams' (316).

The Battle of the Greeks and the 'Amazins' that Christina so fruitfully misreads in this sequence establishes from the beginning a series of circular intersections with the Shakespearean canon.

The Shakespeare play which commences with reference to the battle of the Greeks and Amazons is *A Midsummer Night's Dream*.[7] That comedy's events are framed by scenes in an Athenian court ruled by Duke Theseus. We see him impatient on the brink of his wedding to an Amazon Queen:

> Now, fair Hippolyta, our nuptial hour
> Draws on apace. Four happy days bring in
> Another moon – but O, methinks how slow
> This old moon wanes! She lingers my desires
> Like to a stepdame or a dowager
> Long withering out a young man's revenue.
>
> (1.1.1–6)

The origin of Theseus and Hippolyta's marriage in war and bloodshed would have been common knowledge to an early modern audience versed in classical literature, but it is also rendered explicit by Theseus's claim: 'Hippolyta, I wooed thee with my sword,/ And won thy love doing thee injuries' (1.1.16–17). Geraldo de Sousa has demonstrated how the mythical reputation of the single-sex Amazonian community, with its reputation for self-mutilation (the left breast sheared to accommodate the bow of archery), contributes to an investigation throughout *Dream* of questions of gender and power (1999: 10). Female actors in the role of Hippolyta have a number of choices when they perform this scene. They can represent Hippolyta as a broken woman, a prisoner of war subject to Theseus' patriarchal rule. Alternatively, at this stage in the play at least (she does consent to marriage by the end), she can be interpreted as a figure of resistance, one who questions Theseus' will (McGuire, 1996: 155). This is frequently conveyed to audiences wordlessly via a sympathetic response to Hermia's request to marry the man she loves against her father's wishes.[8]

What is indisputable in *Dream* is that Theseus' court serves as a space of patriarchal domination and control. Egeus, in appealing to the Duke to force Hermia to marry Lysander, begs 'the ancient privilege of Athens' (l. 41):

> As she is mine, I may dispose of her,
> Which shall be either to this gentleman
> Or to her death, according to our law
> Immediately provided in that case.
>
> (1.1.42–5)

Theseus upholds and endorses this patriarchal edict, stressing that to Hermia, her father 'should be as a god' (l. 47). He curbs its arbitrary cruelty only to the extent that he orders that, if Hermia refuses to marry Lysander, she should be cloistered in a nunnery rather than executed.

Early modern audiences would also have been only too aware of Theseus' dubious personal reputation in affairs of the heart: he was the archetype of the male seducer. Rescued from the labyrinth and the Minotaur by Ariadne, he promptly deserted her for her sister Phaedra. In much the same way, he deserted the Amazonian Queen Antiopa for her sister Hippolyta. This reputation for betrayal is mentioned by Oberon at the start of Act 2, when he is answering Titania's jealous questioning of his own love for the 'mortal' Hippolyta:

> How canst thou thus for shame, Titania,
> Glance at my credit with Hippolyta,
> Knowing I know thy love to Theseus?
> Didst thou not lead him through the glimmering night
> From Perigouna whom he ravishèd,
> And make him with fair Aegles break his faith,
> With Ariadne and Antiopa?
>
> (2.1.74–80)[9]

The double standards of Theseus' patriarchal society are clear. The ill-used power of patriarchs would have been further emphasised for contemporary audiences by the nomenclature of Hermia's father – in the myths, Aegeus was the name of Theseus' own father. The duke's sympathies are intuitively placed with the paternal side (Hodgdon, 1996).

In Trapido's novel, this complex web of associations with *Dream* and that play's own mythical sources helps to establish readers' understanding of Christina's difficult relationship with Joe. Wondering how Amazons would have breastfed twins, she is answered by his curt statement that the Amazons 'weren't particularly maternal' (4). Christina's reaction to this is to see Joe in strictly masculine terms: 'her father, like the Greeks, was emphatically perpendicular … even there, in the museum, he seemed to her closer to the ceiling than to the floor' (4). At this stage, Christina is still under the false impression that Joe is her biological father. Trapido, however, plants several clues to raise readers' suspicions that Joe is simply one of several 'nearly fathers' that Christina encounters in the course of her growing up. These include the juggler whom she meets as a little girl, who, with his Hallowe'en hat and perpendicular appearance, alerts us to carnivalesque aspects of the narrative. These elements of carnival provide their own intersections, structural and stylistic, with the paradigms of Shakespearean comedy and criticism, as we shall see later.

It is not until the close of Part 4 that the reality of Christina's paternity begins to dawn on her. Judith Campbell, wife of Christina's university supervisor – who, with her height, confidence and bisexual orientation, provides a direct challenge to that aforementioned equation of perpendicularity and masculinity, and therefore to essentialist notions of gender and heterosexuality – questions Christina's physiognomy. The shape of her cranium casts doubt, it seems, on her claim to have been born prematurely. Judith's queries send Christina off on a wild-goose chase in the presumption that Roland Dent must be her real father, but such are the twists, turns and intersections of *Juggling* that by the time she does meet her true father (Matthew Riley, a Cambridge college fundraiser, identifiable by the Born Lump on his ear) the issue no longer seems of importance. In this way, the narrative steadily erodes the certainties of patriarchal rule in much the same way as the vicissitudes of love in Shakespeare's comedies enable all kinds of empowering inversions.

The extent to which patriarchy is challenged by the end of the comedies has been a point of critical debate. In *As You Like It*, Rosalind surrenders her enabling disguise and resubmits herself to her father's – and, by extension, her husband-to-be's – guidance, but the subversive epilogue which she articulates and which, after all, instructs women in the audience to 'like as much of this play as please you' (l. 11), and the manner in which she has tutored that husband, Orlando, in a more equitable and realistic life-partnership, must give us pause.[10] In *Love's Labour's Lost*, the challenges set the men by the Princess and her ladies establish a newly defiant note, and serve to resist the conventional closure of romantic comedy. In *Twelfth Night*, Viola, though matched with Orsino, remains in her subversive costume of the boy-page (Greenblatt, 1997: 1762).

Dream offers similar ambivalences. The humiliation of Titania by Oberon, forced as she is, in a grotesque rewriting of Ovidian metamorphosis, to couple with an ass, has been seen by some feminist critics as indicative of a more general degradation of powerful women in the play (Hackett, 1997). This is in part Trapido's reading, at least in so far as we can associate her with the analysis of the comedies that Christina produces (and Hugo plagiarises) for her Cambridge supervision essay:

> The Comedies take as their subject what people seem to care about most. That is the business of getting it together with a member of the opposite sex. In this they are just as abrasive and cruel as life. The sexes are matched in a constant state of war. The war is represented by the words. The quick-fire banter between men and women is a mating dance and a metaphor for the act between the sheets, in all its violence and joy... In the conflict of gender, the women win the war of the words, but the men will win the battle. (219–20)

'Like the stuff of Shakespeare comedy': structure, echo and expectation

Christina's free-form essay on the comedies provides an intriguing template for Trapido's own interest in Shakespearean appropriation, and the forms and structures which such an act of appropriation might take. The question of the happy ending is clearly a crucial one: the artificial nature of that comic convention is one that Shakespeare recognised, and even celebrated:

> The Comedies are a better sort of tragedy because they make us laugh and because the characters stay alive. Survival is admirable. It is more difficult than death, since it takes more energy and guile. The Comedies send us home feeling happy, because we believe that we have witnessed happy endings. What we have really witnessed are sexy endings; visionary endings; endings frozen in a moment of precarious, brilliant symmetry, like a rain of fireworks in a prison yard. The Comedies climax on a moment of upbeat that is balanced between all time and no time. Their reality is forever and never. (217)

Juggling is self-conscious about its own efforts at closure. The novel's structure signals its dramaturgic origins: the narrative is divided into five parts, mimicking the five-act structure of a Shakespearean play, but there is also an epilogue – 'or what you will' – which deliberately recalls the subversive addenda to plays such as *As You Like It* and *Dream*.

A recurring joke in *Juggling* is that Trapido, like Shakespeare in *As You Like It*, will in her own 'fifth act' produce a novelistic equivalent to the 'second son of old Sir Rowland de Boys', a figure intended to tie up loose ends and provide the proverbial happy ending. When Roland Dent, who seems significantly named in this respect, proves not to be Christina's father, the way is clear. That it is Roland, rather than any son of his, who provides the life-partner for Christina is, however, intriguing. This displacement keeps – albeit in a suppressed way – the implications of incestuous father–daughter relationships present in the reader's mind. Incest as a topic has entered the novel in a more explicit form in the shape of Zuleika/Miffy, Judith and Father Zak's child, a product of their illicit sexual encounter as siblings. Incestuous readings of Shakespearean relationships have featured in many feminist re-visions of his canon. Trapido both allows for and diffuses the potentially tragic consequences of this theme in her own feat of narrative juggling.

Trapido's central theme is clearly the loss of childhood. Part 1, 'Lying Down and Standing Up', makes reference both to the (nearly) perpendicular and horizontal positions of the Greeks and Amazons, and to six-year-old Christina's movement into individual consciousness. The encounter with the juggler, which brings out her relatives' latent fears about sexual attack, and is significantly placed at the close of the first chapter, marks an ending as well as beginning: 'It was something like the beginning of the end of childhood' (34).

Subsequent chapters deal with comparable moments of growth and loss in the lives of other characters such as Peter, Jago and Victor. These moments are frequently described in terms of cor-poreal dismemberment – 'He had lopped off the limb of his own infancy' (54) – and often involve a failure of family structures. Christina seeks a 'nearly father' in the juggler; Peter finds himself struggling with a stepfather in the form of Roland Dent; and Jago is separated from his twin, Victor, by the divorce of their parents. The echoes of Shakespearean comedy are once again informative: the protagonists of *As You Like It*, *Twelfth Night*, and *Dream* are frequently the product of dysfunctional or aberrational family structures. Rosalind has a banished father, Duke Senior, and a surrogate parent, her uncle Duke Frederick, who in turn seeks to banish her. Her mother is never mentioned; presumed dead, she is one of Shakespeare's many absent mothers who have proved such fertile creative soil for women writers. Viola is, like her play counterpart Olivia, mourning a dead father and a presumed dead twin brother; Hermia (another motherless character) is forced to reject her father in choosing to follow her heart (she has a tragic counterpart in Desdemona's stance against Brabanzio in *Othello*).

Sigmund Freud's notion of the 'family romance' has heavily influenced psychoanalytical criticism of Shakespearean drama, and been fruitfully applied to several appropriations that themselves concentrate on family structures.[11] Freud's notion of the psychosexual fantasies woven by children, in which they dream of alternative parentage (often of higher social status) or delegitimise rival siblings, would seem apposite for a reading of the complex family relations depicted in *Juggling* (Freud, 1971: 235–41). The young Christina is obsessed with Pam's adopted status. As Freud observes:

> A younger child is very specially inclined to use imaginative stories ... in order to rob those born before him [/her] of their prerogatives ... An interesting variant of the family romance may then appear in which the hero [/ine] ... returns to legitimacy ... while his [/her] brothers and sisters are eliminated by being bastardised. (1971: 240)

The inverse of this Freudian paradigm is detectable in Christina's plot trajectory, although a related drive may also stand behind her desire to be proactive in arranging for the abortion of Pam's child. It is certainly this event which promotes Christina's severance from parental authority.

If Shakespearean romantic comedies provide a perfect analogy for Christina's post-Freudian maturation into a point of estrangement from her 'parents', plays such as *The Tempest* and *The Winter's Tale*, the so-called late romances, offer templates for the discovery of identity that Christina is engaged upon. But the comedies specifically, from *The Two Gentlemen of Verona* through *Dream* and *The Merchant of Venice* to *The Winter's Tale*, concern themselves with the pressures placed on childhood – invariably same-sex – friendships by the pressures of heterosexual marriage and social expectation. Proteus and Valentine betray each other in *Two Gentlemen*; in *Dream*, Demetrius, Lysander, Hermia and Helena hurl invective and abuse at each other in the course of their forest adventures; Bassanio and Antonio face the ultimate test of their love in the wake of Shylock's and Portia's interventions in their lives in *The Merchant of Venice*; and jealousy between those formerly 'twinned lambs' (1.2.69), Polixenes and Leontes, propels the tragedy in the first half of *The Winter's Tale*. Trapido echoes these concerns in *Juggling* by means of the choice forced on Jago by Peter and the onset of puberty: after the campground cruelties of Pongo and Stet (themselves a prefiguring of later, darker group cruelties in the form of the Hallowe'en rape of Pam), Peter tells Jago he must choose between him and his new-found friends. Jago, rejecting Peter, feels he has no choice. This episode is again described in the narrative in terms of dismemberment, and it is no coincidence that the significant intertext in this passage is William Golding's parable of children's cruelty to fellow children, *Lord of the Flies* (80).

The second part of *Juggling*, entitled 'Leaning Forward', marks the entry of the novel's young protagonists into adolescence, as they head off to boarding school. This is a transitional moment, indicated not least by Christina's liminal age of thirteen, but also by the increasing demarcation of gendered worlds and subjects. In one telling scene within the school building, Joe and the ever-confident Jago bond over a discussion of *Hamlet* and Eliot's theory of the Objective Correlative (Trapido, 1995: 112; Eliot, 1932: 145). In stark contrast to this, when Christina asks the meaning of the same theory, Joe enacts his power as denying patriarch, laughing at her inquiries (117). A further example of male bonding asserting itself to the exclusion of Christina, and once again enabled by the medium of Shakespeare, occurs in Part 3 when Jago and Roland unite in opposition to her interest in possible connections between mathematics and the sonnets. Jago dismisses Christina's connection of the galliard, a matrix and the sonnet structure as 'girlie' (168), although in his stance of (male) intellectual superiority he misses entirely her admirable ability to cross the boundaries between poetry, dance and science.

Part 3 is titled 'Tumbling' and, like the central plateau of much Shakespearean drama, it contains the central events of the novel (Holland, 1997: 4): these include the Hallowe'en rape of Pam, but also Christina's restorative encounter with Dulcie Jackson. The 'tumbling' movement is, then, a sexual fall of sorts but also a movement that carries the body forwards. Part 4 sees Christina aged eighteen and attending Cambridge University. She both enjoys and endures the independence and new forms of authority that constitutes. The title of this section indicates the complex negotiations that her new existence demands: 'Balancing'. Here Christina finds her voice (not least in the academic essay on Shakespeare already quoted), yet also recognises her loneliness: 'I am a survivor from three sets of four' (210). If we accept the sonnet matrix discussed above, Christina fails to see here that three quatrains will be followed not by a lone individual but by a pair, a rhyming couple(t). The reader retains a sense of structure and expectation throughout (awaiting the 'second son of Rowland de Boys'), even when the protagonist has discarded hers.

In the dramatic, and Shakespearean, scheme of things we might expect the fifth act to provide a dénouement or resolution of some sort. In terms of the novel's extended time-scheme, the children with whom we began have come full circle. In some cases – Pam and Jago, for example – they are parents themselves. Victor and Jago, those twins who were in the best Shakespearean tradition separated at birth (one thinks of the sundering shipwrecks of *The Comedy of Errors*, *Twelfth Night*, and *Pericles*), are reconciled. The other reunion – and one that both raises and disappoints in the reader the expectation of a father–daughter reconciliation in *Juggling* to mirror those of Pericles and Marina, and Leontes and Perdita, in the late Shakespearean romances – is that of Christina and her natural father. By the time his identity becomes clear to Christina, it is no longer significant ('Some schmuck' (300)).

Trapido cares deeply about the structures and movements of her intricate dance of a novel. In 'Epilogue; or, What You Will', she addresses the reader directly, just as Rosalind and Puck address their audiences: 'So what has happened to them? Did the frame freeze? Did the balance hold? No, of course not. Well, yes and no' (301). In this privileged glimpse into a future beyond the remit of the novel, we see Pam and Jago married and living with baby Bruno in Italy (there is a circularity here, if we recall Pam's own Italian origins). Peter and Victor are happily paired off. Trapido takes great pleasure in telling us this, asserting the author's power to determine the characters' fate:

Peter was never marked out for Christina, for all that symmetry, colour-
coding and all the physical correlatives seemed to point so conven-
iently in that direction. Colour-coding is, after all, not necessarily a
highly successful basis for permanent living-together relationships, and
sometimes, as in *Twelfth Night*, for example, it is employed merely to
mark out links between siblings, especially twins. (301–2)

Peter and Christina have been twinned throughout the narrative,
but as kindred spirits rather than intended lovers – an idea made
explicit in the final part of the novel, when Christina dresses in
Peter's clothes. Various other couplings have occurred: Dulcie and
Alice (incest of a sort, as Dulcie observes); Gentille and Hugo;
Judith and Joe; and, of course, Christina and 'old Sir Rowland de
Boys' himself. But this is another narrative balancing act, a moment
caught in freeze-frame. When in her next novel, *The Travelling
Hornplayer*, Trapido explores the lives of Ellen and Lydia Dent,
Roland's twin daughters, readers learn in passing of further com-
edies and tragedies in Christina's life (including the miscarriage of
her own twins).

In structuring the course of her narrative in terms of five acts
and an epilogue, and ensuring that certain events unfold at specific
points within that structure, Trapido makes more than a passing
gesture to a particular brand of Shakespearean literary criticism
which dominated thinking in the 1950s and 1960s, Structuralism,
and the writings of one of its chief exponents, Northrop Frye. In
his still-salient account of Shakespearean comedy in *A Natural
Perspective*, Frye suggested that three main movements were
common across the plays (1965: 72–115). In the first movement of
each, an anti-comic world of restrictive laws was represented. In
Dream, that would constitute Athenian society and the restrictive
patriarchal rule of Theseus; in *As You Like It*, the usurping rule
of Duke Frederick; in *Love's Labour's Lost*, the briefly lived reign
of abstinence evoked, and as soon revoked, by the King of
Navarre's edict. The central movement of such plays invariably
involves an escape into a comic or 'green' space, an antithetical
site of holiday, which often entails a confusion or obliteration of
identity leading to sexual and/or social development. The forests
of *Dream* and *As You Like It*, and in some respects the world of
Illyria in *Twelfth Night* (an 'escape' into a new community for the
shipwrecked Viola), provide exactly these environments for shifting

identity: Hermia, Helena, Demetrius and Lysander find themselves
worked upon by Puck and his love-in-idleness; Rosalind, Celia
and Viola proactively assume disguises.

In a Structuralist reading, the final movement provides a reconciliation of sorts, and often a return to a changed version of the
original environment. Frye talks of this in terms of the discovery
of identity, on either an individual or a social level (1965: 78).
Again, *Dream* and *As You Like It* very obviously fit into this
pattern of return; *Twelfth Night* and, before it, *The Comedy of
Errors* deal with comparable themes of family reunion (a structure
Shakespeare would poignantly echo in late plays, such as *Pericles*
and *The Winter's Tale*).

The comedies and late romances are informing texts for
Trapido, as much as they were for Frye in establishing his structural account of Shakespearean drama. Trapido seems to fashion
Juggling quite deliberately from comparable structural material.
Joe's patriarchy provides the restrictive starting point – Christina's
chastisement for spending time with the juggler (she gets a beating)
is just one case of its anti-comic, anti-holiday stance. Boarding
school (by necessity, a milieu away from parents and family structures) provides the space for the necessary refashionings of identity
that Frye's structure demands, as well as the central act of moral
and sexual confusion in the horrifying rape. Christina obliterates
her former self in almost clinical style, the androgynous result
linking her in the reader's mind to the boy-actors who played
Shakespeare's heroines (123). The resolution (or, at least, the resolution as we choose to believe in it at a given moment of the
'performance') to the novel has already been discussed, but the
relevance of Frye's comedic structure persists. Christina quite
literally returns to earlier shaping environments (her boarding
school), but as a changed individual and in an altered state (she
will be there as Roland's wife, not pupil).

Frye's patterning of Shakespearean comedy has proved an informative one for literary critics accounting for these plays, often
in a productive combination with the work of his contemporary,
C. L. Barber, as well as that of the Russian theorist Mikhail
Bakhtin. Both Barber and Bakhtin were interested in central
moments of 'holiday' and release in the midst of restrictive or
normative societies, as depicted in the literature produced by those

societies. Barber was responsible for describing Shakespeare's comedies as 'festive comedies'. His relating of those texts of escape into the greenworld of May Day and Midsummer to the actual rituals and customary practices of Elizabethan and Jacobean England has in turn encouraged critics to reapply to the Shakespearean *oeuvre* ideas on 'carnival' that Bakhtin developed in relation to the writings of Rabelais (Barber, 1972 (1959)); Bakhtin, 1984 (1965)). Festive readings of Shakespeare have dominated recent decades, and it is no coincidence that several of the writers I will be exploring in the course of this book – Trapido, Angela Carter and Kate Atkinson among them – have been deeply influenced by these modes of criticism.

Barber felt that Shakespearean comedy's interest in the rituals and landmarks of an agricultural calendar – events such as Valentine's Day, Hocktide, May Day, Whitsun Ales and Midsummer – was in itself a nostalgic social mode (1972: 16). Shakespeare had been part of that rural migration to the cities that stamps itself on the nostalgic interest in folklore in plays such as *Dream* (Holland, 1995: 21). It is clear that customary occasions such as May Day (when young people went into the woods on the premiss of gathering flowers, an act which nevertheless facilitated romantic liaison and erotic encounter), the fertility rites of Midsummer and the wintertime festival of Twelfth Night, when servants were allowed to rule the household for the day, help to shape and influence the images and themes of Shakespearean comedy, but they also have a narrative function in *Juggling*. For example, Judith, a figure of inversion and challenge in the novel, is described in carnivalesque (and Amazonian) terms (195). The fact that the reader's (and Christina's) first encounter with her is on a festive occasion, a party, brings into play all the complex ideas of subversion and release that Barber and others associate with such topics in a Shakespearean context.

Carnival, though, has its own associations with the grotesque and excessive, as Bakhtin's politically informed criticism has been important in demonstrating, and there is a darker carnival at the heart of Trapido's festive novel. Part 3 focuses on Hallowe'en, or All Souls' Eve – 31 October, when all the evil spirits do their worst in advance of the reassertion of control by the good forces of All Souls' Day. Jago becomes interested in the socially subversive possibilities of the festival after hearing a clergyman's objections broadcast on the radio (125). He subsequently persuades his acolytes or 'groupies' to join him in donning gruesome costumes and terrorising the neighbourhood for the evening.

This Hallowe'en carnival carries the usual potential for liberation in disguise: we are told that 'Jago's disguise consisted almost entirely in altered speech and body language' (136). But it also involves the implicit challenge to authority and establishment institutions that early modern events such as the Feast of Fools contained: Jago takes grim delight in offending householders with anti-Semitic and anti-Catholic references. Under the haze of alcohol, that identity-altering substance, the groupies carry out their ultimate violation of the festive occasion: the rape of Pam.

The alternative possibilities of carnival, liberation and violation, will prove instructive in later readings of novels such as *Wise Children* and *Human Croquet*. The ironies persist in Trapido's dark version in that the result of the attack is Pam's pregnancy and the positive presence in her life of baby Bruno. What is inescapable, however, in the description of the rape is its association with oral violation. The prose dwells on Stet's disguise as a Mummy (another grim inversion of the novel's interest in parents and nearly-parents: Stet will become a father, of sorts) and, in particular, his costume's 'ugly, reptilian suck-hole' (150). Elsewhere in the novel, carnival's more usual association with the orality of eating and drinking comes to the fore: Joe is commonly associated with food in the narrative (tellingly, he makes pancakes – alimentary emblems of the carnivalesque spirit of consumption – but in a manner that seems to repel Christina, using ricotta cheese, or 'sloppy stuff', as Granny P calls it (19–20)). Pam and Christina's childhood is described as carnivalesque in spirit, although that, too, is not without its problems: 'life for the girls had a great deal going for it. The spirit of it was expansive. By most people's standards it was like Christmas every day. But something in the air of it made Christina prickly. There was something that gave her an edge' (8). It is the 'edge' in carnival that Trapido chooses to place at the heart of her novel.

The setting of Part 3 has kinship with the labyrinthine woodlands and moral mazes at the centre of Shakespearean comedy, but the anxieties that remain latent in *Dream*, and even *Two Gentleman* (where rape is attempted but forestalled), are fully realised here. Pam's character parallels not only Silvia and Hermia but the violated Lavinia of Shakespeare's brutal early tragedy *Titus Andronicus*. Lavinia's tongueless and dismembered condition (her hands removed by her violators so that she may not write of their crime; her tongue removed so that she may not voice it) re-emerges in this context. Pam is silenced by her traumatic experience, a fact which clearly unnerves Jago, who is the passive audience for this criminal act. Shakespeare's own intertextual reference for this plotline was the rape of Philomel by Tereus in Ovid's *Metamorphoses*: raped in woodland, Philomel is transformed into a nightingale, and can only sing of Tereus' violation. Lacking even this transformative recourse in *Titus Andronicus*, Lavinia points to Philomel's informing narrative in a copy of the *Metamorphoses*. The cultural valence and significance of literature and ongoing acts of appropriation by women are acted out for all to see on the Shakespearean stage.

A Shakespeare of one's own?

Trapido is self-conscious not only in her appropriation of Shakespeare but in her appropriation of male-authored, male-performed (at least in their own time) dramatic texts to speak to a quintessentially female experience, and to speak to that experience in a non-dramatic narrative form. There is a deliberate claiming of Shakespeare for the realm of women's writing, both critical and fictional.

A common feature of Shakespeare's romantic comedies is to display the education, usually by a female protagonist, of a male suitor on the topic and practice of love: one thinks of Rosalind instructing Orlando in the realities of love rather than the worn-out clichés of Petrarchan sonneteering: 'Men have died from time to time and worms have eaten them, but not for love.' (*As You Like It*, 4.1.92–3); or of Rosaline educating the cynical Biron in *Love's Labour's Lost*. Christina receives a comparable education in *Juggling* from Trapido's own outspoken heroine, Dulcie Jackson. Fittingly, Dulcie enters the narrative in its central movement and in an appositely Shakespearean, theatrical context: the two girls meet in the lavatories during the interval of a Royal Shakespeare

Company production of *The Winter's Tale* at the Barbican theatre, London. Dulcie provides another of the novel's Amazonian icons: 'Atalanta in Calydon' (173). Her appearance and bawdy street-level language are an education for Christina: theatre has, in its age-old capacity, provided the space for cross-class and cross-cultural interaction of the most productive kind.

Dulcie offers a highly idiomatic précis of Shakespeare's magical and mysterious late play:

> Right. So there's this woman, then, right? And she's the queen. And her husband's fuckin slung her in prison, all right? And it's because she's got fuckin pregnant and he reckons the kid ain't his. So when it's born he fuckin takes it right? And he gets this geezer to dump it in the forest to get fuckin ate by wild bears and that, all right? (174)

Not averse to contemporary resonances – 'It's like my cousin's last week' (174) – the ensuing discussion between Dulcie and her companion, overheard in best theatrical tradition by Christina, introduces the latter to the idea of arranging an abortion for her violated sister. This idea draws her into conversation with Dulcie, causing them both to miss the play's second half. Had they seen the second part of *The Winter's Tale*, the girls would have witnessed the play leaping sixteen years, courtesy of a personified Time, to reach a grown-up Perdita engaged in the joyousness and flirtation of the Bohemian sheep-shearing festival. More significantly, perhaps, the fifth act would have shown them Perdita (the lost one) reunited with her father, Leontes, and her mother's statue miraculously (or not, depending on interpretation) come to life. As Dulcie says: 'It's all about that baby, isn't it? The one that was supposed to have been got rid of. It's all about how she grows up beautiful and marries the prince and all that' (176). Christina misses the relevance to her own and Pam's situation, but the reader may not. Pam will indeed bear the child and marry a 'prince', at least in the form of Christina's self-assigned Prince Charming, Jago. *The Winter's Tale* recurs in several women novelists' appropriations of Shakespeare: Carter, as we shall see, undoubtedly uses it in structuring her fifth-act family reunions and reconciliations, however parodically, in *Wise Children*.[12] In Trapido's novel of severed families and lost children, the relevance of this late play is clear. Again, Christina sees only the analogy with those around her, not herself, yet in some sense she is the lost daughter who finds true identity by the close.

Dulcie, who helps Christina to effect that self-discovery, is intelligent, black, working-class and lesbian. In *Juggling*, she represents a strident and persuasive alternative to the oversimplistic gender binaries established in the opening pages. By going to live with Dulcie's East End family and attending a London state school, Christina, like Perdita, finds herself raised in an alternative family and social structure, one to which she may or may not have been born (readers of *Temples of Delight* will remember Matthew Riley's working-class origins). As with Perdita, however, everyone seems quicker to recognise a potential in Christina than in those around her: in this way, Trapido exposes the class rigidity which permeates *The Winter's Tale*, and deems Perdita's relationship with the disguised Florizel acceptable only because she is a princess herself by blood. *Juggling* makes blood, in the end, count for very little, at least in terms of personal relationships; but it does acknowledge that in the institutions which structure our lives, not least educational establishments, the case may be very different.

In *Juggling*, Dulcie is appalled by everything that Cambridge University represents. Her first sight of child choristers and mullioned windows is enough to dissuade her from applying for an assisted place. She is menaced by the number of signs exhorting her to 'Keep Off the Grass' (209). Controls of this nature and ancient architecture are anathema to Dulcie's experience, but all too familiar to Christina from her public-school days. Cambridge, by the very fact of its appearance, seems welcoming only to the select few.

While Trapido never makes the connection explicit, Dulcie's experience of Cambridge calls to mind one of the more famous female outbursts in print against the male bastion of privilege and exclusivity that the University represented, at least in her own time: Virginia Woolf's *A Room of One's Own*. That essay, originally delivered as a series of papers on the topic of 'Women and Fiction' to Girton and Newnham Colleges, then all-women institutions, begins with Woolf seated on the edge of the Cam, having interesting thoughts. She then makes her way across the college backs, only to be borne down on by repressive male authority in the uniformed shape of a Beadle:

> It was thus that I found myself walking with extreme rapidity across a grass plot. Instantly a man's figure rose to intercept me. Nor did I at

first understand that the gesticulations of a curious-looking object, in a cut-away coat and evening shirt, were aimed at me. His face expressed horror and indignation. Instinct rather than reason came to my help; he was a Beadle; I was a woman. This was the turf; there was the path. Only the Fellows and Scholars are allowed here; the gravel is the place for me. (Woolf, 1993: 5)

This passage prefigures other moments in the essay when Woolf finds herself barred from the full experience of a Cambridge scholarly life, be it in the libraries or the food halls; these feed into one of her most famous rallying cries: 'Literature is open to everybody. I refuse to allow you, Beadle though you are, to turn me off the grass. Lock up your libraries, if you like; but there is no gate, no lock, no bolt that you can set upon the freedom of my mind' (Woolf, 1993: 68–9). Trapido takes up that rallying cry in the assertive shape of Dulcie, who, while rejecting the world of academe as such, is last seen in the novel proper (that is, prior to the revisions of the Epilogue) juggling in the middle of a quadrangle lawn. The earlier father-figure juggler of Christina's desires has metamorphosed into the feminine and subversive form of Dulcie, and even the imperatives of Christina's real patriarch – Matthew Riley, the new college fundraiser who gruffly shouts at Dulcie: 'Off the *gruss* ... *Cun't* you read?' (299) – cannot dispel the significance of the moment. The implicit misogyny of the stressed pronunciation merely confirms the feminist significations.

No student of women's fiction can forget that it is in the course of *A Room of One's Own* that Woolf offers her own fictional alternative to Shakespeare: his sister, Judith, who shares his wit, talent and perception, and longs to be an actor:

She picked up a book now and then, one of her brother's perhaps, and read a few pages. But then her parents came in and told her to mend the stockings or mind the stew and not moon about with books and papers ... She had the quickest fancy, a gift like her brother's, for the tune of words. Like him, she had a taste for the theatre. She stood at the stage door; she wanted to act, she said. Men laughed in her face. (1993: 43, 44)

Numerous women writers have found the figure of 'Shakespeare's sister' an alluring one. Critics have also been encouraged to look for the women hidden in the parish registers and literary margins of the Elizabethan and Jacobean age. Although historical scholarship has in some respects proved Woolf wrong about the absence of women writers in that era, we should not ignore her skill in identifying the research topics of the later twentieth century:

> What one wants ... and why does not some brilliant student at Newn-ham or Girton supply it? – is a mass of information; at what age did she marry; how many children had she as a rule; what was her house like; had she a room to herself; did she do the cooking; would she be likely to have a servant? All these facts lie somewhere, presumably in parish registers and account books; the life of the average Elizabethan woman must be scattered about somewhere, could one collect it and make a book of it. (1993: 41)

This is not quite the remit of Trapido and her sister novelists in appropriating Shakespeare, but they, too, are engaged in an act of reclamation, recovering marginal, even offstage female characters and imposing a female perspective on some of the plotlines. They speak to, and through, Shakespeare from their own very deter-mined subject positions, from a room of their own. Like Christina Angeletti and Dulcie Jackson, they learn to juggle in tandem and not to keep off the grass.

Notes

1 The exception appears to be her second novel, *Noah's Ark* (1984), which remains integral to itself, but that is not to say this will not be revised by future productions. Katherine, Jonathan and Roger from *Brother of the More Famous Jack* (1982) reappear in *The Travelling Hornplayer* (1998). *Temples of Delight* (1990) acts as a prequel to the events of *Juggling* (1994), and the twins, Ellen and Lydia Dent, who figure in *The Travelling Hornplayer* are bit-part players in *Juggling*, the children of Roland Dent, who ultimately marries that novel's pro-tagonist.

2 For a useful overview of this movement, see Veeser (1989, 1994).

3 In real life, Mary had committed matricide (Wolfson, 1990: 19). Hers is also an example of authorship that was effaced from the publica-tion for a long time.

4 On this topic, see Bevington (1996).

5 On postmodern fiction, see Hutcheon (1988a, 1988b); McHale (1990), and Botting (1999).

6 See Trapido (1982: 124), where there is an extended reference to *The Taming of the Shrew*.

7 The characters also appear in Shakespeare's later collaboration with John Fletcher, *The Two Noble Kinsmen*.

8 This was evident in the most recent big-screen version of the play (dir. Michael Hoffman, 1998). In the New Victoria Theatre, Newcastle-under-Lyme production in 1999, directed by Chris Monks, Hippolyta,, as well as glaring at Theseus to convey her view in scene 1, appeared in the hunting scene in Amazonian armour. I am grateful to Chris Monks for his discussion of these topics.

9 These details would have been familiar to Shakespeare's audience from Plutarch's *Life of Theseus*.

10 Erickson, who prefers the contained reading of Rosalind's achievements in the play, reads the Epilogue as merely a continuance of the 'phasing out' of Rosalind, in that it reminds the audience of the boy-actor beneath the costume and therefore, by extension, the all-male cast (1991b: 164).

11 See Barber (1972). Most importantly, Chedgzoy (1995) has used the Freudian paradigm to read texts from Gus Van Sant's 1991 film *My Own Private Idaho* to Angela Carter's *Wise Children*.

12 Jane Smiley has suggested that it is the Shakespeare play she would most like to work with in the future: (Smiley, 1999: 178). It is not a purely female prerogative to demonstrate an interest in the familial themes of this play: in *Tree Surgery for Beginners* (1998), Patrick Gale rewrites the Freudian family romance of *The Winter's Tale* in the context of a modern plotline of jealousy, suspected murder, death of children, and – in a truly Shakespearean flourish at the end – the reunion of long-lost twins. Gale's protagonist, Lawrence Frost, is alliteratively connected to his literary archetype, Leontes, although he shares the fate of false imprisonment with Hermione. With a wry glance at his own act of appropriation, Gale has his main character undertake a life-changing cruise (the duration of the novel is sixteen months, as opposed to the sixteen years of the source-play) on the *SS Paulina*, but Paulina's guiding presence in the play is registered elsewhere in the novel both in the form of Lawrence's remarkable mother, Dora, and his eventual life-partner, the transsexual Lala/Serena. It is the latter who, in a fantastic episode with an escaped tiger, provides the novel's parodic version of that all-too-famous stage direction from the play: '*Exit pursued by a bear*'.

TWO

'We dearly love the Bard, sir': Angela Carter's Shakespeare

Angela Carter (1940–92) enjoyed a lifelong literary flirtation with Shakespeare – with both the works and the very idea of the man. Several of her books are shot through with Shakespearean allusion. *The Passion of New Eve* is ostensibly a text about the power of cinematic illusion and the possible empowerment for women involved in the recognition that gender is a construct: that all gender is – to appropriate Judith Butler's terminology – performance (Butler, 1990). Nevertheless, the novel's narrator is fascinated by that archetype of gender-bending, Shakespearean cross-dressing.[1] A number of Carter's short stories deploy Shakespearean texts for both tragic and comic effect, most notably in the *Black Venus* collection (1985): 'Overture and Incidental Music for *A Midsummer Night's Dream*' provides a comic, carnivalesque prequel to the 1599 Shakespearean comedy, and 'The Cabinet of Edgar Allan Poe' has a woman actor (the American Gothic writer's mother), famous for her Ophelia and Juliet, commemorated in a funeral ceremony shaped by Shakespearean language and tragic convention:

> They told her children that now she could come back to take no curtain-calls no matter how fiercely all applauded the manner of her going. Lovers of the theatre plied her hearse with bouquets: 'And from her pure and uncorrupted flesh May violets spring.' (Not a dry eye in the house.) The three orphaned infants were dispersed into the bosoms of charitable protectors. Each gave the clay-cold cheek a final kiss; then they too kissed and parted, Edgar from Henry, Henry from the tiny one who did not move or cry but lay still and kept her eyes tight shut.

When shall these three meet again? The church bell tolled: never never never never never. (Carter, 1985: 55)

Each of the four major tragedies has a sedimentary presence here: the oration over Ophelia's corpse in *Hamlet* is quoted directly; the children's cold kisses on their mother's corpse echo Othello's on Desdemona's 'alabaster' skin; the question of when the three children will meet again reworks the witches' cries in *Macbeth*; and the church bells seem to toll out Lear's pentameter recognition of the finality of Cordelia's demise. In this passage the seed of a larger flowering of Shakespearean allusion in Carter's late novel, *Wise Children* (1992), can be seen.

Lorna Sage has acknowledged that *Wise Children*'s narrative: 'is littered with allusions that disseminate Shakespeare, spread him around, reinvent him as a latterday demotic' (1994a: 56).[2] An indication of Carter's complex operations on her critics is that Sage qualifies her description almost as soon as it is made, suggesting that Carter's relationship with the Bard is less one of re-invention than one of reclamation, an act that strives to 'restore him to his pre-canonised self' (1994a: 56). Carter saw the pre-canonised Shakespeare as a champion of popular culture and of illiterate and semi-literate communities. In her view, the Victorians who sanctified him had much to answer for. She lamented the academic narrowness with which his works were hedged in:

> intellectuals ... are still reluctant to treat him as popular culture ... You mention folk culture and people immediately assume you're going to talk about porridge and clog dancing, there's this William Morris and Arnold Wesker prospect, truly the bourne from which no traveller returns. Shakespeare, like Picasso, is one of the great hinge-figures that sum up the past – one of the great Janus-figures that sum up the past as well as opening all doors towards the future. (Sage, 1994a: 56)

Carter laid great store by hinge-figures and hinge-moments, on thresholds and limits, between-time periods (*Nights at the Circus* is self-consciously set on the eve of the twentieth century, and Kate Webb has described *Wise Children* as a 'cuspy, millennial novel' (1994: 288)) and social boundaries. Her lifelong interest in the cross-dressing motif is just one example of her complication of the thresholds between masculinity and femininity. Shakespeare's plays also dealt with comparable issues of sexuality and performance, social and geographical boundaries, and other kinds of liminal experiences to do with time and the potential in our lives for the magical, supernatural or otherworldly. They therefore offered Carter a perfect vehicle for the exploration of these themes. Like that of several of the other women writers who are the focus of this book, Carter's intertextuality was not restricted to Shakespeare; her works pay homage to Milton, Dickens, Joyce, and European writers such as Rilke, Mallarmé and Baudelaire, as well as film, fairytale, folklore, Gothic, and science fiction. This chapter is an attempt, however, to register, through a sustained reading of *Wise Children*, just how central a hinge-figure Shakespeare was for her, and why.[3] Lizzie, that social ideologue and alternative mother-figure who is so significant a presence in the life of giantess trapeze artist Fevvers in *Nights at the Circus*, might almost have been voicing Carter's own view when she declared: 'We dearly love the Bard, sir' (Carter, 1984: 53).[4]

Twins and travesties

The Freudian family romance – a theory itself frequently negotiated through Shakespeare, as we saw in Trapido's deployment of the paradigm in *Juggling* (see Chapter 1) – is undoubtedly one of Carter's main concerns in *Wise Children*. The novel is narrated by Dora Chance, one of – now elderly – twin sisters who made their career in music hall and pantomime. The popular cultural English theatrical domain stands in an antithetical relationship in the novel (at least at first) to the profession of their Shakespearean tragedian father, Melchior Hazard. *Wise Children* explores the petty comedies and tragedies of familial relationships.

The choice of twins is itself Shakespearean in association. From the shipwreck-sundered master–servant pairs of *The Comedy of Errors*, through the similarly fissured Viola and Sebastian in *Twelfth Night*, to the emotional twinning of Polixenes and Leontes in *The Winter's Tale*, Shakespeare was fascinated throughout his career by the intensity of identification between the two halves of this biological relationship. He was the father of twins who were untimely parted: Hamnet and Judith. The former died at the age of eleven in 1596 in a drowning accident, a family trauma which influenced the writing of both *Twelfth Night* (where, in true comic tradition, the twin brother does not die, but is reborn into Illyrian society along with his identical sister) and *Hamlet*, where the play's eponymous prince evokes the lost son of the playwright. A tragic drowning does occur in that latter play, but is displaced on to the female character of Ophelia (5.1.146–54).

Carter's protagonist twins, like those of Trapido, are both similar and not the same. *Wise Children* has only one narrator; Nora is voiced via the mediating rhythms of Dora's narrative. Despite the novel's fun with the twin sisters' ability to engage in 'bed-swaps' of the kind inaugurated in Shakespearean 'problem plays' such as *Measure for Measure* and *All's Well That Ends Well*, the narrative is careful to stress the distinctions between their characters. This is achieved partly through one of Carter's favourite tropes of dressing up: one twin wears Shalimar perfume, the other Mitsouko. Of course, surface affectations are easily swapped and used in the process of disguise, as is true in the case of the bed tricks of *Wise Children*. It is typical that Carter should invoke a binary only to deconstruct it at the next turn: in itself a very Shakespearean gesture. And in truth, Nora proves not to be Dora's only 'twin' in this self-multiplying text: the first wife of Mrs Genghis Khan, the Hollywood film director who directs the Hazard–Chance ensemble in a disastrously over-the-top cinematic version of *A Midsummer Night's Dream*, undergoes plastic surgery to look like Dora, and therefore remarry her ex-husband in her stead.

The novel's opening revels in the establishment of informing but ultimately unsustainable binaries:

> Good morning! Let me introduce myself. My name is Dora Chance. Welcome to the wrong side of the tracks.
>
> Put it another way. If you're from the States, think of Manhattan. Then think of Brooklyn. See what I mean? Or, for a Parisian, it might be a question of *rive gauche, rive droite*. With London, it's the North and South divide. Me and Nora, that's my sister, we've always lived on the left-hand side, the side the tourist rarely sees, the *bastard* side of Old Father Thames. (Carter, 1992: 1)

The city of London, topographical centre of *Wise Children* not least because it is the Chance twins' birthplace and home, is divided into North and South by the geographical boundary of the river. As a result, all kinds of class assumptions are attached to a person's provenance. As Dora says, the twins derive from what has long been regarded as the poor sister (note the gender) of the richer North: the place the tourists never visit, 'the *bastard* side' of the Thames. There are contributing historical factors to the North–South divide, which serves in the novel as a metonym for the wider North–South divide within English culture (I am deliberately using the adjective 'English' here, since it seems to me that England is Carter's focus).

In the sixteenth and seventeenth centuries, when London began to emerge as a city with genuine force, defining itself as an urban site with a particular political and civic identity (the display of the Lord Mayor's Shows and the appointment of a city Recorder were manifestations of this), the area that constituted the city proper was the area north of the Thames, within the city walls. Today, this is often referred to as the 'Square Mile', the established business district of the capital. The area to the south of the river, while notionally under city control, was outside the full jurisdiction of the London authorities and, as a result, became a harbour for criminals, prostitutes, and illegal or illicit operations. This was known as the 'Liberties'. The commercial theatres of London, which followed the building of the Theater in 1576, clustered in this locale due to the freedom from strict building regulations which were in operation in the city. The Globe, the Hope, the Rose and the Swan, all theatres for which Shakespeare wrote, established themselves on the south side of the river, in Southwark, on Bankside (Mullaney, 1988). Carter is clearly attracted by the Bard's South London connections, and by the early modern theatre's association with the illicit or illegitimate.[5] It is part of the joke that Nora and Dora reside at 49 Bard Road, Brixton, an observation that in part parodies the tendency of late-twentieth-century British housing developments to name streets after the canonical greats of English literature ('Wordsworth Way', 'Coleridge Close', and so on).[6] There is also the embedded recognition that the 'bastard side of the ... Thames' was the Bard's provenance. In this way, too, Carter claims Shakespeare for popular culture; Nora and Dora's life as travelling players in vaudeville and on music hall stages is likened to the popular open-air amphitheatres and companies of Bankside which staged *Hamlet*, *Romeo and Juliet* and *As You Like It*.

Wise Children both establishes the North–South divide as denoting the legitimate and illegitimate, and then indicates its disintegration:

> Once upon a time, you could make a crude distinction, thus: the rich lived amidst pleasant verdure in the North speedily whisked to exclusive shopping by abundant public transport while the poor eked out miserable existences in the South in circumstances of urban deprivation condemned to wait for hours at windswept bus-stops while sounds of marital violence, breaking glass and drunken song echoed around and it was cold and dark and smelled of fish and chips. But you can't trust things to stay the same. There's been a diaspora of the affluent, they jumped into their diesel Saabs and dispersed throughout the city. You'd never believe the price of a house round here, these days. (1)

The passage quoted above commences with the fairytale rhetorical construction 'Once upon a time', which may serve to inform us that binary distinctions are only ever helpful thinking tools, and cannot be sustained in reality. Social problems such as marital violence and drunkenness are scarcely contained by geography. Legitimate and illegitimate, north and south, male and female, British and Other, are all binaries placed under pressure in this novel, as is the reputation of Shakespeare.

Dora and Nora's illegitimate status aligns them with the theatrical type of the bastard. Alison Findlay has indicated that there was an increased concern about bastardy in the early modern period and that the resultant social anxiety can be registered in the preoccupations of its drama: the subject features in nearly a hundred extant plays from the period (Findlay, 1994: 5). Of specifically Shakespearean bastards, a list which includes Don John in *Much Ado About Nothing* and 'the Bastard' in *King John*, one of the most infamous is Edmund from *King Lear*. His Act 1 Scene 2 soliloquy, invariably delivered from a downstage position and with the actor dressed in the black garb of the malcontent (a related stage type), has become almost an essentialist expression of the bastard's theatrical role:

> Thou, nature, art my goddess; to thy law
> My services are bound. Wherefore should I
> Stand in the plague of custom, and permit
> The curiosity of nations to deprive me,
> For that I am some twelve or fourteen moonshines

Lag of a brother? Why bastard? wherefore base?
When my dimensions are as well compact,
My mind as generous and my shape as true,
As honest madam's issue? Why brand they us
With base? with baseness? bastardy? base, base?
                              (1.2.1–10; conflated text)

The bastard is a challenger of conventions (in Edmund's case, primogeniture) and a figure who places the audience in a complex position of intimacy with his or her machinations.[7]

Dora shares none of Edmund's scheming villainy, though in her first-person narrative intimacy with her readers we may find a novelistic parallel to the downstage delivery of a soliloquy (Peach, 1998: 152). However, her bastard status, and in particular her father Melchior's ongoing refusal to accord his out-of-wedlock daughters anything more than a secondary role compared to his 'official' offspring, clearly dominates Dora's troubled sense of self throughout the novel.[8]

A series of defining events in Dora's life, recalled in her memoir-like narrative, involve encounters with her father – or, at least, the idea of her father. Melchior as patriarch is an emblem of a series of alternative values to those embodied by the twins. This is expressed in their antithetical career trajectories. While the Chance sisters sojourn in music halls and pantomime, their generic domain undoubtedly that of comedy, the 'official' Hazards are connected throughout to mainstream, 'legitimate' theatre.

If Dora's narrative consciously eschews the tragic tone:

Sad. Nothing more than sad. Let's not call it a tragedy; a broken heart is never a tragedy. Only untimely death is a tragedy. And war, which, before we knew it, would be upon us; replace the comic mask with the one whose mouth turns down and close the theatre, because I refuse point-blank to play in tragedy. (153–4)

Melchior's career is patterned by his performances in the Shakespearean tragedies, from *Macbeth* to *King Lear*: 'Tragedy, eternally more class than comedy' (58).[9] Clare Hanson has argued that the comic genre undoubtedly represents the world of femininity and endurance in the novel, while the tragic embodies the masculine and warrior ethic, but the tragic–comic binary cannot hold either (1997: 68). The iconic crown which Melchior's own father, Ranulph, wore as Lear, and which is carried in talismanic fashion

out of the flames of the Twelfth Night party, a fire which destroys
the Hazard family's sub-Elizabethan kitsch manor house, proves,
like the house, to be a fake, constructed of paper. Ironically,
Melchior's greatest success in a Shakespearean production is when
he performs alongside his illegitimate daughters in the musical
revue *What You Will* (Carter punctuates the revue's title differently across a dozen or so references, enacting the carnivalesque
refusal of this performance to be categorised or epistemologically
defined).

If tragedy and comedy cannot hold, then what remains is a
hybrid form, the mongrel form of 'tragicomedy' that Sir Philip
Sidney was so set against in Shakespeare's day (Sidney, 1960). As
Kate Chedgzoy has shown, *Hamlet* is one of the major shaping
texts of *Wise Children*. Most significantly, Tiffany's sub-Ophelia
tragedy is rewritten with a happy ending. The pregnant Tiffany
does not drown herself but, instead, reappears in the novel's own
fifth act (like Trapido's *Juggling*, Carter's novel is self-consciously
structured in five parts with an epilogue, and even includes a
dramatis personae) (Chedgzoy, 1994). Of the comedies, *Dream* (as
we shall see later) was as important to *Wise Children* as it had been
to Carter throughout her career. But in truth, the novel finds its
real analogue neither in comedy nor in tragedy but in the hybrid
form of the late romances (classified in Shakespeare's time as comedies, but with their own particular brand of miracle and magic):
in particular in *Pericles* (which, alongside *Hamlet*, contributes to
the incestuous subtexts of the family relations related in the novel),
The Tempest and *The Winter's Tale*.

All of these plays depict in some fashion the relationship between fathers and daughters – the driving force, as we have identified it, of Dora's narrative in *Wise Children*. Pericles and Marina
are, like those aforementioned twins of earlier Shakespearean plays,
parted by shipwreck (a destiny embedded in Marina's nomenclature) but reunited in Act 5. Prospero and Miranda's solipsistic
relationship is part of the complex web of family relations depicted
in *The Tempest*, and in *The Winter's Tale* we have a precursor of
Tiffany, an onstage rejected pregnant woman (Hermione) whose
seeming tragedy is averted miraculously in the statue scene of Act
5. Her supposed 'bastard' daughter Perdita is reunited with her
parents by the close (Neely, 1999).

All these playtexts are part of the creative maelstrom which constitutes Carter's burlesque novel. At the beginning of the narrative, Dora reflects on the miniature tempest that is whipping up the litter in the London streets:

> There goes the wind, again. Crash. Over goes the dustbin, all the trash spills out ... empty cat-food cans, cornflakes packets, laddered tights, tea leaves ... What a wind! Whooping and banging all along the street, the kind of wind that blows everything topsy-turvy. (3)

This will be the same whirlwind that blows Uncle Peregrine back into everyone's lives on his hundredth birthday, an event shared with his twin, Melchior. (Theirs is another case of sameness and difference: Perry and Melchior might have invented the phrase 'chalk and cheese'.)

Perry returns carrying another of the novel's numerous sets of twins. Tristram, the recalcitrant father of Tiffany's child, is the son of Melchior and his third wife. He is also the incestuous lover of his aunt Saskia. It is Tristram's twin, Gareth, a priest in South America, who, according to Perry (who has been there on an exploration – remarkable enough for a supposed centenarian), has fathered these twins. The babies are found in Perry's jacket pockets (fittingly enough for this novel of binaries: one in the left-hand pocket, one in the right-hand pocket). What differentiates them from those twins that have gone before is that they are, like Viola and Sebastian, or even Hamnet and Judith, one of either sex. In them rests a sense of balance, and an optimism for the future.

Birth is a potent force in *Wise Children* – as, indeed, is rebirth. Nora, who has always yearned for a child, is rejuvenated by the opportunity for motherhood at seventy-five provided by Gareth's twins. Dora's lack of excitement continues to demarcate the twins even at the end of the novel. Some have linked this optimism to Carter's own failing health when she was writing *Wise Children*, but an obvious literary source for these motifs of rebirth and reconciliation exists in the late Shakespearean 'family romances'.[10]

Family affairs: patriarchs and absent mothers

The nature and structure of the Shakespearean family have been the focus of considerable critical discussion. Coppélia Kahn has stressed the patriarchal conception of the early modern family, and indicated how this is reflected in the *dramatis personae* of plays such as *Lear*, where the queen, mother to Goneril, Regan and Cordelia, is conspicuously omitted. That omission is deliberate to the extent that Shakespeare reduces an opening and lengthy lament on her death to a single mention in his adaptation of his source-text, *The True Chronicle History of King Leir* (Kahn, 1986: 33–49). Absent mothers 'populate' the Shakespearean canon: mothers are 'lost' in plays from *The Comedy of Errors* through to *Pericles* and *The Winter's Tale*; comic heroines such as Rosalind and Viola do not even speak of theirs; and Miranda's father Prospero, like Lear, tries to be both parents in his daughter's mind (like Lear's wife, in *The Tempest* Prospero's is mentioned only once (Orgel, 1986: 50)[11]).

Unsurprisingly, perhaps, absent mothers have proved to exert a peculiar fascination in women's rewritings of Shakespeare, and Carter is no exception. Critics, such as Nicole Ward Jouve and Lorna Sage, have argued that the absent mother is a defining feature of Carter's *œuvre*: 'mother is a missing person' (Sage, 1994a: 6; Jouve, 1994). This has origins other than purely Shakespearean – absent or surrogate mothers are a common motif of fairytale and folklore (it is perhaps no coincidence that Shakespeare's sources for plays like *Lear* were folkloric) – and Sage has suggested that Carter's own political biography may be telling in this respect, in that a defining feature of feminism was the rejection of maternal and traditional values by radical daughters (1994a: 6–7).

Carter is, however, clearly struck by the poignant figure of the absent mother in Shakespeare: 'has it ever occurred to you to spare a passing thought to the character of the deceased *Mrs* Lear? Didn't it ever occur to you that Cordelia might have taken after her mother while the other girls ...' (224–5). The effect of this absence in the plays, as Stephen Orgel has outlined in a discussion of *The Tempest*, is to push the maternal presence into other channels, ghostly or otherwise:

> The absent presence of the wife and mother ... constitutes a space that is filled by Prospero's creation of surrogates and a ghostly family: the witch Sycorax and her monster child Caliban ... the good child/wife Miranda, the obedient Ariel, the violently libidinised Ferdinand. The space is filled, too, by the whole structure of wifely allusion and reference: widow Dido, model at once of heroic fidelity to a murdered

husband and the destructive potential of erotic passion; the witch Medea, murderess and filicide; three exemplary goddesses ...; and Alonso's daughter Claribel, unwillingly married off to the ruler of the modern Carthage and thereby lost to her father forever. (1986: 51)[12]

All these figures, these alternative mothers, have been of interest to female appropriators: we will explore reclamations of Sycorax and Claribel, as well as Miranda, in later chapters focusing specifically on novelistic adaptations of *The Tempest*. These figures are not Carter's concern *per se*, but surrogate matriarchs certainly are – from Lizzie in *Nights at the Circus* and Aunt Titania in 'Overture and Incidental Music in *A Midsummer Night's Dream*' through, perhaps most importantly, to Grandma Chance in *Wise Children*. She constitutes Carter's twentieth-century version of the fairy godmother, and embodies the power of a family founded on genuine affection as opposed to biological connection: '"Family," I say. Grandma invented this family. She put it together out of whatever came to hand – a stray pair of orphaned babes, a ragamuffin in a flat cap. She created it by sheer force of personality' (35). Peregrine plants the suspicion at the close of the novel that Grandma Chance may have been the twins' biological mother all along – 'has it ever occurred to you that your mother might not be your mother?' (222) – but Dora seems to dismiss this further twist to her life-story. Perry's following statement sums up the guiding spirit of the novel: 'Mother is as mother does' (223).

Biological mothers are mentioned in *Wise Children*, most significantly Melchior's actor-mother Estella, but often in the context of failure: Estella's carnivalesque promiscuity (a fact which links her to the Falstaffian Peregrine) contributes to her death when the jealous Ranulph (himself a cheap reworking of parts he has played such as Lear, Othello and Leontes) shoots himself, Estella, and her lover Cassius Booth while on tour. The implication of this is that Melchior's own legitimacy as Ranulph's son is also in doubt. Elsewhere in *Wise Children*, Saskia and Imogen reject their mother in violent fashion, pushing Lady Atalanta downstairs and disabling her for life; and Lady Margarine, Melchior's third wife, has an obsession with her son Tristram that verges on a Gertrude-like intensity.

The one positive representation of the matrilineal in the novel must be the pregnant Tiffany. A resoundingly corporeal presence in the midst of Tristram's hideously tacky television game show,

'Lashings of Lolly', she paraphrases Ophelia's desire to redeliver remembrances to Hamlet. Casting aside her symbolic daffodils, she declares:

> 'Off with it! You only lent it to me! Nothing was mine, not ever!'
>   And [she] stripped off her Number 69 shirt, threw it to the floor and trampled on it. It was a shock to see her breasts under the cruel lights – long, heavy breasts, with big dark nipples, real breasts, not like the ones she'd shown off like borrowed finery to the glamour lenses. This was flesh, you could see that it would bleed, you could see how it fed babies. (46)[13]

Carter saves Tiffany from Ophelia's suicidal fate, reversing what Adelman has called the 'end-stopped genre of tragedy' (1994: 73).[14] Maybe in that final act the absent mother is returned to the novel.

The matrilineal in its affective role seems perhaps most dominant in the form of Nora and Dora's adoption of Gareth's illegitimate babies. Noticeably, though, the South American mother of these twins goes unlamented: 'who she was or where they both were do not belong to the world of comedy. Perry told us, of course, because we were family, but I don't propose to tell *you*, not now' (227). But the absence of mothers also draws attention in Shakespearean drama to the presence of fathers – Duke Senior, Lear, Prospero – and many of these patriarchs prove as flawed as Carter's biological matriarchs. Lear unreasonably asks his daughters to be mothers: to be the care and nursery of his old age, and to love him all. Prospero is a control freak who manipulates Miranda and her suitor to answer his dynastic ends as much as he does the 'subjects' of 'his' island such as Caliban and Ariel. In the dramatic soliloquy 'Ye elves of hills, brooks, standing lakes and groves' (5.1.33–57) – a direct appropriation of a speech early modern audiences would have known as one of Medea's, a figure elsewhere in the play more closely allied to the absent Sycorax, witch-mother to Caliban ('This island's mine, by Sycorax my mother' (1.2.334)) – Prospero seems to draw into himself Sycorax's (and Medea's) potential for black magic alongside his more countenanced white form of the art. In turn, the feminine, maternal aspects of his psyche are indicated. Of course, in so far as at the end of the soliloquy he determines to drown his book, this absorption of the feminine and the Other by Prospero has been seen as a self-cancelling or containing gesture; but the speech and its associations have served to nuance the paternalistic note sounded by his belated acknowledgement of what he has created in Caliban: the potential for rebellion and conspiracy: 'This thing of darkness I acknowledge mine' (5.1.278–9). In the strict terms of the play, Prospero has never met Sycorax, although there are many parallels between them, not least in terms of magical practice and banishment. By means of this speech, however, Prospero almost claims to be Caliban's father, acknowledging a shared parenthood with Sycorax. This reinterprets Caliban's sexual desire for Miranda, the root cause of his punishment by Prospero at the start of the play, as incestuous.

Incest (along with rape) has been identified as a significant subtext to a number of Shakespeare plays, including *Lear* and *The Tempest*, as well as being an overt theme in *Hamlet* and *Pericles*. Carter takes the tragic impetus of those themes in Shakespeare, and, as with her rewriting of the fifth acts of tragic drama, finds potential comedy in the inversion and multiplication of the incest taboo. Tristram's sexual liaison with his aunt Saskia and Peregrine's affair with his twin brother's wife (a recognition of what Adelman has described as the 'legacy of *Hamlet* (1994: 193)) are simply the most obvious examples. The tendency of Hazard patriarch-actors to marry the Cordelias from their productions of *Lear* (Melchior does so in direct imitation of his parents, Ranulph and Estella) can be read in quasi-incestuous terms, and Lady Margarine's 'unnatural' obsession with Tristram is a further comic reworking, as is the revelation in the closing pages of the novel that Peregrine may have seduced a thirteen-year-old Dora (221).

While Dora appears to repeat this incestuous act with her uncle some sixty years later in a bedroom above the ballroom where the Hazard/Chance clans are gathered, Nora's position is equally significant. She was 'Sitting on our dad's knee, like a good daughter ought to on her old man's birthday' (221). Carter is deeply aware (as is Dora) of the sexually-charged nature of the image, as well as its comedy (Nora is seventy-five and Melchior is a hundred, after all). In some respects Dora's entire narrative has been charged with a quasi-sexual desire for her father. Excited encounters with him (often hedged around with sexual encounters with others – not least the bedroom romp with the waiter that inadvertently causes the Twelfth Night fire) are the defining features of this daughter's life; unlike Cordelia's or Desdemona's situation, there is never a husband or 'divided duty' here.

The potency (literal and symbolic) of Melchior Hazard is persistently questioned by the operations of the narrative. He is implicitly linked to the castrated grandfather clock that stands in 49 Bard Road. In a wonderful version of castration, Grandmother merely has to touch the clock and its balls drop off, and Dora acknowledges that the hopes and desires she has invested in her father may well be equally vulnerable:

> 'Nora ... don't you think our father looked two-dimensional, tonight?'...
>
> 'Too kind, too handsome, too repentant. After all those years without a word... he had an imitation look, even when he was crying, especially when he was crying, like one of those great, big, papier-mâché heads they have in the Notting Hill parade, larger than life, but not lifelike.
>
> Nora sunk in thought for a hundred yards.
>
> 'D'you know, I sometimes wonder if we haven't been making him up all along ... If he isn't just a collection of our hopes and dreams and wishful thinking in the afternoons. Something to set our lives by, like the old clock in the hall, which is real enough, in itself, but which we've got to wind up to make it go. (230)

The empowerment of the female sex which this passage constitutes scarcely needs highlighting. Maternity is sure, while paternity is anything but. Carter is well aware, in invoking this theme, of yet another novelistic appropriation of Shakespeare, and *Hamlet* in particular: James Joyce's *Ulysses*. The Chance twins' names are highly un-Shakespearean in this Shakespeare-drenched novel: 'Nora' may well be a direct nod to Joyce's own wife, Nora Barnacle. Webb has suggested that Dora is named for one of Freud's famous psychoanalytical case studies: Freud's Dora had incestuous desire for her father, which she transferred to a string of father substitutes, and in some respects Dora's narrative is like Freud's Dora's spilling out of family secrets, although in this instance the reader displaces Freud as receiving therapist or auditor (Webb, 1994: 294).[15]

The wider sub-Freudian question Dora and Nora debate in relation to the theme of family undermines even the certainty of maternity, however. Considering the South American babies, Nora reflects: 'Think about it ... We can tell these little darlings here whatever we like about their mum and dad if Perry doesn't find them but whatever we tell them, they'll make up their own romance out of it' (230). Dora's response is telling: 'thinking of the twins put me in mind of something more pressing than family romances' (230). Her concern is their own advanced age for the task of parenting, but she alludes directly to the Freudian family romance in expressing this.[16]

The Hazard family in the novel is described as the Royal Family of theatre, and Carter is not averse to a few comic comparisons of their dysfunctional family soap opera with that of the real-life House of Windsor. In the end, however, it is theatricality that is at the heart of her engagement with both Shakespeare and the concept of family. Biological loyalties prove as much a matter of performance as anything in this world theatre.

Dreamworks: theatre, film and *A Midsummer Night's Dream*

The 'legacy' of *Hamlet* – with its dysfunctional families, incestuous, Oedipal subtexts, and its own cross-dressing stage history – is clearly writ large on the narrative of *Wise Children*. Chedgzoy has identified the role of Hamlet as one with a long history of female performances, and Carter pays homage to this legacy of the feminised prince in her account of Estella (1994: 256).[17] But another text acts as a shaping signifier in *Wise Children* – appositely so in view of Carter's interest in comic inversion and subversion: *A Midsummer Night's Dream*. Carter stressed her special penchant for the play: 'I like ... *Dream* almost beyond reason, because it's beautiful and funny and camp – and glamorous, and cynical' (Sage, 1994a: 56).

Dream appears in *Wise Children* in several different guises, reflecting the novel's wider interest in a variety of different media: from theatre and music hall, to film and television. In true Shakespearean fashion, the novel has its own play-within-a-play: the Hollywood film spectacular version of *Dream* that Melchior and his family troop off to California to make in the 1930s. Several critics, including Roger Apfelbaum, have noted the similarity between this extravagant (and, in retrospect, highly kitsch) production and a genuine Hollywood cinematic interpretation of the play: Max Reinhardt and William Dieterle's 1935 film for Warner Brothers, starring James Cagney (as Bottom) and Mickey Rooney (as Puck) (Apfelbaum, 1998: 183–93; Hackett, 1997, 64–6). Gary Williams has described the sheer bravura of Reinhardt/ Dieterle's *mise en scène* for their Shakespeare film, which was made in the midst of the Great Depression, and as Nazi ideology began to gain hold in Germany, as the ultimate form of escapism (1997: 179). At a running time of 140 minutes, this was one of the first full-length movie versions of Shakespeare with sound. It recast many of the stars from Reinhardt's 1934 Hollywood Bowl production of the play:

> The film was seen by some critics in 1935 as a throwback to nineteenth-century romantic stage traditions for the play. The early motion pictures were the natural offspring of the nineteenth-century pictorial stage and its star system. Hollywood built its empire on lavish, illusionistic spectaculars and attractive personalities. (Williams, 1997: 179)

The visual was certainly prioritised in the Reinhardt/Dieterle film. There were lavish ballet sequences (filmed to complement the movie's Mendelssohn soundtrack, a further gesture towards nineteenth-century conventions of staging the play), and the Athenian forest was created by means of 'sixty-seven truckloads of trees and shrubbery, [which] included a transplanted redwood tree, a pond and a stream, all arranged over sixty-six thousand square feet' (Williams, 1997: 179). It is this oddly neo-realistic approach to filming Shakespeare's play of dreams, magic and illusion that Carter so shamelessly parodies in the Hollywood sequences of *Wise Children*:

> The wood near Athens covered an entire stage and was so thickly art-directed it came up all black in the rushes, couldn't see a thing, so they sprayed it in parts with silver paint to lighten it up ... What I missed most was illusion. That wood near Athens was too, too solid for me. Peregrine, who specialised in magic tricks, loved it just because it was so concrete ... But there wasn't the merest whiff about of the kind of magic that comes when the theatre darkens, the bottom of the curtain glows, the punters settle down, you take a deep breath ... none of the person-to-person magic we put together with spit and glue and will-power. This wood, this entire dream, in fact, was custom-made and hand-built, it left nothing to the imagination. (124–5)

A film set, in a conscious allusion to *Hamlet*, appears just 'too solid'. If we read this passage in isolation, it would be easy to assume that Carter valued theatre over and above the cinema as a medium. In truth, film was a form which impacted upon her writing throughout her career, from *The Passion of New Eve* onwards. Laura Mulvey has explored this fascination, seeing in it a fundamental interest in the powers of transformation: 'Transformations and metamorphoses recur so frequently in Angela Carter's writing that her books seem to be pervaded by this magic cinematic attribute even when the cinema itself is not present on the page' (1994: 230). There is, of course, the case to be made that these metamorphoses are, on occasion, as much Shakespearean and Ovidian as they are cinematic (it is no coincidence that *Dream* is one of Shakespeare's most Ovidian-influenced texts), but Mulvey is right to note that Carter's relationship with cinema was a nuanced one. Carter recounted her childhood experiences of the form: 'It seemed to me, when I first started going to the cinema intensively in the late 50s, that Hollywood had colonised the imagination of the entire world and was turning us all into Americans. I resented it, it fascinated me' (Mulvey, 1994: 232). The paradox inherent in her response to film and its relation to US cultural domination feeds into the complicated portrayal of the form in *Wise Children*. Carter had a productive liaison with cinema, seeing her short story 'The Company of Wolves' successfully adapted for the big screen. Perhaps it is Hollywood in particular that is the focus of her scorn (or pastiche) here. There is a destructive force at work in Hollywood: Genghis Khan, with his tyranny and his casting-couch mentality, is just one embodiment of this, and Gorgeous George's appallingly unfunny performance as Bottom represents a comparable British decline of fortunes in the face of advancing capitalism.

Carter's novel seems, ironically, to gain in relevance in the twenty-first century when big-bucks, big-name Shakespeare films are undoubtedly the order of the day. Yet there is a value and a magic intrinsic to film to which Carter is not immune: early on in *Wise Children*, Nora and Dora are contacted by a doctoral student of Film Studies who wishes to interview them about the Hollywood *Dream*. Dora is struck by the longevity of the piece, the survival of that particular part of their lengthy careers. From this perspective, the ephemerality of theatre seems a downside:

It took me donkey's till I saw the point but saw the point I did, eventually, though not until the other day, when we were watching *The
Dream* again in Notting Hill, that time, couple of batty old tarts with
their eyes glued on their own ghosts. *Then* I understood the thing I'd
never grasped back in those days, when I was young, before I lived in
history. When I was young, I'd wanted to be ephemeral, I'd wanted the
moment, to live in just the glorious moment, the rush of blood, the
applause. Pluck the day. Eat the peach. Tomorrow never comes. But,
oh yes, tomorrow *does* come all right, and when it comes it lasts a
bloody long time, I can tell you. But if you've put your past on celluloid, it keeps. You've stored it away, like jam, for winter. That kid came
up and asked for our autographs. It made our day. I could have wished
we'd done more pictures. (125)

This passage is another rich example of Carter's deeply intertextual
and punning narrative style: Dora's Cockney rhyming slang
'donkey's ears/years', her means of marking time, is also a reference to Bottom's metamorphosis in the play; 'Eat the peach'
alludes to T. S. Eliot's dramatic monologue 'The Love Song of J.
Alfred Prufrock' – a monologue which features a speaker who, like
Dora, is looking back on the missed opportunities of his life, but
one which also appropriates Shakespeare in subtle and elusive
ways.[18] The element of the spectral or the ghostly in the celluloid
vision should be noted. Watching an old movie, one sees a spectral
image of oneself. Shakespeare and early modern drama had their
own interests in ghosts, but there is a case to be made here that
Carter's precise understanding of the spectral is a postmodern,
post-Freudian and post-cinematic one. In noting her links to
Shakespeare, as we are here, it would be wrong to deny those
elements that also differentiate her, situating her within her own
time and historicity.
    In contrast to film, Carter recorded her objections to TV: 'Tele-
vision has extraordinary limitations as a medium for the presenta-
tion of imaginative drama of any kind. It has an inbuilt ability to
cut people down to size, to reduce them to gesticulating heads or,
in long shot, to friezes of capering dwarfs' (Mulvey, 1994: 242).
Wise Children enacts these views in the damning version of the
television game show that is Tristram's capitalistic 'Lashings of
Lolly'. The fact that Melchior is prepared to appear on this
travesty (and, indeed, in several commercials) tarnishes the high
cultural armour he has established around his career, and raises

for the reader the question of whether Dora and Nora aren't indeed better arbiters of taste. In a short story published in *American Ghosts and Old World Wonders*, Carter described TV as a 'secular' medium (1993: 85).[19] The magical or quasi-religious power of performance is reserved for theatre and celluloid in her work, albeit in sharply differentiated manifestations.

Carter had explored the rich complexities, both sexual and illusionistic, of *Dream* in that earlier short story 'Overture and Incidental Music for *A Midsummer Night's Dream*'. Linden Peach discusses the significance of the title:

> It is important to appreciate the full implications of the relationship between the two texts which Carter encourages us to question by calling her story an 'overture and incidental music.' An 'overture' is normally an introduction, which reverses the chronological relationship between the two texts, and does not have to have a close relationship in style to the main piece of music. Carter is really saying that *A Midsummer Night's Dream* is predicated on an absence. (1998: 146)

While these observations are helpful, they fail to notice the specific allusion in Carter's title to Mendelssohn's music for *Dream*, which became virtually standard in nineteenth- and early-twentieth-century adaptations of the play in the theatre, in ballet and on film. For Carter, Mendelssohn's music represents the harnessing of Shakespeare to a false Victorian ideal:

> Such is the English wood in which we see the familiar fairies, the blundering fiancés, the rude mechanicals. This is the true Shakespearian wood – but it is not the wood of Shakespeare's time, which did not know itself to be Shakespearian, and therefore felt no need to keep up appearances. No. The wood we have just described is that of nineteenth-century nostalgia, which disinfected the wood, cleansing it of the grave, hideous and elemental beings with which the superstition of an earlier age had filled it. Or, rather, denaturing, castrating these beings until they came to look just as they do in those photographs of fairy folk that so enraptured Conan Doyle. It is Mendelssohn's wood. (Carter, 1985: 69)[20]

'Overture and Incidental Music' is narrated by the Golden Herm, Carter's subversive version of another of Shakespeare's famous unseen or absent characters, the Indian Boy over whom

Oberon and Titania quarrel. The boy became a regular stage presence in the age of the British Empire, and was also an exotic screen focus in Reinhardt/Dieterle's 1935 film (Williams, 1997).[21] In Carter's hands, she or he becomes a medium for the exploration of sexual ambivalence: '"Boy" again, see; which isn't the half of it. Misinformation. The patriarchal version. No king had nothing to do with it; it was all between my mother and my auntie, wasn't it?' (Carter, 1985: 66).

Carter made a career out of questioning 'The patriarchal version', as Herm terms it, and not just of Shakespeare. Sage observes of *Black Venus*: 'she is mischievously engaged in supplementing the canon – writing *round the edges* of the known', noting how she 'resurrects ... materials that didn't quite make it into the record, and voices we didn't get to hear. She inserts apocryphal episodes into various ready-made traditions ' (1994a: 44). It is a method which, as we shall see, is typical of the women writers this book concerns itself with: writers such as Carter, Marina Warner, Jane Smiley and Gloria Naylor are concerned with absent mothers, daughters, and sisters in Shakespeare; with reclaiming their voices, and rewriting the patriarchal versions of the playtexts as they stand. One of the interesting differences between them, however, may lie in their attitudes towards Shakespeare. For Smiley, the relationship, at least so far as *King Lear* is concerned, is not a fond one: she writes against Shakespeare; and Naylor, from her African-American female position, may argue for something similar in terms of her acts of resistance and revision. For Carter, however, there appears to be something festive, celebratory even, in her reclamations: the fact that she 'resurrects' rather than revises the source-texts would suggest that the values she accords to them – of sexual diversity, of fantastic possibility, of liberatory potential for low culture and the working classes – are elements she feels to be inherent within the texts themselves. For Carter, Shakespeare was a metonym for theatre, and theatre was something she accorded a deep value to, in life as in art.

If anything is pastiched in *Wise Children*, it is not Shakespearean drama, or even the early modern period with its boy-actors and 'double-drag', but, rather, the cultural construct of 'Shakespeare' in which subsequent ages have participated. When Melchior takes his family to Hollywood to assist in his venture into movie-making, he ensures that the twins carry with them a casket of earth from Shakespeare's birthplace:

> Look at the headline: 'New York welcomes Shakespeare treasure.' Sub-head: 'Twins bear precious gift.' See that thing in Nora's arms, that looks like a decapitated doll? You'll never believe it. It was a pot, a sort of jar, about the size of the ones they use for ashes in the crematoria, and it was hollow inside and in the shape of a bust of, that's right, William Shakespeare; our father had had it specially made, in Stoke-on-Trent, and the bald patch lifted off, that was the lid. (112–13)

Readers are reminded of the sacred ceremonies and the ritualising of theatre that was indulged in at the memorial service for the Shakespearean actor and filmmaker Sir Laurence Olivier in the UK in 1989 (and Melchior clearly has elements of Olivier in his character, along with aspects of Orson Welles and other eminent Shakespeareans of stage and screen). In Westminster Abbey, a procession of actors carried talismanic stage properties, crowns, laurel wreaths, and scripts, in a manner akin to religious relics, behind Olivier's coffin, which was adorned with a crown woven of flowers directly mentioned in Shakespeare's plays (Garber, 1993: 32–4). Here, though, this reverence is rendered grotesque and carnival-esque. Melchior's intentions are little different in their misplaced idolatry to the shrine Nora and Dora's Mexican maid establishes around the jar in their 'Forest of Arden' motel. Carter brilliantly undermines Melchior's grandiose dreams when the earth that is eventually scattered on the film set of *Dream* proves not to be the 'authentic' Stratford-upon-Avon variety (which has been ignomini-ously used by Daisy Duck's cat as a litter tray) but fakery from the motel. The casket of earth is also a signifier of the very differ-ent genre of Gothic fiction: Shakespeare is rendered one of the 'undead' just as much as Dracula in Bram Stoker's classic text. This is another deliberately comic version of the ghostly and the spectral that reduces 'Shakespeare as commodity' to a false icon, fit only for cats to pee on. The empty nature of such idolatry is brilliantly exposed, but this does not necessarily mean that Carter did not value the Shakespearean playtexts which, in her account, have little to do with such egotistical and nationalistic exercises as Melchior's transportation of Old World values to the New.

The carnivalesque, magic realism, postcolonialism,
postmodernism and the unreliable narrator:
Carter's complex *bricolage*

I want to close this chapter by examining the specific narrative
strategies deployed by Carter in her novel, since they serve to
open up a series of points of comparison and connection for the
narrative techniques of writers and appropriators studied throughout this book. Sage has written of *Wise Children*: 'When [Carter]
made parenthood her theme, it was parenthood literary, literal and
lateral, with twins as mirrors to each other, illegitimate histories,
left-handed genealogies, a whole carnival of the dispossessed' (Sage,
1994a: 54).[22] *Wise Children* is regularly described as a 'carnivalesque' novel; Carter's writing certainly adheres to the carnivalised
style that Bakhtin identified (Dentith, 1995). Peach has suggested,
however, that 'the source of the carnivalesque element in *Nights at
the Circus* and *Wise Children* was undoubtedly Shakespeare rather
than Bakhtin' (1998: 145).

The novel shapes itself around various festive occasions which
offer a comparable social and communal potential to Shakespearean
fifth acts, when a host of often disparate characters are brought
into collision on the stage. But these events also model themselves
upon the ritual bases of Shakespearean comedy, from May Day
ceremonies to Twelfth Night rituals of temporarily inverting the
household hierarchy. We open and close on a joint birthday –
Dora's and Nora's, and Melchior's and Peregrine's – shared,
appositely enough, with Shakespeare himself: 23 April. As Webb
has noted, the events of the novel occur in a single day, inasmuch
as they occur in Dora's recall of them on her birthday. Webb says
that this is like 'all the best modern fiction' (1994: 280), and Joyce's
Ulysses is clearly an important referent here once again; but so,
too, is the dramatic genre which Carter is so explicitly invoking
and appropriating in the course of *Wise Children*. Events occurring
in a single day observes one of the central Aristotelian dramatic
unities. April 23 is also St George's Day, effortlessly linking notions
of the English patron saint with the English patron playwright.
Carter is typically denigrating of such patriotism; the decline of
Gorgeous George, on whose tattooed body the British Empire is
mapped and marked, serves as a metonym for the decline of British

Imperialism *per se*. The same impulse that drove Ranulph Hazard to take Shakespeare to the colonies, much as zealous missionaries took Christianity, is swallowed up in the voracious capitalist and cultural appetite of Hollywood and US domination at the heart of the novel.

Elsewhere we have May Day birthdays and Twelfth Night parties. Saskia and Imogen are 'darling buds of May'. The phrase is from Sonnet 18: 'Rough winds do shake the darling buds of May' (l. 3), but would have been familiar to British readers in 1992, when the novel was first published, as the title of a popular television series, itself an adaptation of H.E. Bates's Larkin family novels. Shakespeare's process of filtration into British culture is a long and winding road, as Carter brilliantly reflects. The multiple wedding in Hollywood, which ends up as a series of complicated disguises and disruptions, is another carnivalesque social gathering in the novel, although the ultimate has to be the fifth-act reunion of all the characters at the close: an event which allows for tempests, treachery, poisonings, incest, births, and rebirths in truly Shakespearean spirit.

We have already described how Peregrine, one of the central figures of carnival (and, indeed, theatre) in the novel, makes his dramatic final entry in the form of a Shakespearean tempest, but he also arrives in a cloud of butterflies:

> In on the wind that came with Perry blew dozens and dozens of butterflies, red ones, yellow ones, brown and amber ones, some most mysteriously violet and black, tiny little green ones, huge flapping marbled blue and khaki ones, swirling around the room, settling on women's bare shoulders, men's bald spots. Nora and I got a couple each in our hair. (207)

Carter's intertextual reference here is not Shakespearean, but – fittingly, since it is from South America that Peregrine and his butterflies have travelled – the Colombian novelist Gabriel García Márquez. Márquez – and, in particular, his novel *One Hundred Years of Solitude* – is often credited as the creator of a genre popularly known as 'magic realism': in *One Hundred Years*, one character's appearance in particular, even when he is merely a ghostly apparition, is always heralded by a cloud of yellow butterflies. The term 'magic realism' was first coined by Franz Roh in

1925 to refer to post-expressionist art. It is now used rather loosely
to categorise any writing with a fantastic element or aspect in the
midst of an otherwise realistic narrative, and has fallen out of
critical favour as a result.[23] For David Lodge, magic realism was
produced by historical and social conditions: writers such as
Márquez, Günter Grass in Germany, or Milan Kundera in the
former Czechoslovakia have 'lived through great historical con-
vulsions and wrenching personal upheavals, which they feel cannot
be adequately represented in a discourse of undisturbed realism'
(Lodge, 1992: 114). Late-twentieth-century feminist writers might
claim a comparable sense of upheaval and change, although Lodge
sees the form in this respect as imported rather than spontane-
ously achieved.

Women writers such as Carter and Trapido (Peter's levitational
capacities in *Juggling* are deployed as part of the comic structure of
that text) frequently use the form in a self-conscious manner which
verges on pastiche. *Wise Children* is happy to allow for the possibility of magic and the fabulous – as indeed was Shakespeare in
plays such as *Dream*, *The Winter's Tale*, and *The Tempest* (perhaps
significantly, some of the most central texts in Carter's novelistic
appropriation of Shakespeare) – but the text also invites readers to
be self-aware about the wish-fulfilment involved in these exercises
of thought. In the novel, Peregrine, along with his mother Estella,
is an embodiment of carnivalesque corporeality; he is compared to
Shakespearean comic characters of feasting and revelry such as
Falstaff and *Twelfth Night*'s Sir Toby Belch, and seems to grow to
giant proportions as the novel proceeds (he is compared at various
points to a 'polar bear' (62) and a block of flats (206)). Peregrine
is also associated with magical properties and the fantastic: not just
those butterflies, but the whole series of appearances and vanishing
acts he carries out during the course of the novel's complicated
events ('here today, gone tomorrow' (19)), his magic tricks, and his
seeming ability to defy age. Peregrine is a Prospero figure, embodying that character's capacity for both magical and theatrical
manipulation of events. Tellingly, when he is offered a walk-on
part as Falstaff in the musical Shakespearean revue that proves
such a hit for the Hazards and Chances, he declines, preferring,
like Prospero, to pull the strings from the wings. When he deserts
the film set in Hollywood, the entire spectacle collapses. The con-

nection Carter makes, through the figure of Perry, between magic
and theatre – the art of illusion – is again central; magic is Shakespearean, because it is inherently theatrical. When Carter does
indulge in magic realism, it is with the metatheatrical frame-
breaking consciousness that has so regularly been accorded to the
Bard's own works.[24]

Linden Peach has persuasively argued that in Carter's hands,
'intertextuality becomes a boldly thematised part of her work', but
so too has the act of writing narrative in itself (1998: 4). Dora
Chance's lively but shifting, and at times deliberately misleading,
memoir of her life provides a fascinating example of the complexities of first-person narration and the concept of the 'unreliable
narrator' (Lodge, 1992). At the start of the novel, Dora – celebrating, as she so eagerly informs us, her seventy-fifth birthday –
appears to be in the attic of 49 Bard Road, sorting through the
mementoes and memories of her life, sifting through photographs
and souvenirs (2). Immediately, alongside the contrast between
photographic or material record and the filing cabinet of the mind,
the issue of selective or failing memory is raised, as is a first-
person fictional narrator's implicitly subjective and personally
biased stance. Carter is invoking the model of oral histories that
became an important part of the academic discipline of History, as
well as of communal and personal records in the late decades of
the twentieth century; yet she also destabilises the validity which
that link would seem to accord to Dora's 'voice'; by the close of
the novel, we seem to have shifted locale to the local pub:

> Hard to swallow, huh?
>   Well, you might have known what you were about to let yourself in
> for when you let Dora Chance in her ratty old fur and poster paint, her
> orange (Persian Melon) toenails sticking out of her snakeskin peep-
> toes, reeking of liquor, accost you in the Coach and Horses and let her
> tell you a tale. (227)

As with Laurence Sterne's eighteenth-century fictional autobiography *Tristram Shandy*, which Sarah Gamble has rightly
identified as another of Carter's crucial intertexts here, Carter
leaves us with at least the possibility that the entire narrative of
Wise Children has been a 'cock and bull story', a drunken fabrication (Gamble, 1997: 172). Certainly, she uses this fact to cast doubt

– as Trapido did in *Juggling* – on the fixity of the happy ending. The fifth-act reconciliations of the novel are humorously modelled on those of Shakespeare's late plays: 'truthfully, these glorious pauses do, sometimes, occur in the discordant but complementary narratives of our lives and if you choose to stop the story there, at such a pause, and refuse to take it any further, then you can call it a happy ending' (227). In retrospect, Dora has been building dramatic pauses of this nature into her narrative from the beginning. Early on in her recounting of Tiffany's part in the story, she used the video remote-control to 'freeze-frame' events.

The resistance of closure which is implicit in Dora's placing of a question mark alongside the happy ending of the narrative, reworking the delicate balance of the juggling act that Trapido saw as the distinctive feature of Shakespearean comedy, is typical of Carter's *œuvre* as a whole. *The Passion of New Eve*'s ending in birth (that is to say, in a metaphor of new beginnings) is repeated here: one example of the resistance to linearity which will be seen to characterise so many of the novels examined in this book.

As Carter's multivalent appropriation of Shakespeare rewrites the tragic genre into a comic, or more accurately tragicomic, mode, so she quite literally offers alternative endings to canonical play-texts at the end of her highly playful novel. Gorgeous George gets the best punchline of his career when he leans over to Saskia and rewrites her personal history in one fell swoop: 'Don't worry, darlin', '*e's* not your father!' (213):

> What if Horatio had whispered that to Hamlet in Act 1, Scene 1? And think what a difference it might have made to Cordelia. On the other hand, those last comedies would darken considerably in tone, don't you think, if Marina and, especially, Perdita weren't really the daughters of… (213)

The 'patriarchal version' is once again being questioned. Dora even permits herself a brief fantasy as to what might have happened if, in the midst of the sexual act, she and Perry really had, quite literally, brought the house down:

> What would have happened if we *had* brought the house down? Wrecked the whole lot, roof blown off, floor caved in, all the people blown out of the blown-out windows … sent it all sky high, destroyed all the terms of every contract, set all the old books on fire, wiped the

slate clean. As if, when the young king meets up again with Jack Falstaff in *Henry IV, Part Two*, he doesn't send him packing but digs him in the ribs, says: 'Have I got a job for you!' (221–2)

In the end, though, this remains at the level of the hypothetical: Carter may toy with the idea of burning all the old books, all the master texts and patriarchal versions, in her re-vision of Prospero's epilogue, but she doesn't. She recognises, like her unreliable narrator, her limits. *Wise Children*, for all its iconoclasm, in the end – in what Steven Connor has so aptly termed 'fidelity in betrayal' (Connor, 1996: 167) – returns us to the Shakespearean family, warts and all.

Notes

1 Carter (1982 [1977]). See, for example, the scene where Eve/Evelyn dresses once again in masculine attire: 'it seemed at first glance, I had become my old self ... But this masquerade was more than skin deep. Under the mask of maleness I wore another mask of femaleness but a mask that now I never would be able to remove ... I was a boy disguised as a girl and now disguised as a boy again, like Rosalind in Elizabethan Arden' (132).

  In making the link between *The Passion of New Eve* and Shakespeare, I am anxious to stress that in many ways the novel distinguishes between the media of cinema and theatre. Carter's novel is heavily influenced by 1970s psychoanalytical film theory, which suggested that spectators were inevitably involved in forms of cross-gender identification as they watched movies. This is distinct from responses to theatre, since cinema's construction of stars manufactures intimacy through mechanical techniques such as editing and sound manipulation. Despite this, however, Carter's playful allusion to *As You Like It* in the passage quoted above raises the spectre of theatre's own blurring of gender boundaries, albeit in the context of the 'arid pastoral' that Eve/Evelyn describes as her/his experience.

2 The importance of Shakespeare to Carter's version of 'double-drag' is lucidly articulated by Warner (1994: 248).

3 I am laying no claims to originality in making this connection. Other significant readings of *Wise Children*, not least in terms of the Shakespearean context, include Chedgzoy (1995: 49–53); Gamble (1997: 169–84); Peach (1998); and Webb (1994).

4 Shakespeare is one of several authors referred to in the course of this densely allusive novel – there are traces of *Hamlet*, *King Lear*, and *Othello*, among others – but his explicit association with London life

in Lizzie's mind does link to Carter's own perceptions of the dramatist.

5 In a 157_ Edict, Elizabeth I classed travelling players in the same category as beggars, vagrants and petty criminals: mobility seemed to be a prime cause of anxiety, as it left people outside the usual parish controls and parameters of justice. See Carroll (1996).

6 Kate Atkinson mocks the same tendency in *Human Croquet*: see Chapter 3. There is a Shakespeare Road, rather than a Bard Road, in Brixton. This reveals a typical Carter strategy of making direct reference to something/someone real, and yet not real. A comparable move can be seen in the naming of her Hollywood film director Genghis Khan, clearly recognisable as expatriate 1930s film director Max Reinhardt. Elsewhere in her *œuvre* she appropriates by approximating: real films, sometimes film versions of original plays or books, are 're-fictionalised' in interesting ways. Reinhardt's 1935 spectacular version of *Dream* in *Wise Children* is a case in point.

7 Findlay has shown that the bastard as villain was one of the most common stage figurations of the type (1994: esp. 222 onwards).

8 My use of inverted commas should indicate that Melchior's 'official' role in the siring of Saskia and Imogen is disproved: they are really the children of his twin, Peregrine.

9 Interestingly, he never plays in *Hamlet*: one might speculate that the comic, and indeed feminine, proximities of that text – evidenced in *Juggling* by Christina's special allowance for *Hamlet* in her veneration of the comedies – disturbs him. That his mother, Estella, had herself been a successful 'Hamlet in drag' (12) may add to the ambivalence of the role for the hypermasculine Melchior.

10 One critic to make this claim is Jouve (1994: 169).

11 Film versions of the play have exhibited an interest in this shadowy figure: Peter Greenaway's avant-garde 1991 version, *Prospero's Books*, not only brings her onscreen but gives her a name, Susannah.

12 On the Dido myth and its relevance for *The Tempest*, see Brotton (1998) and Burden (1998).

13 Adelman has suggested that Shakespeare's plays, even the late romances, 'bear the signs of Shakespeare's ambivalence towards the maternal body' (1994: 37).

14 Adelman (1994: 73). Hackett suggests that 'maternity is a theme and a problem in Shakespeare's late plays' (1999: 25), and argues that tragicomedy, which I have suggested here is Carter's particular emphasis in appropriating Shakespeare, can be seen as a maternal genre. See also Wilcox (1994).

15 In a British context, DORA was also the acronym for the 1914 'Defence of the Realm Act', which was regularly portrayed in caricature as an elderly lady. If Carter is aware of this context, it lends further irony to the character. I am grateful to Helen Stoddart for this information.

16 Several critics note the Freudian aspects of Carter's novel. See Webb (1994: 292) and Chedgzoy (1995).

17 Chedgzoy speaks of the 'complex relationship between masculine cultural authority and the production of Hamlet [in the eighteenth and nineteenth centuries] as a liminal and feminised figure' (1994: 256). Actors including Sarah Siddons, Charlotte Cushman and Sarah Bernhardt all played the role. Twentieth-century examples include Frances de la Tour and Diane Venora: see Thompson and Taylor (1996: 42–3). Interestingly, Gary Williams has identified a comparable acting history for the role of Oberon the fairy king in *Dream*; Lucia Vestris being one of the most famous (1997: 93).

18 The most relevant example is Prufrock's self-deprecating statement 'I am not Prince Hamlet, nor was meant to be/Am an attendant lord' (Eliot, 1985: 16), although with a typically arrogant reflex action, he later claims the all-knowing role of Shakespearean Fool for himself. (Eliot's use of the upper case is surely the significant point). This poem and its *Hamlet* ruminations have been reworked in the context of another novel appropriation of Shakespeare, Alan Isler's brilliantly witty *The Prince of West End Avenue* (1994).

19 Note that the modern ghosts of the New World are very different to the Old World manifestations (Carter, 1993: 85). The story concerned is 'The Merchant of Shadows', which makes its own nod to Shakespeare despite the cinematic subject (another ageing female film icon, akin to Tristessa in *The Passion of New Eve*). There may be an embedded allusion to Orson Welles's famously incomplete film version of *The Merchant of Venice*, recently discovered in archival fragments. The narrator of this story researches in the archives for his thesis, and forms a parallel with the student who visits Nora and Dora in *Wise Children*.

20 The fairies witnessed by Conan Doyle were, of course, a clever piece of fakery, created by teenage girls: this notorious event is explored in Bown (1996).

21 Williams (1997) is invaluable in tracing a sexually ambivalent history for the play, not least in terms of the interpretation of Oberon, which clearly lends credence to Carter's concerns.

22 On Carter's narrative strategies, see Sage (1992: 168–78).

23 Peach argues that the term is usually – lazily – invoked to describe non-European or North American writing from Nigeria to South America (1998: 8).

24 On metafiction, see Currie (1995).

THREE

Kate Atkinson in
the House of Arden

Kate Atkinson's second novel, *Human Croquet* (1997), picks up where her Whitbread-Prize-winning debut, *Behind the Scenes at the Museum* (1995), left off – with a sarcastic, witty young female first-person narrator and a complicated *mélange* of personal and national histories.[1] Relating the adolescent world of Isobel Fairfax, the novel concerns itself in part with her attempt to solve the mystery of her mother Eliza's disappearance. That search leads to the discovery of family and neighbourhood secrets, including suspected murder (by Isobel's father, Gordon, or their neighbour, Mr Baxter) and incest (which also implicates their neighbour), in the midst of a narrative that moves in and out of not only different historical time-schemes but also parallel universes. Shaping intertexts include *As You Like It* and *A Midsummer Night's Dream*, and in that respect *Human Croquet* would seem to take up the baton from novels such as *Juggling* and *Wise Children*, using Shakespeare's work as it does to enable a series of reflections on identity and history.

In a strategy akin to Trapido's and Carter's in their novels, the carnivalesque provides Atkinson with an important means of engaging with the patterns and rituals of Shakespearean comedy. We start the novel on our narrator Isobel's sixteenth birthday. As in *Wise Children*, birthdays prove auspicious occasions and, as in *Juggling*, sixteen is an auspicious age, marking a movement into a more adult, certainly more sexualised, stage of life. As Isobel reflects, the significance of this age has its own textual provenance in fairytale and myth:

It's the first day of April and it's my birthday, my sixteenth – the mythic one, the legendary one. The traditional age for spindles to start pricking and suitors to come calling and a host of other symbolic sexual imagery to suddenly manifest itself, but I haven't even been kissed by a man yet, not unless you count my father, Gordon, who leaves his sad, paternal kisses on my cheek like unsettling little insects. (Atkinson, 1997: 23–4)

The date is equally significant. Isobel's birthday falls on the first of April, April Fool's Day, and the possibility therefore remains in the more sceptical reader's mind that the entire narrative is an elaborate hoax. Isobel's is a very knowing voice; there is at times a self-consciousness that seems untypical of a sixteen-year-old, and readers trained on the verbal tricks and turns of postmodernism, with its knowing narratives, might therefore be being primed to read subtextually. There may be an incestuous or Oedipal context in Gordon's 'sad, paternal kisses': certainly, the word 'insect' is often used as a literary anagram to this end in novels ranging from Trapido's *Juggling* to A. S. Byatt's *Angels and Insects*. At other times, however, Isobel – in her self-centred account of the world around her, and her failure to understand certain (often socio-sexual) issues – confirms our expectations of her age.

Other significant events in the novel take place on festive dates or in the midst of communal events. Hallowe'en, Christmas Eve and Midsummer are all significant dates in *Human Croquet*. Towards the close of the narrative (inasmuch as an ending is possible in these texts, which are so aware of closure as construct) Isobel has slept through much of April following her birthday, and woken to find herself at 23 April. This is yet another birthday, but this time it is Shakespeare's, the same date Carter chose for the tempests and revelations of *Wise Children* and the joint birthdays of her twin protagonists. The subsequent apparition of the 'man himself' on Isobel's bed seems an almost inevitable, and certainly longed-for, moment.

Shakespeare is clearly at the heart of this forest-arched novel. *Human Croquet*'s central locale is a magical household called Arden, a knowing reference to the forest of *As You Like It*. The early modern dramatist functions as both character and ghostly presence throughout. But Shakespeare is not the sole intertext of this allusion-soaked narrative. Apart from his forest comedies, *As You*

Like It, *Two Gentlemen*, and *Dream*, the most overt intertext (although Atkinson never explicitly mentions its author) is E. Nesbit's 1908 children's book *The House of Arden*. That novel, a text of absent fathers and time travel, clearly serves as a template for Atkinson's plotline. Elfrida and Edred find their true inheritance (the Arden family birthright, but also, in the process, their father) through a series of time-travelling incidents in part enabled by a magical white mole (a heraldic emblem from the family coat of arms). For Atkinson, it is almost as if in *Human Croquet* Shakespeare provides the same magical presence as the 'mouldiwarp' of Nesbit's story. The House of Arden magically embodies the Fairfax family history across the generations and ages within its constantly permeable walls.[2]

Echoes of the Bible, fairytales, the poetry of Yeats, C. S. Lewis's children's book *The Lion, the Witch and the Wardrobe*, Charlotte Bronte's *Jane Eyre* and many others weave in and out of the limber sentences of Isobel's first-person narrative.[3] The effect, as with Carter and Trapido, is to offer the reader a complex *bricolage* whereby the textual allusions to the past complicate the present, and break down or fissure any firm sense of boundaries or parameters. This, in the process, affects our sense of time and temporality, history, and genre, as much as that of the narrator.

Isobel commences her narrative with a sense of certainty that is surprisingly short-lived: 'Call me Isobel. (It's my name.) This is my History. Where shall I begin?' (11). Her mock-heroic invocation of Herman Melville's *Moby Dick* ('Call me Ishmael') in the certainty of her nomenclature, and in her conviction that History (note the upper case) can be defined and described, is immediately called into question by her own doubt about the starting point of any such narrative. As it is, Isobel opts to begin not at the beginning of her personal narrative but, rather grandiosely (perhaps indicative of her sixteen-year-old mind's overweening sense of ambition), at the beginning of Time. The echoes of Genesis are unmistakable: 'Before the beginning is the void and the void belongs in neither time nor space and is therefore beyond our imagination' (11). Immediately juxtaposed with the Bible is that other desert-island text, the *Complete Works of Shakespeare*; *Lear* is evoked in the course of Isobel's reflections: 'Nothing will come of nothing, unless it's the beginning of the world' (11).[4]

The first chapter of *Human Croquet*, 'Streets of Trees', offers a breakneck-paced history of the world, albeit one viewed from a curiously localised English perspective. From atoms and nuclei through 'Forests of giant ferns' (12), we move through the stone, bronze, and iron ages, to a medieval landscape of coppiced wood-lands, bodgers and charcoal-burners. The world of Shakespeare's plays is also already beginning to blur the boundary line between fact (history?) and fiction:

> But there was a secret mystery at the heart of the heart of the forest. When the forest was cut down, where did the mystery go? Some say there were fairies in the forest – angry, bad-tempered creatures (the unwashed children of Eve), ill-met by moonlight, who loitered with intent on banks of wild thyme listening furiously to the encroaching axes. Where did they go when the forest no longer existed? And what about the wolves? What happened to them? (Just because you can't see something doesn't mean it isn't there.) (13)

That latter statement, alerting the reader to look beyond the sur-face or obvious in this novel of red herrings and blind alleys, forms a refrain of sorts throughout the narrative. In this passage the world of magic, forests and parallel worlds that Shakespeare's *Dream* so vividly portrays, and that will prove so important to this novel, has also entered the reader's consciousness.

'There is no clock in the forest': concepts of time and history in *Human Croquet*

The forest does indeed lie at the heart of this novel. Isobel's family home is called Arden, embodying the tendency of modern housing developments to enshrine the memory of the very things their construction has destroyed in street and house names like 'Chest-nut Avenue' and 'Holly Tree Lane'. Arden's 'Tudorbethan' archi-tecture exposes the false histories such developments offer. It is built on the site of the Elizabethan Fairfax Manor which had, in its own turn, cut through whole swathes of the Great Forest of Lythe to establish an enclosed estate for the courtier Sir Francis Fairfax. The history that the 'Streets of Trees' offers is, on closer inspection, highly destructive. The Great Forest shrinks to Bos-crambe Woods, which is in turn encroached upon by the voracious demands of the Industrial Revolution and, ultimately, swallowed entirely by a modern housing estate: 'The forest of trees had become a wilderness of streets' (19).

The house of Arden seems to contain within itself its own locational history, the potential for magic, and the power to disorientate which is constantly associated with the forest throughout. It appears to conspire against those who resist its power, including the 'Debbie-wife', as Isobel calls her stepmother, who seeks to domesticate and control it:

> Arden has her in its thrall. 'This house,' she complains to Gordon, 'has a life of its own.' 'Possibly,' Gordon sighs. The house does seem to conspire against her – if she buys new curtains then a plague of moths will follow, if she puts down lino, the washing-machine will flood. Her kitchen tiles crack and fall off, the new central-heating pipes rattle and moan and bang in the night like banshees. If she polishes everything in a room then the minute she leaves, the particles of dust will come out of their hiding-places and regroup on every surface, sniggering behind their little hands. (We must imagine those things we cannot see.) The dust in Arden isn't really dust, of course, but the talcum of the dead, a frail composite waiting to be reconstituted. (43)

This omnipresence of the past in Arden is part of its supernatural qualities. Time is not linear in this space; as Isobel reflects later in the novel, with a sidelong glance at Hamlet's experience of Elsinore: 'The time is seriously out of joint in Arden, I fear' (271). Her experience of time travel and time-warps ensures that the reader, too, loses any certain sense of historical 'time'. We move, as the narrative subheadings tell us, in and out of 'Past' and 'Present', but both of those concepts prove to be highly unstable. The 'Past' is, at given times, the late sixteenth century, the 1920s, Isobel's own past or that of her parents. The 'Present' is no more fixed, since Isobel experiences one Christmas Eve four times over with subtle differences on each occasion (one version seems to be either a fantasy or wish-fulfilment of an ideal parallel world – the alternative subheading 'Maybe' alerts us to the confusion), and the 'Past' of various times appears to throw up ghosts or objects into that space. Shakespeare is an important player in this blurring of time-scales: his works are just some of those objects that persist and endure in the late twentieth century of the novel – and potentially beyond. Like Isobel's Aunt Vinny, Shakespeare's plays outlast the end of the millennium.

To emphasise the uncertainties of time, Isobel persistently puns on commonplace statements we make about the concept and the metaphors we attach to it: 'But time has already begun to fly' (20); 'We're taking a shortcut, to save time (but where will we put it?)' (69); 'I should never have tried to kill time. I wasted it and now it's wasting me' (143); 'Time had flown' (184); 'If I could go back in time (which I can, of course, I know)' (203); 'Time playing tricks, eh?' (232); 'each time the details are different' (278). Time was a central Shakespearean theme, and some of these statements are direct allusions to his plays; for example, to Richard II's declaration: 'I wasted time and now doth time waste me' (5.5.49). John Kerrigan has demonstrated how alternative notions of time – clock-defined, the seasons, human lifespans and literary immortality – provide many of the themes and images of the Sonnets (1995); and in one late play, *The Winter's Tale*, we have the personified figure of Time as a Chorus brought onstage to inform the audience that the events have leapt sixteen years to when Perdita is a young woman of sixteen (that auspicious, cuspy age once again):

> I that please some, try all; both joy and terror
> Of good and bad; that makes and unfolds error,
> Now take upon me in the name of Time
> To use my wings. Impute it not a crime
> To me or my swift passage that I slide
> O'er sixteen years and leave the growth untried
> Of that wide gap
>
> (4.1.1–8)

It is no coincidence that when Isobel's narrative throws up its own abandoned baby, she wishes to call it Perdita.

One remarkable passage associates Arden with the natural world and therefore with a cyclical rather than linear sense of time:

> Time had flown. Seven years of it. Eliza was never coming back, she may as well be as dead as Gordon.
> Arden was in decay, there was wet-rot in the floors and dry-rot in the stairs. The windows stuck, the doors jammed. The wallpaper peeled. The dusty drops of the Widow's chandelier were laced with gossamer cobwebs and chimed and tinkled in the fierce draughts that gusted through Arden, as if Boreas and Eurus were holding a competition somewhere in the vicinity of the front hall or the great eagle Hraesvelg was flying up and down just to annoy them.

> While all the other houses on the streets of trees were being mod-
> ernised and brought up to date, Arden had remained untouched since
> the master-builder nailed in the last slate himself.
> The garden had become home to toad and frog, mouse and mole
> and a million garden birds. The nettles were waist-high, the soil lat-
> ticed with ground-elder and a tangle of brambles was slowly clawing
> across the garden towards the back door. The Widow would have had
> a fit. (184)

Another crucial intertext here is Virginia Woolf's modernist
masterpiece *To the Lighthouse*, where the central 'Time Passes'
section, which touches on momentous world events such as the
decimation of the Great War, embodies the passing of time in the
reassertion of Nature through the cracks and fissures of the lighthouse's edifice. Arden is 'timeless' in linear human terms, resisting
the process of modernisation that adapts all other houses on the
streets of trees; but, like Woolf's lighthouse, it is a world in which
the cyclical time-scale of the natural world holds sway, permeating
the structure.

Clock-based time is a human construct; natural time is what
wins out in this novel, as so often in Shakespeare's plays. There is
'no clock' in the Forest of Arden in *As You Like It*, despite
Rosalind's obsession with time and the hour (3.2.275–6). Tellingly,
when *Human Croquet* envisages the end of the world, it is with a
dense narrative of natural splendour:

> Imagine the wood at the end of time. A great green ocean of peace. A
> riot of trees, birch, Scotch pine and aspen, English elm and wych elm,
> hazel, oak and holly, bird cherry, crab apple and hornbeam ... And,
> finally, the wolves come back. (342–3)

Many late-twentieth-century women's novels adopt a circular
rather than linear time-frame. *Wise Children* and *Juggling* exploit
images and ideas of circularity, and related patternings can be
traced in several *Tempest* appropriations: Marina Warner's *Indigo*
moves in and out of 'Then' and 'Now', allowing the two to
permeate and pervade each other in similar ways to Atkinson's
deployment of 'Past' and 'Present'. Gloria Naylor's *Mama Day*,
Iris Murdoch's *The Sea, The Sea*, and Leslie Forbes's *Bombay Ice*
all demonstrate a cyclical and potentially matrilineal concept of
time and history.

The circularity of *Human Croquet*'s narrative is best evidenced
by the opening and closing chapters: both are titled 'Streets of
Trees', and begin and end in the forest. The forest of the novel, as
in Shakespeare's comedies, is not always benign; it often seems to
manifest a malevolent force. The site in which numerous people
'vanish', from Mary Fairfax through to Eliza, it is also a location
steeped in death and violence. In that respect, Atkinson pulls into
the English woodland the more malevolent forces of Northern
European forests and their function in fairytales: the very world
which, Carter felt, the sentimentalised nineteenth-century versions
of Shakespeare suppressed. Eliza is brutally murdered in the forest,
setting off a chain of events that have deeply harmful effects on
Isobel's life and psyche; Malcolm Lovat, in the Christmas Eve
sequence, seems to be preyed upon by forest forces. This malign
atmosphere is not always present: Lady Fairfax feels that peace
reigns in the forest rather than in her lordship's disordered, unnatural household where incest rules, *Hamlet*-esque, over the 'sty'
(329). But, more often than not, the forest, as in Shakespearean
comedy, forces people to confront sometimes unpalatable truths,
and re-emerge with changed personalities.

The picnic that constitutes Eliza and Gordon's misplaced
attempt to play 'Happy Families', an attempt to conform to some
picture-book ideal of the family ('wicked stepmother' Debbie does
something similar when she clings to a 'strict blueprint' of family
life in Arden against all odds (43)), ends in a gruesome pantomime
of lost children, a found shoe and a sleeping beauty. 'Babes in the
Wood' and 'Hansel and Gretel', itself a formative text in *Behind
the Scenes at the Museum*, are intertexts, but so too are the darker
subtexts of many Eastern European children's stories: the sleeping
beauty here turns out to be Isobel and Charles's murdered mother.

A sense of time vanishes in the forest at this point (114), and a
clear sense of family history disappears along with it.[5] The
children, repressing any clear memory of finding their mother's
corpse (the lost time in the forest and the fairytale constructions
Isobel places upon the event leave them confused as to whether it
was dream or reality), are told that their mother has simply van-
ished ('up sticks and left with her fancy man', according to Vinny
(27)), and spend much of their young lives eagerly anticipating her
return. Their father's sudden disappearance soon afterwards is

explained away by his death; a fact that requires rewriting when he unexpectedly returns with a new wife after a several-year sojourn in the Antipodes. The past is constantly being rewritten in this novel. Gordon's disappearance invites the reader to assume that he murdered Eliza and his sudden confession to Isobel later in the novel would appear to confirm that reading of events. But, as ever, 'appearances are deceptive'. It turns out – from a revelatory moment in the narrative when we, as readers, are allowed a glimpse of something the far-from-omniscient Isobel can never have seen – that Eliza died from a subsequent attack, not Gordon's original physical quarrel with her. The murderer is someone called 'Peter' and readers are invited to speculate that this may refer to the Fairfaxes' neighbour Mr Baxter, with whom Eliza may, or may not, have been having an affair. Isobel's brother Charles is constantly seeking the reason for his red hair, which does offer visual links to the Baxter baby, but the mystery at the heart of the forest and the novel is never solved. Identities remain free-floating and speculative, as do sexual liaisons.

What Eliza's death does is to cast a shadow over all other events. As Isobel acknowledges in discussing her childhood: 'Absence of Eliza has shaped our lives' (27). Atkinson's novel is another text fascinated by the trope of the absent mother. If this were an appropriation of a late romance, we might expect a fifth-act reunion, and Eliza's return, for which Isobel so ardently wishes. That Isobel calls her own daughter Imogen and wishes to call the surprise baby Perdita hints at her longing to be a participant in that kind of Shakespearean plotline. Elsewhere in the narrative, the proliferation of surprise 'motherless' babies ('A BABY!') alludes to the fate of the unseen Indian boy in *Dream*. Eliza's pregnancy is directly compared to that of Titania's female soulmate: 'Eliza drifted into the shop, as pregnant as a full-blown sail' (88; 2.1.131–3). As it is, all romantic options are forestalled by the narrative, and Eliza remains resolutely elusive within it. Romantic descriptions of her are merely a product of Isobel's fertile mind and deep emotional needs: it is here that Shakespearean texts help to shape her imaginative desires. The truth is far less picturesque; the section on Eliza's life is seedy and violent, and destabilises any secure sense of her identity the reader may have acquired from the preceding narrative.

Shakespeare's own identity and role in 'History' is equally slippery within the narrative of *Human Croquet*. A clear distinction
appears to be made between man and works. Isobel, working on
her homework in the 1960s (another transitional historical moment), idolises the Bard: 'Imagine meeting Shakespeare! But then
what would you say to him?' (60); and the fanciful scene in which
he appears to her, and they make love amid a scent of cloves,
seems equally a product of her febrile imagination. The 'real'
Shakespeare is, in Mary Fairfax's terms, a 'weasel' who 'gabbles
like a goose' (329). 'History' is what you make of it in this novel,
and Shakespeare the man has been as subject to romanticised
rewritings as his all-pervasive texts (Holderness, 1988; Taylor,
1990). He is as bound up with concepts of Englishness and identity
as the Lady Oak that manifests such power over events in *Human
Croquet*. It is no coincidence that initials rumoured to have been
carved by Shakespeare (although possibly belonging to a William
Stukely) are embedded in its bark. Shakespeare was, notoriously, a
reviser of older texts, and Atkinson is aware of her own work
coming at the end of a very long tradition of rewritings and myth.

Ovid, metamorphosis, Shakespearean comedy
and the fragile self

Intertextuality is an important factor in the tapestry of histories
and time-frames that Atkinson weaves in *Human Croquet*. While
allusions and half-echoes of Shakespeare extend to all areas of his
canon, from the tragedies to the late romances, engaging most
obviously with Shakespeare's lifelong reflections on the complicated
entity of the family and its impact on individual identity, it is
clearly Shakespearean comedy that is central to her conception.
The forest worlds of several comedies are foregrounded as points
of reference in the novel. Isobel's significantly-named household
contains within itself the sense of Shakespeare's Forest of Arden;
the forest-based rape that is forestalled in *Two Gentlemen* is imaged
in Isobel's experience of the Walshes' Christmas Eve party; and
the Lythe players recall Peter Quince's theatrical mechanicals in
their less than accomplished attempts to stage *Dream*. But Atkinson
recognises in very subtle ways, ways that have important

consequences for the magic realist aspects of her narrative, that
Shakespeare – in creating at the heart of his comic dramas these
locations, places which allow for liberation from social convention
and the discovery of new identities and perspectives, and which
are, potentially at least, a site of magic – had an important intertext
of his own: Ovid's *Metamorphoses*.

Jonathan Bate, our own era's most eloquent voice of Shakespeare's Ovidianism, has explored the Bard's lifelong engagement
with Ovid's works, in particular the *Heroides* and the *Metamorphoses*. Bate sees this operating at the level of direct allusion and
more embedded 'affinity' (1993). In the case of *Dream*, he suggests
that this play, in particular, may be described as 'a displaced drama-
tization of Ovid' (1993: 131). In the fifth act of *Dream*, Quince's
men stage their overliteral interpretation of the story of Pyramus
and Thisbe (from Book 4 of *Metamorphoses*). It is less this overt
Ovidianism that concerns Atkinson when she is appropriating
Shakespearean comedy than what Bate identifies as the 'dispersal'
of Ovid throughout the play, and Shakespeare's revision and rewriting of his source (1993: 132).

Many of the stories embedded within the twists and turns of
the narrative of the *Metamorphoses* concern the effects and impacts
of sexual and erotic desire. Transgressive sexuality and unnatural
love of various kinds is the focus, and, more often than not, the
victims are female. Rape, frequently in a woodland setting, and
incest are the darker tragic subtexts of the generic mix of Ovid's
text. Bate has suggested, however, that the tragic element remains
subtextual: 'metamorphosis lets the characters off the hook: they
are arrested in the moment of intense emotion and released into a
vital, vibrant, colourful world of anthropomorphic nature' (1993:
49). Characters are transformed into running brooks, trees, stones
and statues. The influences on Shakespeare's dramatic transformations are obvious: Bottom translated into an ass in the midst of the
woods in *Dream*; Hermione's statue in *The Winter's Tale*; the magic
of *The Tempest*. But there are more prosaic versions of those
Ovidian metamorphoses in the disguises of Rosalind and Viola,
and the havoc wrought on the lovers in the midst of the forest in
Dream by Puck and his 'love-in-idleness'.

In the case of *Dream*'s lovers, Shakespeare's direct invocation of
Ovid is a conscious inversion. Helena, in pursuit of Lysander,

articulates this fact: 'The story shall be changed:/ Apollo flies and Daphne holds the chase' (2.1.230–1). The story she is rewriting in the midst of her actions is from Book 1 of the *Metamorphoses*: Jove's son, Apollo, grows enamoured of Daphne, the mortal child of Perseus, as a result of Cupid's interventions. She, however, rejects the attention of all men and chooses to join Diana's virgin huntresses in the forest. Apollo, seemingly unable to control his desires, pursues her through briar and glade, pausing only to voice concern for the scratches and scars she is receiving in the course of her flight. Ovid's deeply erotic narrative of the chase compares Daphne to a hunted hare, pursued by hounds (it is an image of the hunt that solicits empathy with the hunted, and one that recurs frequently in the *Metamorphoses*). When Apollo finally catches her, however, the forces of metamorphosis intervene and protect Daphne from the rape to which so many other women are sub-jected by Apollo's father in the course of the text:

> Scarce had she made her prayer when through her limbs
> A dragging languor spread, her tender bosom
> Was wrapped in thin smooth bark, her slender arms
> Were changed to branches and her hair to leaves;
> Her feet but now so swift were anchored fast
> In numb stiff roots, her face and head became
> The crown of a green tree; all that remained
> Of Daphne was her shining loveliness.
> (Ovid, 1986: 17)

It is no coincidence that the texts Isobel is working on for school are *Twelfth Night* (on which she writes an essay with the topic 'Appearances are deceptive', which could serve as a subtitle for the personal narrative she is giving the reader) and the *Metamorphoses*:

> I have to translate Ovid. In *Metamorphoses* you can't move for people turning into swans, heifers, bears, newts, spiders, bats, birds, stars, partridges and water, lots of water. That's the trouble with having god-like powers, it's too tempting to use them … at every opportunity – Debbie would have been turned into an ass long ago, and Hilary would be hopping about as a frog.
> And me, I am a daughter of the sun, turned by grief into something strange. For homework, I'm translating the story of Phaethon's sisters … who mourned so much for their charred brother that they turned into trees – imagine their feelings as they found their feet were fast to the earth, turning, even as they looked, into roots. (146–7)

The emotive tone of Isobel's translation is commented on by her teacher, but it is the reading we might expect from a sixteen-year-old, tormented by her own unrequited passion for Malcolm Lovat.

Metamorphosis is part of the hyperreality of Arden and Boscrambe Woods in *Human Croquet*. The full moon that shapes and guides Shakespeare's moonstruck *Dream* both inspires and disorientates Isobel. The moon, like the forest with which it is so intimately associated, causes the loss of 'points of reference' (49), and becomes in this almost a paradigm for Atkinson's slippery narrative. It carries Isobel into the midst of a suspiciously Ovidian *mise en scène*: 'A moment longer and we will be running for the woods, bows and arrows in our hands, hounds at our heels, converts to Diana' (49).

Isobel's experience at the Walshes' Christmas Eve party is a further Ovidian moment. Richard Primrose, piqued by Isobel's lack of erotic interest in him, has spread malicious rumours of her sexual availability. The adolescent males at the party seem to close in on her like a pack of hunting hounds: 'the baying pack now close in on me in a way that's really quite frightening' (237). Apollo's pursuit of Daphne is reworked in a modern context:

> I set off again at a gallop, the two boys hallooing and tantivying behind me. I notice a big silver birch growing by a perimeter wall and veer over to it … I'm done for … I feel sick from exertion and can't raise a scream no matter how hard I try. It's like being trapped in a nightmare. I lean against the trunk of the silver birch gasping for air like a dying fish and send up a small silent plea for help. Why do I have no protector in this world, someone watching over me? (238–9)

Isobel's 'silent plea' is a direct equivalent of Daphne's prayer in the Ovidian narrative, and, like hers, it is answered:

> I can't even move, my legs feel as though they're full of lead shot and my feet are rooted to the ground. One of the boys, Geoff, I think, runs straight up to me and stops, the mad Dionysian light in his eyes turning to confusion. He seems to look right through me … [Clive] puts his hand out onto my left shoulder and leans his weight against it as if I'm just part of the tree.
>
> But when I glance down at his hand, I see that where my left shoulder should be, where my right shoulder should be – where my entire body should be, in fact – is the silvery, papery bark of the birch. My

arms are stiff branches sticking out from my sides, my previously bi-
furcated legs have turned to one solid tree trunk. I would scream now,
but my mouth won't open. Call me Daphne. (239)

That final knowing nod to Ovid reminds us of the firm sense of
identity that Isobel had at the start of the narrative, and retrospec-
tively undermines it. It is a comic moment and Atkinson does, in
a manner akin to Ovid and Shakespeare, use the metamorphic idea
to swerve away from tragic potential. In Trapido's *Juggling*, Pam is
less fortunate. Daphne's precoital metamorphosis is something of
a rare occurrence in Ovid's narrative; unlike other heroines, she is
not forced to undergo the identity-testing trauma and body-altering
act of rape. Death and trauma in *Human Croquet* are frequently
distanced from readers, because they remain unsure what is fact
and what fiction (for example, Malcolm Lovat repeatedly encounters death in his car, only to survive in the narrative; Mr Baxter
undergoes multiple ends) or because it is forestalled in some way.
Eliza's demise remains the one brutal truth at the heart of both
forest and novel, but even that, in Isobel's idealising narrative, is
subject to transformation.

Bate has highlighted the fact that even incest in Ovid is of
interest to the author less for its tragic potential or the shock value
of a taboo subject than as a means of examining the psychological
causes of this most complicated branch of family relations: 'Even
in the case of incest, Ovid is more interested in exploring the
lover's mental state than condemning her' (1993: 53). The archetypal tale is that of Myrrha, mother of Adonis, which comes in
Book 10 of the *Metamorphoses*, where, in a dramatic monologue
comparable to the interiority proffered by a Shakespearean soliloquy,
she struggles with her sexual desire for her father. Incest weaves its
own complicated fibres into the narrative of *Human Croquet*, most
explicitly in the storyline of the neighbours' daughter Audrey
Baxter, but also emerging in several of Isobel's more forthright
imaginings. Sympathising with her brother Charles's lack of
romance, she reflects:

> One solution, I suppose, would be for us to kiss each other, but the
> idea of incest – though quite attractive in Jacobean tragedy – is less so
> on the home front. 'I mean, incest,' I say to Audrey, 'it's hard to
> imagine, isn't it?' (26)

The irony of that last statement becomes clear only on a second reading of the novel, but the incest question stays with Isobel. It is a family legacy of sorts, part of the 'Fairfax curse' mentioned at various stages: Sir Francis Fairfax's relationship with his ward Lady Margaret is clearly of a dubious and certainly violent sexual nature, and Eliza unwittingly sleeps with her father when she is working as a prostitute, although the implications of that act are swerved away from by the narrative's revelation that Eliza/Violet/the da Breville child was purchased in France, possibly from gypsies. One truth is that this novel's and Isobel's narrative penchant for romance (she informs us towards the end that her profession is as an author of historical romances: this ought to give us pause in considering the veracity of what preceded) makes fact impossible to determine, and leaves incest in the realm of the speculative rather than the tragic actual.

Shakespeare's *Dream* makes similar swerves from the tragic potential of its material towards the comic. Hermia is under sentence of execution from her father at the start of the play, and her dream of the serpent in the forest is an indication of the sexual threat her escape into the Athenian woods might represent. The lovers' trials and traumas in the woodland are treated with the pace and wit of comedy: stichomythic exchanges set the tone. No introspective soliloquies are allowed into the forest confines. Yet critics have suggested that tragedy hedges in the play: the Athenian court-world provides the anti-comic world of law and rationalism that Frye saw as the world challenged by the patternings of Shakespearean comedy, but it also provides audiences with the story of Theseus and Hippolyta and their pending nuptials. Theseus, as we saw in Chapter 1, was a mythic archetype of the serial abandoner. Peter Holland has suggested that shadowy subtexts, such as the quasi-incestuous desires of Phaedra and the death of Hippolytus implicit within Theseus' story, would also have affected audience responses to the blessing of his bridal bed with Hippolyta at the end of *Dream* (1995: 59). The tragic potential of Shakespeare's comedies has been a popular focus of late-twentieth-century productions and critical analyses, and Isobel acknowledges this in her essay on *Twelfth Night*. Like Christina in *Juggling*, she thinks that 'Comedy is a better sort of tragedy':

> *Twelfth Night*, I write with a sigh, ... is about darkness and death – the
> music and the comedy only serve to highlight what lies beyond the
> pools of golden light – the dark, the inevitability of death, the way
> time destroys everything. (203)

A reader might expect that the author sympathises with her heroine's point of view here; but on closer inspection, the narrative
trajectory of *Human Croquet* seems to resist this. Death is far from
inevitable in this text, and time is a slippery and labile concept.
This is best embodied in Vinny's life: a potentially magical, witch-
like older matriarch, she has her counterpart in *Juggling*'s Granny
P or *Wise Children*'s Grandma Chance. Vinny endures beyond all
expectation, eventually joining the realm of metamorphosis and
vanishing people:

> Vinny lasted the whole century, outliving both Gordon and Debbie,
> lingering on in Arden with the support of a succession of home helps.
> She celebrated the millennium and a hundred years of Vinnyhood by
> turning into a cat – small, tortoiseshell and disappearing into the night.
> Probably. (339)

Atkinson's invocations and appropriations of Ovid are akin to
some of the more overtly feminist revisions of Shakespeare that
we will explore later in this book – texts like Jane Smiley's *A
Thousand Acres*, with its recuperation of Goneril and Regan from
King Lear, or the voicing of Miranda and Sycorax in several appropriations of *The Tempest*. Atkinson inverts Ovid in order to
empower her women characters, and free them from the cycle of
sexual abuse and subjugation. What is significant, however, is her
choice – or decision – to mediate this through Shakespearean comedy. This is not done to demonstrate an implicit misogyny in
Shakespeare's writings. The novel is careful to distinguish the
works from the man: Shakespeare the man, in the one section of
Human Croquet that is narrated not by Isobel but by the Elizabethan Mary Fairfax, looks in danger of being a serial abandoner
in the mode of Theseus: 'I wished him well, though he was something of a weasel. He had already left wife and children and now
he was leaving us' (333). Elsewhere Atkinson prefers to acknowledge Shakespeare's revisions of Ovid in favour of women.

The notion of Time is central to Atkinson's project of destabilising social and literary norms. The ambitious scope of Isobel

Fairfax's personal history also has intertextual roots in Ovid. The *Metamorphoses* commence with the beginning of time:

THE CREATION
Ere land and sea and the all-covering sky
Were made, in the whole world the countenance
Of nature was the same, all one, well named
Chaos, a raw and undivided mass,
Naught but a lifeless bulk, with warring seeds
Of ill-joined elements compressed together.

(Ovid, 1986: 1)

Of course, this could also be an image of Isobel's own 'mental hodgepodge', as she terms it (38). Atkinson, in her complicated amalgam of Shakespearean and Ovidian themes and motifs, has opted for an unreliable narrator of the highest order: one who was not even alive at the time of certain events she tries to recall, who frequently misinterprets those happenings she was present at, and whose version of those events is coloured both by her sixteen-year-old imagination and by her subsequent profession as a writer of historical romance. Like Carter in *Wise Children*, Atkinson elects in her final pages to suggest to the reader that *everything* that precedes them may be a complicated fiction. The alert reader will already have entertained this possibility: in the opening chapter, Isobel makes a typically confident (overconfident) statement:

But time has already begun to fly, soon Eliza will come and ruin every-thing. Eliza will be my mother. I am Isobel Fairfax, I am the alpha and omega of narrators (I am omniscient) and I know the beginning and the end. The beginning is the word and the end is silence. And in between are all the stories. This is one of mine. (20)

There are several things to say about this extract. The strangeness of a person talking about their own mother in the future tense – 'Eliza will come' – takes us back to the metafictional world of *Tristram Shandy*. Shakespeare and the Bible are present here, too, in the beginning as the word and the end as silence (recalling Hamlet's last phrase). But, most importantly, Isobel proves that she is far from omniscient, and that the version – or even versions – of events that we receive in the ensuing narrative are just one story among many. Like Ovid, Shakespeare and fairytale, we can all endlessly rework our personal histories.

Notes

1 *Behind the Scenes at the Museum* relates the life of Ruby Lennox, but shares *Human Croquet*'s ambitious sense of time-scheme, moving in and out of the complicated past of Ruby's matrilineal forebears. The focus of *Behind the Scenes* is resolutely twentieth-century (the 1953 Coronation and 1966 World Cup are defining moments), but it makes related observations about 'lost women' and 'lost children' from the family past. Many links with the concerns of Carter and Trapido can be traced, not least themes of illegitimacy and dysfunctional families.

2 Atkinson has recently spoken of her obsession with the 'double time scheme' structure. All three of her published novels, including *Emotionally Weird* (2000), feature this structure, as does her first venture into the dramatic medium, *Abandonment*, which previewed at the Edinburgh Festival, August 2000. This foray into drama is a logical extension of the interest in dramatic structures expressed in *Human Croquet*. Interview on 'Front Row', BBC Radio 4, 10 August 2000.

3 The narrator's family name, Fairfax, acts as a multilayered intertext. The male protagonist of *Jane Eyre* is clearly figured in the myths and rumours that accrue around Sir Francis Fairfax in the Elizabethan era: rumours of first wives and mad wives in attics (14). Also relevant is the real Fairfax family of the early modern period, subject of Andrew Marvell's lengthy country-house poem 'Upon Appleton House', written in the 1650s about the regicide Lord Thomas Fairfax. Marvell was temporarily employed as tutor to his children. That poem features a spiritually empowered Mary Fairfax (the name we are given for Sir Francis's young bride (15)).

4 On 'Desert Island Discs', the long-running BBC Radio 4 programme in the UK, where 'castaways' are asked to choose a selection of music plus one book and one luxury they might wish to accompany them to a desert island, guests are automatically allowed two other texts: the Bible and the Works of Shakespeare.

5 Family history is the recurring topic of Atkinson's novels. The *Tristram Shandy*-influenced *Behind the Scenes* begins with Ruby Lennox's conception and 'first day', an occasion marked by the clock on the mantelpiece in an obvious allusion to Sterne. To alert readers to the intertext, Atkinson ensures that Ruby's sister Patricia studies *Tristram Shandy* for her A-level examination (1995: 251). The self-conscious avoidance of voicing family secrets in fireside storytelling provides the frame to *Emotionally Weird*. That text has its own sub-Shakespearean references in the Scottish cleaner Mrs Macbeth, a cat called Goneril, and an overly idealised young man called Ferdinand.

FOUR

'We might as well be time travelling': Shakespeare, narrative and the Möbius strip

> The way we live now, jetting from palmy LaLa Land to gray and frenzied New York City, to azure Venice, the Serenissima of all Serenissime – the most serene republic of our dreams – we might as well be time travelling. And we are.
>
> Erica Jong, *Serenissima*

In a recent interview, Leslie Forbes, author of *Bombay Ice* (discussed in detail in Chapter 7), described her interest in India as a setting for her novels as enabling 'a form of time travel'.[1] Time travelling is a recurring trope of a number of narrative appropriations of Shakespeare. One of the motives behind the appropriation of sixteenth- and seventeenth-century drama in the contemporary novel might be not only that it raises challenging questions about the parameters of genre, but that the comparison – in either an implicit or explicit form – of the contemporary era with the 'past' is a rich seam. For some authors the drive is to find continuities between Shakespeare's age and their own, a version of the 'universalising tendency' which has affected so much Shakespearean criticism and performance. For others it is to register the deep differences, the advances, and sometimes the declines, that have occurred in the interim. But what the imaginative (and sometimes literal) act of time travel facilitates in a surprising number of these texts is the opportunity to evoke the figure of William Shakespeare himself.

We have already explored the complex operations of time in *Human Croquet*, and time and temporality are unifying features of the novels explored in this chapter. What Isobel Fairfax's time travel in Atkinson's novel – with its origins, as we have noted, in the experiences of the child protagonists of E. Nesbit's *The House of Arden* – enables is a one-to-one encounter with the Bard of Avon:

> He's there. He's lying on my bed, one cynical, quizzical eyebrow raised at me, a lopsided smile as he watches me. I know him. I've always known him. Spaniel eyes and chestnut hair. Not yet bald, slightly greasy. Leather boots. Doublet and hose and rather grubby linen. (323)

There is a distinct tone of anti-Bardolatry here. Shakespeare, in Atkinson's version, is a reprehensible figure who, by the end, flees his responsibilities, both practical and moral, by running away with a band of travelling players: 'He had already left wife and children and now he was leaving us' (333). The narrator here (Mary) is somewhat forgiving in her account of this: 'I wished him well, though he was something of a weasel' (333), since she shares with her modern narrative counterpart, Isobel, a sexual attraction to Shakespeare. When the Bard appears in Isobel's bedroom, the outcome of this encounter seems inevitable: 'I take his hand. I let him pull me down next to him. I let him kiss me. He tastes of cloves. We melt into one and time collapses' (323).

Atkinson is not alone in toying with the idea of what it might be like to sleep with Shakespeare. Erica Jong's *Serenissima* (retitled in its US publication *Shylock's Daughter*) weaves an often fantastic plot around this possibility. Interestingly, like Atkinson's (or, more precisely, Isobel's, for we must regard the representation of Shakespeare as mediated through her sixteen-year-old imagination), Jong's Bard is not yet bald. It is as though the image of the man preserved in the Droeshout engraving that accompanied the printing of the 1623 Folio is somehow a problem for those who wish to dwell on his virility. There is a further question of the extent to which we, as posthumous readers, seek to humanise Shakespeare, rendering him a likeable, even sympathetic, figure. Atkinson's slightly gutless 'weasel' plays against the grain of other novelistic representations.

Serenissima is narrated in the first person by Jessica Pruitt, a former Hollywood film starlet, now approaching middle age. In Venice for a film festival for which she acts as a judge, and also to commence filming a cinematic appropriation of *The Merchant of*

Venice (to be called, initially, *Serenissima*, but renamed by the end *Shylock's Daughter*: a curious parallel with Jong's own dual-titled novel), she finds herself succumbing to a fever. In her feverish state she is transported back into a late-sixteenth-century manifestation of the city-republic in which she, as Jessica, daughter of Jewish usurer Shalach, meets and falls for William Shakespeare.[2] Shakespeare is in Italy with Henry Wriothesley, Earl of Southampton, his patron and, according to this narrative, sexual partner.[3] Wriothesley has been posited by critics as the possible subject of the so-called 'Young Man' sequence within Shakespeare's sonnets.[4] Jong's inclusion of the charismatic and sadistic earl in her novel is telling in a number of respects. The dangerous side to his personality (he engages in a violent and possessive form of bisexuality) enables Jong to employ him as a scapegoat figure. Blame for the promiscuous life of prostitutes and pregnant nuns that he and Shakespeare indulge in while in Venice is deflected on to him, preserving the humane version of Shakespeare to which Jong aspires. But this also reveals the way in which her text is shaped by an older form of Shakespearean literary criticism, which might be termed the biographical approach.[5]

This form of interpretation has held particular sway over readings of the sonnets. As Jonathan Bate has observed, the identification of the 'Young Man' as Wriothesley is important to biographical critics: 'The identity of the fair youth matters much more to those who believe that the poems grew from personal experience than to those who believe that they are poetic fictions, influenced more by sonneteering conventions than by life' (1997: 41–2). One of the major connecting threads between the novels and novelists explored in this book is the way in which their readings of Shakespeare, both man and texts, are shaped by twentieth-century critical discourse as much as by personal interpretation. Jong is no exception, but – as Richard Burt has recently expertly demonstrated – she is influenced less by the revisionary readings of postcolonialism, or even feminism (which, in view of her other publications, we might reasonably have expected), than by a rather outmoded form of autobiographical mapping of texts on to life (Burt, 2000: 203–31). Jong's Shakespeare has a lover back in England called Emilia, and readers are invited to identify her with Aemilia Lanyer, poet and daughter of a court musician. A. L. Rowse famously identified Lanyer as

Shakespeare's 'Dark Lady', recipient of that other grouping of poems, positioned later in the sonnet sequence than those addressed to the 'Young Man' (Bate, 1997: 47). Burt is right to identify in this a precursor of the recent popular strain of Shakespearean interpretation which reached its most spectacular commercial heights in the worldwide success of John Madden's direction of Marc Norman and Tom Stoppard's screenplay *Shakespeare in Love* (1998). In that film, as in Jong's novel, we see a pre-famous Shakespeare as a struggling writer and confused lover who has left his wife and children in Stratford-upon-Avon. His sonnets are given specific focus in the shape of Lady Viola de Lessops, Stoppard's fictional version of the Shakespearean muse.[6]

Norman and Stoppard were infamously subject to accusations of plagiarism – or, in more forgiving terminology, appropriations – of their own when that film was released: the subject of the debate was another Shakespeare novel, co-authored by a woman, the 1941 comedy *No Bed for Bacon* by Caryl Brahms and S. J. Simon (real names Doris Caroline Abrahams and Seca Jascha Skidelsky).[7] In that novel, a Lady Viola also dreams of being an actor in the late-sixteenth-century theatre and, by cross-dressing as John Pyk, achieves her aim.[8] In the process, she falls in love with Shakespeare, who proves resistant to her charms, moving her to an apprenticeship in Alleyn's company. Shakespeare nevertheless sits down immediately to write a sonnet directly inspired by Viola at the close. That sonnet is number 18, 'Shall I compare thee to a summer's day?' The same poem was the cause of considerable controversy over its deployment in *Shakespeare in Love*, since it is a 'Young Man' poem, yet in the film it was clearly addressed as part of a heterosexual courtship. Queer theorists have suggested that this moment embodies the film's overall strategy of hetero-sexualising Shakespeare.[9]

Burt, whose article considers another novel which deploys Shakespeare as a character in a generic romance context, Julie Beard's *Romance of the Rose* (1998),[10] provides a robust defence of the value and validity of biographical versions of Shakespeare, declaring: 'it would be a mistake simply to conclude that academics, not mass culture … are in an authoritative position to judge what is and is not really Shakespeare, what is or is not historically accurate and authentic' (Burt, 2000: 206). Nevertheless, there is a tension in Jong's work between the desire – at least, Jessica's desire in her first-person narrative – to deploy Shakespeare as an authenticating intellectual device – she twice mentions, for example, her locker crammed with Shakespeare biography and criticism – and a professed scorn for the academic discipline that produces these materials. Speculating on Shakespeare's 'lost years', she asks:

> Who knew? Shakespeare scholarship was rife with petty academic rivalries, outrageous suppositions, the mad hypotheses of good brains gone bad in college libraries, eaten by the maggots of paranoia and thwarted literary ambitions. Stratfordians said 'the Bard' (How I hate that orotund, pretentious epithet!) was a simple glover's son; anti-Stratfordians made him earl of this or that, because in their snobbery they could not believe that our greatest poet could lack a title. Piffle. (Jong, 1997: 11)

Elsewhere Jessica appears to claim to be the 'authentic reader' of Shakespeare, in particular of the sonnets: 'that curious sequence in which he surely bared his heart. If you read the sonnets carefully, the pain is unmistakeable' (80).

Time travel in this novel is facilitated by illness. The feverish condition which descends on Jessica while she is in Venice is produced in part by her state of melancholy. The personal and familial causes of this melancholia emerge gradually in the novel: separation from her daughter Antonia, the suicide of her mother, inheritance battles and subsequent estrangement from her brother Pip are all causes. But the traversal of time-boundaries is also encouraged by Jessica's profession in the film industry, which makes capital out of a form of time travel. A number of novels which appropriate Shakespearean drama into narrative also toy with a further generic shift into film. *Wise Children* recognises a paradox in the fixity and yet continuity of celluloid existences and versions of Shakespeare; *Bombay Ice* appropriates the melodramatic plotlines of Bollywood films to influence its intricate narrative. Jong's protagonist shares a hybrid cultural identity with *Bombay Ice*'s Ros Benegal. Both are of mixed parentage: Ros has Indian, English and Scottish roots; Jessica has three stepfathers from different European backgrounds. This adds to a sense of instability of self in both. In addition, as an actor, Jessica is peculiarly open to ideas of role-play and shape-shifting: 'So I wished, knowing that all time was eternally present and that we can, any of us, slip into other times, other modes of being, just by wanting to badly enough, just by believing that they are still there, lingering in the air' (108).

Jessica's Shakespearean namesake was another of Shakespeare's female shape-shifters, a cross-dresser who escapes her father's house in the midst of the Venetian carnival, disguised as a boy, and into the arms of her Christian lover Lorenzo. *The Merchant of Venice* is unusual in the canon for having two parallel stories of cross-dressing: Portia and Nerissa also disguise themselves as lawyers. Jessica is a complex heroine in both Shakespeare and Jong. In Shakespeare, she deserts her father and religion for Lorenzo. This act takes on a particular air of callousness when she leaves her house in Canareggio, the ghetto area of Venice where entrances and exits were strictly regulated, 'gilded' with her father's ducats. Later, in an exchange with Tubal, Shylock learns of other precious items his daughter has wrested from him: 'A diamond gone that cost me two thousand ducats in Frankfurt ... Two thousand ducats in that and other precious, precious jewels' (3.1.71–4). It would be easy to condemn Shylock here for caring more for his ducats than for Jessica, but there are more poignant losses registered. Tubal tells him that one trader showed him 'a ring that he had of your daughter for a monkey' (3.1.98–9). The exchange seems particularly brutal when Shylock reacts: 'Out upon her! Thou torturest me, Tubal. It was my turquoise. I had it of Leah when I was a bachelor. I would not have given it for a wilderness of monkeys' (3.1.80–2). We have a glimpse here of an alternative Shylock and another life. Leah, his dead wife, is mentioned only once (appropriators, as with Lear's wife or Prospero's, are fond of making much of this moment), but in this mention we are shown a single parent, and someone who has experienced great loss. Interestingly, Jong's Jessica seems in this to have more kinship with Shylock than with her play-namesake. Jessica, too, has lost a fortune, partly through a passivity and professional blindness to the world around her. By the end of the novel she is seeking ways to redress that and to become a financial benefactor, founding a New Globe on Southwark's Bankside.[11]

Jessica's melancholy nevertheless echoes something of her stage counterpart's personality. In the exquisite scene that opens the final act, Jessica and Lorenzo gaze at the moonlight and remember other romance pairings:

LORENZO: The moon shines bright. In such a night as this,
            When the sweet wind did gently kiss the trees
            And they did make no noise – in such a night
            Troilus, methinks, mounted the Trojan walls,
            And sighed his soul toward the Grecian tents
            Where Cressid lay that night.

JESSICA: In such a night
            Did Thisbe fearfully o'ertrip the dew
            And saw the lion's shadow ere himself,
            And ran dismayed away.

                                       (5.1.1–9)

Their examples are hardly reassuring in terms of future projections for their relationship. These are all tragic pairings: Troilus and Cressida; Pyramus and Thisbe; Dido and Aeneas; Medea and Jason. As Gross notes, in this scene audiences cannot escape 'undertones of regret, of a recognition that life will always have hurtful possibilities' (1994: 60).[12]

Some of those hurtful possibilities were enshrined, for twentieth-century productions of *The Merchant of Venice*, in audience knowledge of the dark legacy of the Holocaust. If Jong's biographising of Shakespeare is defensible, some of Jessica Pruitt's self-pitying parallels between her condition and that of the Jewish nation are more offensive. Reflecting on the Shakespearean connections of her name, Jessica observes: 'I always found it strange that I, who felt almost like an imaginary Jew (the very definition of the outsider), should be named for the young Jewess who renounces her faith and her father for a facile Christianity and a foppish young man' (8). Later she will talk about the acting profession as a kind of continuous exile, mainly due to its jet-setting lifestyle: 'But of course it is also a curse because it necessitates a kind of constant exile. If I feel the history of the Jews in my blood … perhaps it is because the Jew is the quintessential exile' (55–6). Of course, the reader should not associate Jong herself with the self-indulgent – even crass – views of her narrator but there are problems in this narrative with the harnessing of the Jewish experience to the personal self-pities of a wealthy Hollywood star.[13]

Subtler evocations of *The Merchant of Venice* can be found in Caryl Phillips's *The Nature of Blood* (1997) which in its own 'time-travelling' narrative – it moves in and out of first-person voices from sixteenth-century Venice to 1930s Germany to postwar Cyprus (site of refugee camps in advance of the formation of the Israeli nation) – touches on the questions of identity and ethnic belonging that undoubtedly exist in Shakespeare's controversial play. Phillips's novel appropriates another Shakespearean text which was partially set in Venice (and Cyprus), *Othello*, thus brilliantly melding the experience of a dislocated African general in the 1500s with the Jewish diaspora of the early twentieth century. *The Nature of Blood* conjoins and juxtaposes the white ash of burned sixteenth-century Jews with the gruesome traces of former existences in the Nazi concentration camps. The motive for the burning of Servadio the usurer and the others is a false Christian-promulgated rumour of child sacrifice: a similar plotline is deployed in Jong's novel, but the context is less sensitively drawn, verging at times on the grotesquely ridiculous in the case of the tower of oversexed nuns.

Alan Isler's connected series of novellas, initially gathered together under the title *Op. Non Cit.* (1997), though later retitled *The Bacon Fancier* (1998), also includes a series of first-person narrators stretching across four centuries. The first story in the sequence, 'The Monster', has an unnamed Jewish usurer as narrator, but embedded references to Leah, pounds of flesh, and various trials against one Asher Bassan (later renamed Antonio Bassanio, a melding of two characters from the play) make it clear to the reader what the Shakespearean subtext or pre-text for this story is.[14] Returning home after a successful second trial in which he employs Antonio's own lawyer against him, this Shylock finds his daughter gone: 'I had a daughter Jessica once' (Isler, 1997b: 22).

Where Jong's novel holds more interest is in its construction of Shakespeare as an authority figure, but also as a compensatory parent. This Shakespeare, despite his sexual philanderings, is one who pines for his children back home. Jessica, of course, has the historical hindsight he cannot share that his son Hamnet will die. In a parallel move, in the text, she is haunted, Hamlet-like, by her own deceased mother: 'If parents die in their own good time, we learn to shed them and go on; if they take their own lives untimely,

they cling to us forever, whispering their good-bys' (7). Shakespearean texts and acting in Shakespeare have been compensatory
mechanisms throughout Jessica's life: 'Shakespeare was my home,
my substitute mother … my escape' (8).[15] This reliance on Shakespeare takes on a physical 'reality' when the writer enters her life.
Her encounter with him enables her to rationalise her childhood
and adult traumas: 'Childhood, like a bell, calls us back again and
again. "Ding-dong-bell," says Shakespeare. Full fathom five thy
childhood lies, of its bones are coral made' (29). Echoes and para-
phrasing of *The Tempest* allow an element of the later plays'
dominant themes of family reconciliation to influence Jong's
narrative here.

Shakespeare as a key to the resolution of childhood trauma is
also the founding idea of a remarkable recent book for young people
by Susan Cooper, entitled *King of Shadows* (1999). The first-person
narrator in this instance is a contemporary US actor called Nat
Field, who finds himself on a transatlantic adventure, coming to
London to perform with the self-styled Company of Boys (an
obvious allusion to the boys' companies of Shakespeare's time) at
the New Globe Theatre.[16] The company is to stage *Dream* and
Julius Caesar in the resonant wooden O of the Southwark play-
house. There is certainly a sense in which the deep history of
London functions much as Venice's does in *Serenissima*, beckoning
the narrator across the ages and blurring supposedly finite lines
between past and present. What might be a tourist-brochure cliché
takes on a very specific resonance for Nat when he finds himself
transported back in time to 1599. Once again the promoting event
is an illness, a fever, but this time a direct swap takes place between Nat and his sixteenth-century namesake, actor Nathan Field,
who finds himself with bubonic plague in an isolation ward in
Guy's Hospital. There is a touching scene where the distressed
boy, confused by the unfamiliar electronic paraphernalia that
surrounds him, is soothed by a nurse who sings him the lullaby
from *Dream*: in a curious twist of fate, she has been singing this
song in an early-music group.

Both 1599 and 1999 are dates and cultural moments freighted
with meaning. In 1599, the turn of a glorious century, *fin-de-siècle*
anxieties about the succession were rife. Elizabeth I was an ailing
and ageing monarch. The year 1999, full of millennial expectations

and attendant anxieties, has already figured in Atkinson's *Human Croquet*, and will resurface in Gloria Naylor's take on *The Tempest*, *Mama Day*. Time travel seems particularly possible at what Angela Carter would call these 'cuspy' moments.

For the 1999 Nat Field, theatre is clearly a compensatory entity: 'This company is a family, a big family', he says early on (2). Nat is, like several Shakespearean protagonists – Viola, Caliban, and, to all intents and purposes, Rosalind and Hamlet – an orphan. His mother died of cancer and his father committed suicide, unable to bear the loss. As with Jong's Jessica, there is a deep-seated resentment of this on the part of the bereaved child, the one left behind to bear a double loss. Theatre is a means to forget for Nat, a site of escapism and role-play: 'It would be better in London, it would be better in the Company; I wouldn't be Nat there, I would be Puck' (12). Of course, this lack of parents also renders him oddly akin to the changeling boy of *Dream*.

The boys rehearse both *Dream* and *Julius Caesar*, and there are revealing allusions along the way to *Henry V* and the part of the boy in that play. But it is *Dream*'s story of magic, transportation and transformation that forms the major subtext to *King of Shadows*.[17] The title refers to Puck's description of Oberon in the play: 'Believe me, king of shadows, I mistook' (3.2.348), and elsewhere 'shadows' refer both to the fairies and to actors more generally: 'If we shadows have offended/ Think but this, and all is mended' (Epilogue, ll. 1–2). Nat plays Puck in both eras, but in 1599 Shakespeare plays Oberon for the special royal command performance of the play that has led to the temporary secondment of Nathan Field from Richard Mulcaster's company, St Paul's Boys.[18] This brings boy and playwright into a relationship akin to the master–servant – but also quasi-father–son – one that pertains between Oberon and Robin Goodfellow in the play proper.

Shakespeare's presence has a huge emotional impact on Nat: 'I looked at the lines on his face, and at his ordinary brown doublet and hose, and I thought: *Don't go, please don't go*. It wasn't because he was William Shakespeare. I just knew that I liked being with him, more than with anyone I knew' (48–9). They share their personal losses: Shakespeare talking of the drowned Hamnet; Nat for the first time opening up about his father's death. Shakespeare provides the perfect therapy.[19] A facilitating device of this emotional and psychological therapy is the sonnets. Here, though, the 'Young Man' becomes a far more innocent version than Jong's sexually charged Earl of Southampton: Nat is given sonnet number 116, 'Let me not to the marriage of true minds/ Admit impediments', as a way of coming to terms with the loss of his father, and a means of asserting enduring love beyond the grave:

> Love is not love
> Which alters when it alteration finds,
> Or bends with the remover to remove.
> O no, it is an ever fixèd mark
> That looks on tempests and is never shaken;
> (ll. 2–6)

Shakespeare calls Nat his 'sprite', and alert readers think of *The Tempest*'s Ariel at this point. The supposition is confirmed when, back in the twentieth century, Arby, the Company of Boys' director, gives Nat a copy of that play along with the sonnets. Readers, like Nat, are being invited to find connections between the sonnets, the plays, and Shakespeare's 'real' experience.

Arby's role is more significant than even this suggests. Initially he seems an archetype – a stereotype, even – of the tyrannical director (Jong has her own variation on this theme in the form of the Swedish director of Jessica's planned film of *The Merchant of Venice*). When Nat returns to his modern existence, however, he is immediately struck by the similarity between Arby's voice and Richard Burbage's (wonderfully, his Globe experiences enable encounters with Burbage, Heminges and Condell, and even Will Kemp). When Arby's real name is revealed to be Richard Babbage, a magical slippage appears to occur. Arby seems to know about Nat's experiences – even, to a certain extent, to have caused them. Nat's time-travelling is described in retrospect as a version of the archetypal quest journey. He was sent back in time to save Shakespeare from coming into contact with Nathan Field when he had bubonic plague. The 1599 Field is, of course, saved by twentieth-century medical advances (there is much in the book intended to make younger readers appreciate the many conveniences of their modern lives, from hospitals and health care to clean water), and goes on to become a fine adult actor. But that, in this bardolatrous book, is not really the point.[20] The point is that Shakespeare is able to go on to write *Hamlet*, *Lear*, *Othello* and other great plays. As Arby informs Nat: 'We think too much about past and present, Nat ... Time does not always run in a straight line. And once in a while, something is taken away in order that it may be given back' (178–9). Arby had been seeking Nat out, pursuing his own quest narrative: 'To find and cast a boy whose name was Nat Field, who had a fierce painful need strong enough to take him through Time' (179). There is, then, a deep desire for connection, with Shakespeare and the past, in all these books that adopt time travelling as their theme or topos. The Shakespeare who emerges from them is a varied one: from the matinée idol of Jong's cinematically aware narrative, or Atkinson's 'weasel', to the humane father-figure of *King of Shadows*. In Cooper's novel, Nat's narrative also invokes the aforementioned Droeshout engraving, but with intentions other than stressing Shakespeare's manliness:

> Will Shakespeare grinned at me. He wasn't a tall man... His hair was receding, leaving lots of forehead like in the pictures you see in books, but he didn't otherwise look much like the pictures at all. There were more lines on his skin, lines from laughing, and a thicker beard. He wore a little gold hoop in his left ear. (46)

The laughter lines are a further humanising impulse, pulling the iconic image of the engraving back into an understandable context. For, in the end, it is iconic images and ideas that these novels play with and test. The concern is not the complex Shakespearean textual and contextual debates of literary criticism which elsewhere exercise writers like Warner, Murdoch, Isler or Phillips; instead it is Shakespeare's popular image and appeal, the same series of icons and familiar allusions that form the warp and woof of Carter's comedy in *Wise Children*.

Shakespeare in Love begins with an image of Will in his study, trying to write. This iconic moment has been the stuff of countless advertising images and posters. It began *No Bed for Bacon*, and Nat Field conjures up the same picture in *King of Shadows*:

> So I found myself living in the house where Will Shakespeare lodged, and where, for the time being, he wrote his plays and his poems. He spent hours at a time sitting in an upstairs room, scratching away with a quill pen, beside a window that looked out on to a crab-apple tree. (77)

King of Shadows closes, however, not on an image of Shakespeare but on an image of theatre. As with Alan Isler's *Hamlet* appropriation, *The Prince of West End Avenue*, we find ourselves on the threshold of performance, waiting for the curtain to rise: 'And from the top window in the little roofhouse over our gallery, the long clear note of a single trumpet rang out, signalling the audience, telling the actors, calling the world to the theatre. In one hour from now, our play would begin' (181). In this respect, as with *Shakespeare in Love*, the end result is less about 'Shakespeare' than the power and energy of theatre. It is the presentness, the immediacy, of theatrical experience that allows the most amazing time travel of all. Our feelings on watching a Shakespearean play, either in the supposedly 'authentic' surroundings of the Globe or in a school gymnasium, are comparable to Jessica's awed response to Venice in *Serenissima*: 'Perhaps the whole present tense has been abolished' (77).

The Möbius strip is a topological surface that can be formed by taking a long, rectangular strip of paper and rotating the ends by 180 degrees with respect to one another, then joining the ends together to form a loop.[21] It is a two-dimensional surface that has only one side.[22] Shakespeare's plays perform the literary equivalent of this, proving able to retain their origins and yet be retranslated and reperformed, seemingly without end, in subsequent ages. Time ceases to matter: like these narratives, we find ourselves caught – wonderfully so – in an endless loop.

Notes

1   *Bombay Ice* is set entirely in Bombay, and relies for many of its plot intrigues on the geography, both cultural and physical, of the city of Mumbai, as it is now known. Forbes's second novel, *Fish, Blood and Bone* (2000), involves historical research by its protagonist into nineteenth-century Indian plant-hunters and botanical artists. The interview referred to was given on British Radio ('Woman's Hour', BBC Radio 4, 20 September 2000).

2   See Gross (1994) on Shylock's name, which is not a common biblical one. 'Shallach' is the Hebrew word for a cormorant. This association would link the naming to Ben Jonson's later bird-like avaricious Venetian lawyers and senators in *Volpone* (1606). In the eighteenth century, a Jacobean pamphlet was discovered which referred to 'cer-

tain prophecies of a Jew called Caleb Shillocke' (Gross, 1994: 4). Jong's nomenclature responds to this vein of scholarship.

Venice is as much a character as Shakespeare in Jong's novel. Her epigraphs from James/Jan Morris and Virginia Woolf's *Orlando* highlight themes of multiple sexualities and time travel, but also the city's reputation for shape-shifting. Venice has featured as a setting for numerous novels of doomed romance, including Henry James's *The Wings of the Dove*, Thomas Mann's *Death in Venice*, directly alluded to by Jessica when she succumbs to a fever after a walk on the Lido, and Jeanette Winterson's *The Passion*. See Belsey (1995).

3   See Bate (1996) and Marrapodi *et al.* (1993).

4   John Mortimer's *Will Shakespeare* (1977) also features the Wriothesley–Shakespeare relationship. In that novel, a further exponent of the 'biographising' approach to the Shakespearean canon, the earl is nicknamed Hal, and at one point dresses as a horse-thief in an obvious allusion to the *Henry IV* plays. Mortimer hints at bisexuality, but again he is anxious (via his narrator, boy-actor Jack Rice) to defend Shakespeare against charges of homosexuality: 'I must agree that Shakespeare, unlike his teacher Marlowe, would rather lie with a girl or a woman, if one could be had' (113).

5   Other novels that play with the Shakespearean 'life' include Robert Nye's *Mrs Shakespeare* (1993) and *The Late Mr Shakespeare* (2000) (which, like Mortimer's novel is narrated by an actor from the King's Men) and David Pownall's *The Catalogue of Men* (2000).

6   A darker version of Shakespeare is offered by Edward Bond in his play *Bingo* (1974), which sees the Bard as a grasping, unsympathetic landholder late in his life in Stratford-upon-Avon.

7   For the background to the novel's composition and subsequent reception, see Ned Sherrin's introduction to the recently republished Brahms and Simon (1999 (1941)).

8   On this theme in Shakespeare, see Howard (1988).

9   I am grateful to Kate Chedgzoy for discussions of this topic, which she addressed in a BBC Radio 4 special on Sonnet 18 in 1999.

10 This novel has an aspiring woman playwright, Rosalind, who crossdresses to achieve her ends within the confines of Elizabethan society. Her best play turns out – rather ironically, in feminist terms – to have been *The Taming of the Shrew*. The novel improvises on the idea that someone other than Shakespeare wrote his plays. Bate (1997) explores this authorship controversy in some detail, but it is noticeable, in historical terms, that only Beard proposes a woman in the ghost-writer's role (65).

In a fascinating article, Laurie E. Osborne has catalogued the wide range of women's romance fiction that deploys Shakespearean reference, quotation and direct appropriation (1999: 47–64).

11 Jong's novel was completed before the New Globe, but there are parallels with the lifelong efforts of the late US actor Sam Wanamaker to

get the project off the ground. His actor-daughter Zoe poignantly
spoke the Chorus in the theatre's inaugural production of *Henry V*.

12 Gross (1994) discusses a twentieth-century dramatic appropriation of
the text that sees Jessica and Lorenzo (and, indeed, Portia and Bassanio) ten years on, and no longer in love: St John Ervine, *The Lady
of Belmont* (1923) (204–6). Jong seems to share an awareness of this,
observing of the operations of Time: 'Do the stars govern these
things? The planets? Are people attracted because their zodiacs are in
a certain alignment at a certain period of their lives? Would Romeo
and Juliet, ten years later, walk by each other with never a flicker?
Jessica and Lorenzo? Portia and Bassanio?' (92).

13 Elsewhere, she compares the treatment of Hollywood actors to that of
those who suffered under the Stalinist regime, describing herself to
Grigori, the Russian poet who is also on the film festival jury, as a
'survivor of a system just as brutal to artists in its own way' (24).
There is the history of McCarthy in the USA, and it is intriguing
that Sam Wanamaker, elsewhere evoked in the novel in the context of
the building of the New Globe, was an exile from the McCarthy
trials. Jong, however, is not explicit enough about those connections
for a reader to be sure that Jessica is not simply being outrageous in
making such analogies.

14 Isler (1997b). Other canonical works, including 'Kubla Khan' and
The Importance of Being Earnest, are evoked in an embedded way in
the accompanying stories, the implication being that Jewish contribu-
tions to the canon have been marginalised, constituting, as it were,
the 'Op. non cit.' of the title. Isler appropriates Shakespeare to great
effect elsewhere, most extensively in his use of *Hamlet* in *The Prince
of West End Avenue* (1994), but his second novel, *Kraven Images*
(1997a), features a Shakespearean lecturer as its protagonist. *En route*
in this picaresque adventure of plagiarism and assumed identity, he
meets two showgirls who plan a stage spectacular entitled *Bardic Fol-
lies*, including racy versions of *Hamlet* and *Antony and Cleopatra*. The
link with Dora and Nora's revues in Carter's *Wise Children* is self-
evident. Isler's latest novel, *Clerical Errors*, includes the discovery of
a lost Shakespearean manuscript (2001).

15 There is a wickedly funny parody of such tendencies in Kenneth
Branagh (dir.), *In the Bleak Midwinter* (1995) (retitled as *A Midwinter's Tale* for the US market) when, in an audition scene, one particularly intense actor (played by Nicholas Farrell) declares: 'Hamlet is
Bosnia … Hamlet is my grandmother.' On the parodic version of the
play this film provides, see E. Smith (2000).

16 Sam Wanamaker is evoked here also: 'An American actor called Sam
Wanamaker spent half his life making a dream come true, making it
possible for Shakespeare's Globe to be rebuilt in this place. So it was
built, and here it is. The place where Nat Field could be brought to
Nat Field. But not by accident' (Cooper, 1999: 179).

17 Adrian Noble's 1996 film version of *Dream* highlighted these links with a framing sequence, itself an appropriation from the traditional Christmas ballet *The Nutcracker Suite*, of a dreaming boy. See Burnett (2000).

18 In terms of historical focus, it is interesting that once again in this appropriation, it is the Elizabethan, early Shakespeare who is depicted (see also *Serenissima*, *Human Croquet*, *Shakespeare in Love*). The Jacobean moment of Shakespeare has been of less concern to novelists and film directors. One explanation is the play on the possibility of an as yet unfamous Shakespeare: it invites readers and/or audiences to feed in their own knowledge of his later life. But it also surely enables the use of the powerful and iconic figure of Elizabeth I. Cooper (1999) makes much of Nat's meeting with the flirtatious and acute queen towards the end of the novel. James VI and I has not had the same romantic history as the Virgin Queen (we need only to think of Lytton Strachey's *Elizabeth and Essex* (1928) and various films leading up to the most recent *Elizabeth* (dir. Shekhar Kapur, 1998)), and therefore seems a less attractive option in historical romances, which these books certainly are.

19 There are intriguing real-life parallels with uses that have been made of Disney's *The Lion King*, itself an appropriation of *Hamlet*, to help young people come to terms with mortality and grief. See Finkelstein (1999).

20 At one point, which stands in contrast to Jong's anti-academe stance, we learn of Arby's reverence for Shakespearean literary critics, one in particular: 'These are Arby's, he's been going mad buying books at the Globe shop. Specially some guy called Andrew Gurr who writes about the Elizabethan theatre – Arby thinks he's God' (164).

21 In Margaret Atwood's *Cat's Eye* (1990), explored further in Chapter 10, the narrator's brother Stephen introduces her to the concept of the strip: 'He thinks I should develop my mind. In order to help me to do this, he makes a Möbius strip for me by cutting out a long strip of paper, twisting it once and gluing the ends together. This Möbius strip has only one side, you can prove it by running your finger along the surface. According to Stephen, this is a way of visualizing infinity' (218).

22 Definition courtesy of the Microsoft® Encarta® Encyclopedia (1993–99).

FIVE

Iris Murdoch and
the theatrical scene

the theatre is essentially a place of hopes and disappointments and in its cyclical life one lives out in a more vivid way the cyclical patterns of the ordinary world.

Iris Murdoch, The Sea, The Sea

The theatrical (sometimes even melodramatic) nature of events in Iris Murdoch's novels – from *Under the Net* (1954) to *Jackson's Dilemma* (1995) – has been noted by many critics. It is perhaps not surprising that Murdoch (1919–99), an academic married to a recognised Shakespearean critic, John Bayley, should have indulged in Shakespearean allusion of a sustained nature throughout her writing career.[1] Her early novels have been described as existentialist fiction, interested in role-play and debate, and the influence on her work of Jean-Paul Sartre, Samuel Beckett and Albert Camus has been well noted. According to the late Malcolm Bradbury, *Under the Net*, dedicated to the French surrealist Raymond Queneau, is: 'In the manner of surrealism ... set in two Londons, one "necessary" and the other "contingent", but also in a mime theatre, a film studio, and in a surreal Paris itself' (1993: 329).

The practical world of theatre was a point of fascination as much as the literary scene; as well as artists and writers, a number of Murdoch's protagonists are actors and directors. This makes some form of Shakespearean referentiality both inevitable and required in her work since in Shakespeare's appearance-and-reality, role-playing-obsessed drama, British society has found its own cultural marker of social role-play.

Bruno's Dream (1969) is one novel that is overt in its Shake-spearean allusions. Will Boase plays the bantering game of Shake-spearean quotation throughout, and the description of his marriage to Adelaide is shot through with a typically Murdochian sense of irony towards those who deploy Shakespeare as an easy, even authenticating, cultural reference:

> Nor did she, as she wept and signed her new name, Adelaide Boase, for the first time, dream of much later and sunnier days, in spite of Will's cantankerous temper, when her tall twins would be up at Oxford (non-identical, Benedick and Mercutio), when Will would be one of the most famous and popular actors in England and a greatly transformed Adelaide would be Lady Boase. (2001 (1969): 260–1)

There is, as Richard Todd has noted, a kind of easy humour in the precocious naming of the non-identical twins, and the reverence with which British society treats the Shakespearean actor (1979: 57).

But for Elizabeth Dipple, the relevance of Shakespeare to this novel goes deeper than mere surface allusion of the kind Will indulges in:

> The Shakespearean connection is sustained not only as a parody of the great comic frames – twins, fools, a duel, reversals – but also in the hilariously tearful marriage of Will and Adelaide with all its attendant ironies, and the projection of twins to be born, Mercutio and Benedick, one tragic and one comic, non-identical, absurd. (1982: 179)

Twins, which we have discussed in the context of other novels by Trapido and Carter, hold a particular interest for female appropri-ators of Shakespeare. They recur with remarkable frequency in Murdoch novels; Edward and Henrietta Biranne receive the accolade of closing *The Nice and the Good* (1968), as images of optimism for the future, and, as well as Catherine and Nick Fawley in *The Bell* (1958), we have the aforementioned Will and Nick in *Bruno's Dream*.[2] Other characters are 'twinned' in a less biological sense, including Morgan and Simon in *A Fairly Honourable Defeat*.

Another pairing or paired relationship by which Murdoch, like Shakespeare, is intrigued is that of siblings. Sororial and fraternal relations figure largely in her heavily populated novels:[3] significant examples would be Bradley and Priscilla Pearson in *The Black Prince*; Rupert and Simon Foster in *A Fairly Honourable Defeat*; and Charles and James Arrowby in *The Sea, The Sea*. Like

Shakespeare's plays, Murdoch's novels evidence a fascination with the institutions of marriage and family, both their fragility and their endurance. In a manner comparable to that of Trapido or Carter, the Shakespearean family romance provides a potent prism for Murdoch's ruminations on these themes.

In Murdoch's *œuvre*, Shakespeare functions as a wide-reaching metonym for the nature of drama or theatrical experience itself. For Bradbury, this becomes particularly pointed in her later work, from *Bruno's Dream* onwards – novels which directly analyse 'Platonic themes of reality, art and deception' (1993: 370–1). 'Now,' declares Bradbury, 'the important analogy was with theatre, particularly the drama of Shakespeare' (371). While it is certainly true that those later novels consciously use the framework of Shakespearean drama, and often specific texts (three of which will be examined in detail later in this chapter), the metaphorical power of the theatrical experience is evident from Murdoch's first novel. *Under the Net* has a remarkable mime-theatre scene, and its first-person narrator, Jake, self-consciously reads events in his life in terms of theatre:

> I wanted to hold on, just a little longer, to my last act. A premonition of pain made me delay; the pain that comes after the drama, when the bodies have been carried from the stage and the trumpets are silent and an empty day dawns which will dawn again and again to make mock of our contrived finalities. (Murdoch, 1982 (1954): 239)

There is also a dramatic element to the way in which Murdoch 'stages' events in her narratives, a cunning attempt to merge the possibilities of the two genres, and to manipulate and invoke the reader of her fiction in a manner akin to the metatheatrical addresses to the audience so common to early modern drama. This, too, may explain her particular fascination with Shakespeare, although critics have noted an additional kinship between her fiction and the postmodern drama of Beckett and others. Spear observes:

> Like the playwright, Murdoch prepares the stage and sets the scene for her dramas, creating a world of 'them' and 'us', enabling us, as audience, to look in upon the lives of her characters, simultaneously knowing that we are being told a story and yet consciously suspending our disbelief and feeling the essential reality of the events that pass before us. (1995: 19)

There is a conscious construction in Murdoch novels of readers as onlookers, as audience to events, and as an active rather than passive audience, of whom judgement, with all its attendant confusions, is demanded. In early modern drama, the particular theatrical manifestations of this requirement include prologues, epilogues and other forms of direct address to the audience such as soliloquy, as well as the trope of the overhearing scene. Narratorial framing materials in several Murdoch novels, such as *The Black Prince* and *The Sea, The Sea*, constitute her version of the prologue/epilogue; and, as in other authors we study here, first-person narration provides a particularly rich means of reconfiguring the dramatic soliloquy in a narrative context.[4] Murdoch has made the overhearing scene a personal trope in her novels, achieving, according to Spear, a 'duality of action' which finds its most obvious analogue in Shakespearean drama:

> This kind of simultaneous duality of action is present in Shakespearean drama when the theatre audience find themselves observing not only the main action of the play but also a group of characters who have become part of a 'subtext' within the play. Such is the eavesdropping scene in *Twelfth Night* … Similarly in *A Midsummer Night's Dream* the action in the woods is regarded with what Hermia calls a 'parted eye,/ When everything seems double…' (4.1.186–7). (1995: 45)

The plays most frequently evoked in these critical comparisons are Shakespearean comedies. The way in which these texts contain the potential for (and sometimes direct subtexts of) tragic events began to hold a genuine sway over literary criticism and theatrical performance, particularly of plays such as *Twelfth Night*, from the 1960s onwards, when the majority of Murdoch's novels were conceived and composed. Comedy and tragedy, as on the Shakespearean stage, seem dangerously allied in Murdoch's fiction. In truth, the entire canon has resonances within her work: both tragedies and comedies deploy the letter device she proves so fond of in novels such as *The Nice and the Good* and *A Fairly Honourable Defeat* (*Twelfth Night* employs this strategy, but also *Hamlet*, *Love's Labour's Lost* and *Romeo and Juliet*); both genres contain examples of overhearing scenes (*Much Ado About Nothing* and *Twelfth Night*, along with *Hamlet* and *Othello*); both genres profess an interest in the themes of cross-dressing and appearance and reality that provide leitmotivs in Murdoch's work. In turn, Shakespeare's late plays are examples of the questions of mysticism and magic, as well as family relations, that her later fiction was to probe.

In this later work, it is claimed, 'Murdoch's fiction was itself turning into a speculative theatre, where narrative is an illusion through which are constructed serious rituals of reality and self-discovery, and where the deceptions involved in creating the illusion are themselves carefully explored' (Bradbury, 1993: 371). By 'speculative theatre', Bradbury appears to mean work in which stories are invented to test ideas. Murdoch's characters engage with this activity as much as the author herself. This chapter concentrates on the three novels Bradbury singles out as the most developed examples of her engagement in this form (and, indeed, with Shakespearean drama): *A Fairly Honourable Defeat* (1970), *The Black Prince* (1973) and *The Sea, The Sea* (1978).

Midsummer magic and motiveless malignity in *A Fairly Honourable Defeat*

The opening words of *A Fairly Honourable Defeat* constitute a name: 'Julius King' (Murdoch, 1970: 11). This name echoes around the opening pages, as various characters discuss the implications of Julius's return to English shores. He is presented as an ambivalent figure – 'He's not a saint' (11) – and his background as an experimental scientist, who worked in the field of biological warfare, is sketched in. A reader who is alert to the Shakespearean resonances and subtexts of Murdoch's writing may find echoes of *The Tempest* here, and Prospero's abjuration of his 'rough magic' in Act 5. Throughout the novel, the portrayal of Julius King, and the understanding of him exhibited by the other characters who populate the scene, is as an enchanter figure, a seducer and a godlike puppeteer of events. All these terms would be equally apposite in a description of Prospero, surely an experimental scientist of sorts in the play proper? King's experimental laboratory, though, is no sea-girt island but London SW10, the familiar cultural geography of 'Murdochland', to use Bradbury's suggestive phrase.[5] The 'defeat' of the novel's title refers to the break-up of the long-lived marriage of Rupert and Hilda Foster (their twentieth anniversary marks the novel's opening) by the machinations of King, who engineers an affair between benign philosopher Rupert and Hilda's emotional sister Morgan (herself a former King sexual conquest). The affair ends tragically with Rupert's drowning. In the process, other loving – albeit flawed – relationships, such as Simon (Rupert's brother) and Axel's are destabilised, though these two do survive.

At the centre of *A Fairly Honourable Defeat*, Ariel's song for Ferdinand, one which falsely described the drowning and sea-bed metamorphosis of his father's corpse, informs Morgan's intense reaction to the power of nature in the railway-cutting scene that she shares with her nephew Peter:

> Full fathom five thy father lies.
> Of his bones are coral made;
> Those are pearls that were his eyes;
> Nothing of him that doth fade
> But doth suffer a sea-change
> Into something rich and strange.
> Sea-nymphs hourly ring his knell
> (1.2.400–6)

Morgan is led through a series of emotional reactions from joy to repulsion at the world which, in turn, leads her into a condition of acceptance – a state of grace, almost. This also throws herself and Peter into a brief but charged erotic encounter (185–93). Peter will later reject the significance of the moment when he uncovers the truth of Morgan's liaison with his father: 'And what you said in the railway cutting just isn't true, I know that now. *Full fathom five* proves nothing, nothing at all. Except that everything's rich and strange all right, rich and strange and foul. And the bells are ringing but they don't sound pretty any more, not any more at all' (363–4).

Within pages, however, the resonance of a father's drowning will become all too real for Peter, when Rupert's body is found floating in the family swimming pool (423). There have been premonitions of this death throughout the novel, from the drowsy bumblebee that falls in during the opening scene to Simon's fear for the hedgehog that regularly visits the Fosters' garden, and Julius's near-drowning. Ariel's song has the status of literary shorthand for the notion or event of death by drowning: T. S. Eliot deployed it to these ends in his long Shakespeare-soaked poem *The Wasteland*; Marina Warner uses it to similar effect in *Indigo*

for Xanthe's death and metamorphosis; and most recently
Arundhati Roy's Booker-Prize-winning *The God of Small Things*
(1998) used the lines as a poetic refrain to indicate the significance, in the Keralan family history recounted there, of a death by
water.

The Tempest is not the only Shakespearean drama informing the
events and relationships of *A Fairly Honourable Defeat*. Numerous
playtexts are evoked in this theatrically self-aware novel. Settings
and events are frequently described as if they were theatrical scenes
or happenings, and characters, as well as readers, regularly adopt
the subject position of an onlooker or overhearer: 'She turned
again to the garden. The sharp division between sun and shade
made it seem far away, separated from her as if by a proscenium
arch' (43). The affair which Julius cynically engineers between
Rupert and Morgan is partly achieved by means of the theatrical
device of a letter, recalling plotlines from Shakespearean comedies
such as *Twelfth Night* and *Love's Labour's Lost*. The tricking of
two lovers into loving because they believe the other to be in love
with them – that is, by appealing to their vanity – recalls the
gulling of Beatrice and Benedick in *Much Ado About Nothing*. The
structures of festive comedy are surprisingly strong in their register
in this dark novel. If Julius King's machinations within his SW10
community resemble in part Prospero's manipulation of the islanders in *The Tempest*, they are also reminiscent of Oberon's love-play
in *Dream*. The sexual androgyny, as well as powerful mastery, of
this potent enchanter figure (Oberon, as we saw in Chapter 2, has
a long history of female performance) can be registered in Julius's
particular interest in fissuring the relationship between Simon
(Rupert's younger brother) and Axel in *A Fairly Honourable
Defeat*.[6] When Julius describes the ease with which this can be
achieved, he hits the note of detachment evident in Oberon's play
with the Athenian lovers, as well as Puck's disgusted observation:
'Lord, what fools these mortals be!' (3.2.115; R. Todd, 1979: 99):
'Human beings set each other off so. Put three emotional fairly
clever people in a fix and instead of trying quietly to communicate
with each other they'll dream up some piece of communal violence'
(427–8). Elsewhere, Julius is even more explicit about his manipulation of events: 'As I told you, it's just a midsummer enchant-
ment, with two asses!' (266).[7]

Oberon, of course, has a servant in Robin Goodfellow/Puck, the woodland sprite of English folkloric imaginations. Julius's plot relies on the vanity of its participants (in particular Rupert and Morgan: Rupert's downfall from his smug position of Platonist philosopher – a curious moment of self-reference by Murdoch? – has been compared to Malvolio's humiliation in *Twelfth Night*). It also requires the unwitting assistance of Simon whose own anxieties and jealousies almost allow Julius's plot to succeed. It is Simon who is the suspicious onlooker to Rupert and Morgan's exchange in the Prince Rupert museum, which Julius has so carefully stage-managed: 'The two chairs which you so kindly rearranged are just a few feet away from us. They should prove irresistible, don't you think? Our puppets are sure to sit on them' (263).

Earlier in the novel, Murdoch has contrived to associate Simon with Puck (and, indeed, Ariel, continuing the Prospero–Oberon parallel) when he playfully wears the flower wreath he has woven for Morgan:

> Simon had put the wreath on. It fitted him perfectly. The tall crown of roses extended the thin lines of his features and lent a sudden ambiguous elfin beauty to his now rather flushed and laughing face. 'Oh Hilda, I must see myself. I do look rather marvellous, don't I, Axel? Who am I? Puck? Ariel? Peaseblossom? Mustardseed?' (134)

Vanity is evident here, too, in Simon's admiration of his resemblance to a Caravaggio model. By complicating our responses to characters in this way, ensuring that no one is entirely 'good' or 'innocent' in this novel, Murdoch retains the opacity of Julius King's actions in readers' minds as well as those of his 'victims'. It is telling that Julius does not endure any punishment in the novel: he ends in a sunlit Paris, and the novel closes, as he reads a restaurant menu, on the phrase 'Life was good' (447). Julius has told Rupert elsewhere in the narrative that evil is 'opaque' (223).

Shakespeare's tragedies, rather than his comedies, are the plays most associated with a philosophical exploration of evil. Macbeth, Lady Macbeth, Edmund of Gloucester, and Claudius are all part of the Bard's ongoing dramatic rumination on the theme. The character most associated with the opacity of evil actions in Shakespeare – with what has famously been described as 'motiveless malignity' – is Iago from *Othello*.[8] It is in Iago that we might want to identify the third Shakespearean subtext to the character of Julius King.

The Iago analogy is not, however, a secure one. The eponymous hero of *Othello* (1603–04) famously does not appear in the opening scene of the play, although his name and various derogatory nick-names resound off the walls of the Venetian *palazzi* which provide the ostensible locale for Iago's public declaration (via his puppet Roderigo) of 'the Moor's' clandestine marriage to Desdemona:

> 'Swounds, sir, you're robbed. For shame, put on your gown.
> Your heart is burst, you have lost half your soul.
> Even now, very now, an old black ram
> Is tupping your white ewe. Arise, arise!
>
> (1.1.86–9)

Othello does not appear until Act I Scene 2, by which time the audience has already been subjected to both Iago's and Brabanzio's prejudiced readings. Something similar is true of the account(s) of Julius King proffered to the reader at the opening of *A Fairly Honourable Defeat*: Rupert and Hilda might be expected to hold a prejudicial opinion of a man who had an affair with Hilda's sister, Morgan, only to leave her once it had led to the break-up of her marriage to Tallis.[9] *Othello* appears to inform the dramatic structure of this opening scene of Murdoch's novel, in that here, too, as in the play ('Tush, never tell me!' (1.1.1)), we enter mid-conversation:

> 'Julius King.'
> 'You speak his name as if you were meditating upon it.'
> 'I am meditating upon it.'
> 'He's not a saint.' (11)

Iago works his poison on Othello by feeding the general's propensity to jealousy. The image the ensign uses for this action (which itself offers a parallel with the murder of Old Hamlet by Claudius in *Hamlet*) is of pouring pestilence into Othello's ear: 'Let's see./ After some time to abuse Othello's ears/ That he [Michael Cassio] is too familiar with his wife;' (1.3.376–8). Telling-ly, when Julius first renders Simon complicit with his intrigues, he does so by whispering in his ear.[10] The Iago reference re-emerges at this point, although it is intriguing that in the same soliloquy

from *Othello*, the world of *Dream*, one of asses and misunderstand-
ings in love, is conjured up, albeit in a tragic context. Murdoch's
implicit connection of the two plays in Julius has roots in Shakespeare's language:

> The Moor is of a free and open nature,
> That thinks men honest that but seem to be so
> And will as tenderly be led by the nose
> As asses are.
>
> (1.3.381–4)

Julius is both Prospero and Oberon, Iago and Othello: the equa-
tions are never exact or complete. This reveals an important fact
about Murdoch's Shakespearean appropriations: they do not function as direct allegories of specific plays but, rather, require the
complexity of readings each play has produced to nuance and shade
the imaginative picture Murdoch creates.

Many of Murdoch's novels interrogate the possibilities and attendant dangers of freedom in a social context. This may explain
the attraction of Shakespearean servant–master relationships, such
as Puck and Oberon or Ariel and Prospero, as templates and allusive frameworks. Murdoch asks the ultimate existential question as
to how honest any of the social parts we play truly are.

Othello is a play that self-consciously evokes and subverts comic
dramatic conventions such as the father-daughter estrangement of
Brabanzio and Desdemona over the contested issue of marriage,
which promotes the action here as much as it does in *Dream*, and
the overhearing scenes in which the audience has privileged
knowledge. In *Othello*, however, Iago carries human propensity to
misunderstand what we are watching or witnessing to its tragic
conclusion when he persuades Othello of the relationship between
Cassio and Desdemona. His assistant stage property in this matter
is the notorious handkerchief. That talismanic prop finds its own
parallels in the malachite paperweight and amber bead necklace
which significantly change hands, and are 'read' and interpreted as
much as the letters by characters in *A Fairly Honourable Defeat*.[11]
Iago engineers overhearing scenes, and so does Julius King – from
the compromising nakedness of Simon with Morgan in King's
own flat to the ultimate staged event of the clandestine museum
meeting (262).

In these instances the reader, like the audience in any staged overhearing scene, has alternative knowledge to the onlooker in the story:

> Just as Shakespeare creates a 'double drama' when he provides his audience with a stage audience as well as a staged action to watch in the eavesdropping scenes ... so Julius ensnares Simon in the eavesdropping scene at the museum and the reader observes a triple action – Morgan and Rupert, Julius's 'puppets', Simon the innocent onlooker and Julius the 'magician'. (Spear, 1995: 69)

When Julius 'discovers' Simon naked in his flat, Morgan (whose clothes he previously cut to ribbons with scissors) is dressed in Simon's clothes. This is just one of a series of invocations of the early modern theatrical convention of cross-dressing that Murdoch was to make (usually in an erotic context) in her Shakespearean novels. The 'twinning' of Morgan and Simon has been hinted at by comments on their similar appearances, and there is a vanity as well as a gender ambivalence in their previous relationship (163). Julius now carries that further, declaring to Morgan: 'you make a lovely lovely boy' (166). This scene prefigures more extended studies of the power games involved in men's attraction to boyish girls in novels such as *The Black Prince* and *The Sea, The Sea* (where the Puck–Ariel comparisons are also relevant).

If Simon and Morgan figure as Puck or Ariel (the fairy associations of Morgan's name – Morgan le Fay – are pertinent here), and Julius embodies elements of Prospero, Oberon, Iago and Othello, we might want to ask what other character comparisons can be found in the novel. On close inspection, several characters hold an Othello-like relationship of vulnerability to Julius-Iago's enchantments and seductions. Simon may be Puck at certain points, but in the museum overhearing scene he is also the jealous Moor. Rupert's pride in his marriage renders him Othello-like in his openness to Julius's insinuations, but so does Hilda's. Axel at times plays the role of jealous and suspicious lover, even constructing himself as noble in the face of events around him (Julius plays on this by contriving secret assignations between himself and Simon, which he then encourages Axel to 'discover').

From her first novel onwards, Murdoch exhibited a fascination with the power of language to conceal as much as reveal. Silence carries a particular charged power in novels such as *The Black Prince*. As Spear notes: 'Language, communication, can all too easily be used to conceal rather than to expose. Both speaker and listener place their own interpretations on what is said, understanding what they want to believe, creating through their use of words a wall of misunderstanding' (1995: 21). In Shakespeare, Murdoch found an obvious kinship with this interest, but the question remained for her whether the transformation of this from a dramatic context into narrative could be achieved only through the self-conscious staging of scenes ('speculative theatre') of which *A Fairly Honourable Defeat* is an exercise in kind. Spear registers a paramount shift in Murdoch's later work, in which: 'The looking-in on little theatrical scenes which is so much part of the actual writing of the earlier novels ... has gradually given way to more deliberate dramatic structuring' (1995: 119). The answer, for Murdoch, to Shakespeare's philosophical metatheatricality, which defined a relationship between audience and text in which the audience was required to move in and out of a position of judgement and ironic awareness, seems to rest – as for so many of the authors studied here – in the complex and wide-ranging possibilities of first-person narration. Perhaps it is no surprise that the Shakespeare plays Murdoch uses to explore the possibilities of unreliable narration in this way are in many respects his most self-consciously philosophical and metatheatrical playtexts: *Hamlet* and *The Tempest*.

'I am not Prince Hamlet': *The Black Prince*

The Black Prince is a novel deeply invested in art and aesthetics. It is one of a number of Murdoch novels narrated in the first person by an artist (*The Sea, The Sea*, her 1978 *Tempest* appropriation, is another, narrated as it is by the retired theatre director Charles Arrowby). *The Black Prince* is narrated by the retired tax inspector – but also writer – Bradley Pearson. The plot concerns Bradley's all-consuming passion for a young woman, Julian, daughter of his chief writing rival, Arnold Baffin. It works itself out through a series of betrayals (including a relationship between Baffin and Pearson's first wife; the unrequited passion of Baffin's wife for

Pearson himself, and the ultimate suicide of Pearson's sister), concluding in the murder of Baffin and the narrator's arrest (despite protestations of innocence).

The novel's title is an allusion to a declaration by Lavatch the clown in *All's Well That Ends Well* that he serves the ultimate of masters: 'The Black Prince, sir, alias the prince of darkness, alias the devil' (4.5.36–7). Bradley Pearson's own initials may connect him in a surface sense to the titular Black Prince, and the allusion to Lavatch's statement may link him further with either the demonic or the foolish: is he, by association, the clown prince of this text, our self-deluded narrator?

The Black Prince's most obvious and sustained Shakespearean intertext, however, is not *All's Well*'s tragicomic tale of bed tricks, but Shakespeare's ultimate philosophical tragedy, *Hamlet*. Onstage in productions of that play there is an obvious 'black prince': the Prince of Denmark dressed in a suit of mourning for his dead father, the 'nightly colour' his mother pleads with him to discard (1.2.68):

> 'Tis not alone my inky cloak, good-mother,
> Nor customary suits of solemn black,
> Nor windy suspiration of forced breath,
> No, nor the fruitful river in the eye,
> Nor the dejected haviour of the visage,
> Together with all moods, forms, shows of grief
> That can denote me truly. These indeed 'seem',
> For they are actions that a man might play;
> But I have that within which passeth show –
> These but the trappings and the suits of woe.
>
> (1.2.77–86)

This connection conjures up a series of associations between the events of the novel and the play's protagonist.[12] The literal text of *Hamlet* is a cause or contributing factor in the coming together of the fifty-eight-year-old narrator and the twenty-year-old daughter of his novelistic rival.[13] Julian Baffin (her androgynous name has its own significations, as we shall see) has played the Prince of Denmark in an amateur production, and her description of the costume she wore for her cross-dressed performance becomes an erotic totem for Pearson. Insisting that she describe this costume, he later convinces himself that this is the point when he fell in love with her: 'Perhaps it was when she said, "Black tights and black velvet shoes with silvery buckles"' (Murdoch, 1973: 205). Her 'dressing-up' in a costume akin to the one she wore for the performance, and her self-conscious pose with a sheep skull, later promote the violent sexual consummation of their troubled relationship (328).

Mediated through the text of *Hamlet*, and Pearson's insistent association of Julian with the eponymous hero, Shakespeare becomes invested with an erotic charge in this novel (Dipple, 1982: 123). This is undoubtedly linked to the androgynous power of the boy-actor in the Elizabethan theatre; when Pearson first sees Julian in the course of the narrative, he assumes that she is male:

> In this mood of rather doom-ridden spiritual lassitude I noticed with only a little surprise and interest the figure upon the other side of the road of a young man who was behaving rather oddly. He was standing upon the kerb and strewing flowers upon the roadway, as if casting them into a river…
>
> The young man was slim, dressed in dark narrow trousers, a sort of dark velvet or corduroy jacket and a white shirt. He had a thickish mane of slightly wavy brown hair which grew well down on to his neck. I had paused and had been watching him for some moments and was about to set off again towards the station when, with one of those switches of *gestalt* which can be so unnerving, I realised … this was in fact no young man but a girl. In the next moment I further realised that it was a girl whom I knew. It was Julian Baffin, Arnold and Rachel's teenage daughter and only child. (So named, I need hardly explain, after Julian of Norwich.) (54–5)

Julian's androgynous nomenclature and appearance lend a quasi-homoerotic frisson to this encounter, which Francis Marloe will, in his subsequent postscript (one of several offered from different characters' points of view – just the most overt of Murdoch's use of destabilising postmodernist techniques in this complex and self-aware novel), ascribe to Pearson's latent homosexuality. Certainly, Julian's persistent association with Hamlet in the text has led critics to comment on the complexity of identifying exactly who the Hamlet-character is in this novel. Is it Pearson, the self-assigned Black Prince, or the twenty-year-old object of his sexual obsessions? In some of their sexually charged discussions of the play, Julian would seem to open up the possibility of Bradley's playing a Claudius-type role. He was sexually implicated with her mother,

Rachel (Gertrude?), before his relations with Julian herself, and
there is certainly an enemy–brother-type construction to be made
of his relationship with her father, whom Pearson jealously claims
as his more successful protégé. By the close of the novel, Pearson
is implicated in Baffin's death (a cynical fabrication by Rachel, at
least in his subjective account), and an Old-Hamlet–Claudius reading of their relationship might seem to be confirmed. Interestingly,
in teasing Julian, Pearson suggests at one point that these two
characters may have been in love: another homosexual reading which
Marloe will ascribe directly to Pearson's relationship with Baffin.

Despite the seemingly incontrovertible association of Julian as
the Hamlet-figure of this novel by critics such as Spear and Dipple,
the passage quoted at length above, which describes Pearson's first
confused encounter with her in the text, surely associates Julian in
the first instance not with the Prince but with his abused lover
Ophelia (Spear, 1995: 76; Dipple, 1982: 44). When Pearson sees
her strewing what are presumed to be flowers into a river-like
roadway, Julian's behaviour recalls Ophelia's onstage mad scene
and offstage drowning:

> There is a willow grows aslant a brook
> That shows his hoar leaves in the glassy stream.
> Therewith fantastic garlands did she make
> Of crow-flowers, nettles, daisies and long purples.
>   (4.7.137–40)

In the play, these actions are a direct result of the murder of
Ophelia's father, Polonius, by her lover, Hamlet. An alternative
construction of the Baffin–Pearson relationship now seems possible.
As if to confirm these Ophelia-associations, we learn from Julian's
subsequent conversation with Pearson that the white fragments
she is seen throwing away are not petals at all, but scraps of torn-
up love letters: 'My lord, I have remembrances of yours/ That I
have longed long to redeliver' (3.1.95–6). Readers later see her
attired in a dress patterned with willow sprays, and in her own
postscript she talks of how the death of her father 'drove me nearly
mad' (408). As with *A Fairly Honourable Defeat*, the links between
Murdochian and Shakespearean characters are persistently labile.

As ever with Murdoch's Shakespearean-influenced texts, a
further series of embedded allusions associate Julian Baffin's story

with *Dream* and the sexually ambivalent power of Oberon the Fairy King. Remembering Julian as a young girl, Pearson describes his friends' daughter as a 'fairy-like little girl' (55), and there is a sense in which his and Baffin's war over her as a possession is akin to the battle in *Dream* over the Indian Boy. Baffin later alludes to the events of Shakespeare's midsummer-based festive comedy: 'Bradley ... what you are saying describes nothing which could possibly have happened in the real world ... it's nearly midsummer and you are, perhaps, reaching the age when men make asses of themselves' (280).

But it is the *Hamlet* framework which remains the most persistent in the novel, even though the *dramatis personae* never function on a one-to-one basis with the Shakespearean original (R. Todd, 1979: 30). Part of Pearson's personal attraction to *Hamlet* (indeed, obsession with: this is a text about obsession, like so many Murdoch novels) is the sheer centrality of the protagonist. There is a case for suggesting that he tries to accord himself a comparable position in this narrative. When he discusses the sonnets and *Hamlet* as those texts in which Shakespeare most overtly inscribed his identity, he seems to be referring to the relevance he finds to himself. There is an egotism at the heart of Pearson's Shakespearean criticism which the alert reader cannot fail to notice. In fact, his reading of Shakespeare is essentially a misreading, one which adopts Shakespeare for selfish purposes. In Murdoch, the identification by characters with Shakespeare is often suspect: it is an indication of self-dramatisation, or – as in Julius King's or Charles Arrowby's case – an attempt to justify the rendering of people as puppets in an egotistical game.[14]

The 'Four Postscripts by *Dramatis Personae*', just one of Murdoch's complex framing apparatuses in this novel, delivered as they are by Christian (Pearson's equally androgynously named first wife, who was engaged in an affair with Baffin, offering the further alternative of reading Baffin and Christian as Claudius and Gertrude), Rachel, Francis Marloe (whose name teasingly contains the suggestion of two of the writers posited as being the 'real' authors of Shakespeare's *œuvre*: Francis Bacon and Christopher Marlowe), and Julian herself, offer the reader alternative points of view that displace Pearson from his self-assigned Shakespearean centrality. The reader's enforced consciousness of the possibility of unreliable narration ensures that irony is the primary operative method in this novel. Dipple describes Murdoch's 'enclosure of a realist tale … by an elaborate system of qualifying forewords and postscripts' (1982: 110). This is further enforced by the Fowlesian intrusions into the narrative of Pearson's direct addresses to the 'dear friend' (a role 'Loxias' later claims as his, though once again there is no textual confirmation of this supposition).

Pearson's text claims all kinds of accuracy and authenticity in rendering its account of the past; yet that very claim undermines the viability of leaving the present behind in an effort to construct the past (something similar operates in the 'Prehistory' and 'History' sections of *The Sea, The Sea*). A further frame to Pearson's narrative is provided by the 'Editor's Foreword' and 'Postscript'. These are authored by one 'P. Loxias', a publisher who appears to have met Pearson following his arrest and trial, and whose acquaintance with him therefore postdates the events being described. Marloe, in his Freudian analysis of Pearson, suggests that Loxias may not exist at all, but is (like Hamlet himself) one of Pearson's constructed *alter egos*. The reader is – frustratingly – given no evidence either way, although Loxias claims in the 'Postscript' to be writing after Pearson's death. This would seem clear enough, except when we consider that he is writing an utterly defensive and supportive piece, a kind of historical reclamation of Pearson, which would render Loxias the Horatio of this tale:

> O God, Horatio, what a wounded name,
> Things standing thus unknown, shall live behind me!
> If thou didst ever hold me in thy heart,
> Absent thee from felicity a while,
> And in this harsh world draw thy breath in pain
> To tell my story.
>
> (5.2.286–91)

So it would be perfectly reasonable to assume that Pearson could have invented this, too.

As in Shakespeare's play, appearance and reality are at the heart of this oblique novel. Pearson's name alerts us to this fact. As well as containing resonances of literary role-play (and his opening discourse is obsessed with the idea of roles) – Pearson = person = persona – it also alludes to F. H. Bradley, author of a philosophical tome on the subject (Dipple, 1982: 110).[15] In turn, of course, this evokes his brother, A. C. Bradley, the nineteenth-century character-based Shakespearean literary critic, whose work Murdoch deeply admired.[16]

The question of appearance and reality is a central operating factor in any understanding of the role of the unreliable narrator in postmodernist fiction. Many of Pearson's less palatable obsessions emerge only accidentally from the reader's engagement with his narrative. His heightened sensitivity to smells – which verges, as the narrative progresses, on repulsion – is just one example of this. Marloe will again confirm the psychological significance of this phobia in his analytical postscript (Murdoch exposes Marloe's own mercenary motives in that he is publishing a sub-Freudian study of Pearson that seeks to capitalise on the scandal surrounding his trial: *Bradley Pearson, Paranoic from the Paper Shop*). Richard Todd has identified a further link with Hamlet in terms of his own repulsion at the 'rank sweat' of his mother's incestuous bed, which he takes as a metonym for the rank condition of Danish society (Todd, 1979: 34). One of the most significant of these repulsions – which further extends the connection with Hamlet, and serves to cast at least some doubt on the objectivity of Pearson's history, in particular his version of Rachel Baffin – is the embedded hatred of women. Pearson – in, as Marloe tells us, a classic Oedipal paradigm – claims to worship his mother, yet has strangely troubled memories of the paper-shop locale in which he and Priscilla passed their childhood (Pearson's sister Priscilla, whose concealed suicide prompts Julian to abandon her love hideaway, is another quasi-Ophelia in this tale). Elsewhere in the novel, older women appear as predators and sirens, figures of hatred and vitriol: 'Ships are compartmental and hollow, ships are like women. The steel vibrated and sang, sang of the predatory women, Christian, Marigold, my mother: the destroyers' (109). Pearson seems similarly to under-estimate the intelligence of younger women, consigning them to a contained notion of innocence: 'my dear Julian, pure ignorant young girls cannot save complicated neurotic over-educated older men from disaster' (196). Hamlet's stereotypical construction of women is instantly recalled: 'frailty, thy name is woman' (1.2.146); indeed, 'frailty' is the very term Pearson deploys in attempting to under-stand Julian's emotional vulnerability when she leaps from a moving car in order to 'prove' her love for him (309).

The Black Prince is a genre conscious text. It begins in, best thriller tradition, with an imagined murder, and ends with a real one. It is also deeply self-referential to its treatment of the events of the plot in quasi-dramatic terms. Murdoch did subsequently adapt *The Black Prince* for the London stage, but it is the theatrical manner with which Pearson constructs his past which gives us most pause, since it questions any claimed objectivity or authenticity in that it draws attention to the acts of creation, selection and ordering. Pearson attempts to claim a sort of immediacy for his narrative (or 'fable' – a term which denies the authentic):

> Although several years have now passed since the events recorded in this fable, I shall in telling it adopt the modern technique of narration, allowing the narrating consciousness to pass like a light along its series of present moments, aware of the past, unaware of what is to come. (11)

But elsewhere the impossibility of this narratorial innocence becomes plain:

> It might be most dramatically effective to begin the tale at the moment when Arnold Baffin rang me up and said, 'Bradley, could you come round please. I think that I have just killed my wife.' A deeper pattern however suggests Francis Marloe as the first speaker, the page or housemaid (these images would appeal to him) who, some half an hour before Arnold's momentous telephone call, initiates the action. (21)

Fiction only ever ascribes an inauthentic order, a beginning and an ending to ongoing events, as Murdoch frequently observed in her fiction. As Pearson remarks, 'Where after all does anything begin?' (21).

The deeper patterns to this novel ultimately, however, derive from Shakespeare, and Murdoch, in deploying Shakespeare's most influential tragic drama, is not oblivious to the downscaling of its themes and events. The three parts of the central narrative certainly map on to the three acts of a play, with the first act introducing us to the characters and relationships, the middle act containing the great defining moment (Pearson's realisation of his love for Julian) and the third act the dénouement or resolution (tragic in this instance). If, as Richard Todd has brilliantly suggested, *Hamlet* is a play not just about revenge but about 'what it is to commit the concept of revenge to drama' (1979: 38),

Murdoch in turn considers what it is to transport those themes into fiction, a bourgeois form and context. She is not afraid to acknowledge the quasi-comic results of that transposition of genre: *The Black Prince* identifies the novel as, in many respects, a form that is resistant to tragedy (more suitable, perhaps, to Murdoch's own favoured mode of irony): 'Almost any tale of our doings is comic. We are bottomlessly comic to each other. Even the most adored and beloved person is comic to his lover. The novel is a comic form' (81). In this respect, perhaps, Murdoch does have the final word on Pearson's pretensions to be Hamlet. He is in too bourgeois a body, context and genre ever truly to achieve that identification. That, perhaps, is – as with Eliot's Prufrock – part of his tragedy.

'Written in water': *The Sea, The Sea* and *The Tempest*

Malcolm Bradbury has described *The Black Prince*, with its 'various narrators and narrative deceptions', as Murdoch's 'most "meta-fictional" novel' (1993: 371), but her 1978 Booker-Prize-winning *The Sea, The Sea* must be a close rival for that title. The role of the unreliable or untrustworthy narrator is central to both: Dipple describes both Bradley Pearson and Charles Arrowby, narrator of *The Sea, The Sea*, as 'maddening' (1982: 275). But whereas *The Black Prince* deploys framing devices, including no fewer than six contradictory postscripts to the main narrative, the generic ambiguities and instabilities of *The Sea, The Sea* are built into its heart.

Arrowby is a retired theatre director who has withdrawn to a remote island community, presumably to live out his days peacefully. During this sojourn, which his narrative recounts in detail, he encounters a former lover, Mary Hartley Smith, and subsequently subjects her and her family to a series of invasions and abductions in an attempt to win her back. Arrowby's efforts fail, but not before he has done considerable damage, both emotional and physical, to those around him, including his own brother and another former partner, Lizzie.

Charles's self-imposed exile has parallels not only to the enforced island occupation of Prospero in *The Tempest* but to a particular strain of criticism of that play which, somewhat sentimentally and self-indulgently (it ignores the fact that Shakespeare continued to work on drama in a collaborative capacity), regards it as the dramatist's farewell to the stage. This problematic association of Shakespeare with his magus-protagonist is clearly one to which Arrowby himself is attracted. Reflecting on his life in the course of the narrative, he describes this time on the island as a fifth act of sorts: 'now the main events of my life are over and there is to be nothing but "recollection in tranquillity"' (Murdoch, 1978: 1). Wordsworth's poetic powers of imaginative reconstitution of events are also invoked here, but Arrowby, born in Warwickshire, near the Forest of Arden, has what can only be described as an obsession with the Bard, frequently reading events in his own life through the prism of particular plays or characters. He self-consciously constructs himself as Prospero, declaring: 'Now I shall abjure magic and become a hermit: put myself in a situation where I can honestly say that I have nothing else to do but to learn to be good' (2). The obvious allusion is to Prospero's fifth-act renunciation:

> But this rough magic
> I here abjure. And when I have required
> Some heavenly music – which even now I do –
> To work mine end upon their senses that
> This airy charm is for, I'll break my staff,
> Bury it certain fathoms in the earth,
> And deeper than did ever plummet sound
> I'll drown my book.
>
> (5.1.50–57)

The alert reader, however – and Murdoch surely always demands alertness of her readers – may also find echoes of another character. This association casts doubt on the self-professed certainties of Arrowby's assigned role. Charles claims that he will 'learn to be good': compare Caliban's promise in Act 5 that he will 'be wise hereafter,/ And seek for grace' (5.1.298–9). What might appear on the surface to be a straightforward analogue between Arrowby and Prospero is diffused and destabilised. Just as the Prospero of the play contains troubling elements of both Sycorax and Caliban (the soliloquy at 5.1 is a direct reworking of a speech by Medea, the herbalist-witch of Ovid's *Metamorphoses* and, elsewhere in the play, a more obvious intertextual counterpart to Sycorax; in Caliban's case, he is the 'thing of darkness' Prospero acknowledges as his own in the fifth act), so Charles is a complex hybrid of these possibilities. The diffusing and hybridising of Shakespeare's *dramatis personae* is a technique that Helen Gilbert and Joanne Tompkins have argued is particularly pertinent to theatrical appropriations of this play (where performative conventions such as role-doubling can be deployed) 'in ways which fictional rewritings of *The Tempest* cannot approximate' (1996: 33). This underestimates Murdoch's comparable form of diffusion of characterology that both enables and invites a complex and insightful consideration of identity.

Genre as much as character is a diffused entity in this novel. Charles appears at the start to be writing a memoir of sorts, but that is rapidly forestalled, most noticeably in a shift of tense which is characteristic of Arrowby's narrative throughout, a confirmation of the confused state of his mind and thinking:

> The sea which lies before me *as I write* glows rather than sparkles in the bland May sunshine … Near to the horizon it is a luxurious purple, spotted with regular lines of emerald green. At the horizon it is indigo … I *had written* the above, destined to be the opening paragraph of my memoirs, when something happened which was so extraordinary and so horrible that I cannot bring myself to describe it even now after an interval of time and although a possible, though not totally reassuring, explanation has occurred to me. Perhaps I shall feel calmer and more clear-headed after yet another interval. (1; emphasis added)

Elsewhere Arrowby states: 'I *spoke* of a memoir' (1; emphasis added), establishing a tension between written and oral, as well as past and present.

The definition of a memoir is 'a biography or historical account'. As a form it is usually inflected by personal knowledge, but it is a nostalgic enterprise, a reflection on what is past, and in that way rather different to a diary, which would be written in the present moment, with a sense of immediacy and without the benefits of hindsight. Bradley Pearson tries to write his narrative as if he were without hindsight in *The Black Prince* – a flawed objective, as we have seen. Charles, too, seems uncertain about the generic status of his literary enterprise:

> I have considered writing a journal, not of happenings for there will be none, but as a record of mingled thoughts and daily observations: 'my philosophy', my *pensées* against a background of simple descriptions of

the weather and other natural phenomena… Of course there is no need
to separate 'memoir' from 'diary' or 'philosophical journal'. I can tell
you, reader, about my past life and about my 'world-view' also, as I
ramble along. Why not? It can all come out naturally as I reflect. Thus
unanxiously (for am I not now leaving anxiety behind?) I shall discover
my 'literary form'. (2)

Anxiety is, in truth, never far from the surface of Charles's fissured
narrative, and by the very next page he is wondering about the
genre of autobiography as his mode: 'To repent of egoism: is autobiography the best method?' (3).

Memoir, diary, journal and autobiography are related – albeit
distinct – forms of life-writing, but at other times in the narrative
Charles is so precise about his culinary activities that the text
seems almost to resemble a cookbook. The shifting of modes and
tenses, and the novel's resistance to closure – 'That no doubt is
how the story ought to end' (477) – which will be discussed in
more detail later, are all evidence of the instability of Arrowby's
position and account.

There are obvious ways in which Arrowby's sojourn at Shruff
End relates to Prospero's time on the island in Shakespeare's 1611
play. The library of books which contributed to Prospero's
alienation from his political responsibilities, and which Gonzalo
the kind counsellor ensured travelled with the deposed Duke of
Milan and his baby daughter on their journey, are recalled in
Arrowby's 'book room'; the 'inner room' of his tower is reminiscent of Prospero's 'cell', one of Shakespeare's most intriguing stage
locations. Arrowby's attitude towards the house is one of coloniser; like Prospero, he asserts (or attempts to assert) control over
his alien surroundings: 'I am very conscious of the house existing
quietly round about me. Parts of it I have colonised, other parts
remain obstinately alien and dim' (17). It is no coincidence that
for him the space resembles a theatre: 'It has the expectant air of
a stage set' (17).

But it is not merely space that Arrowby, and Prospero before
him, seeks to control and manipulate, but history too. Murdoch
emphasises this by calling the three sections of this carefully structured novel (themselves suggestive of the three acts of a play, akin
to the structure of *The Black Prince*): Prehistory, History and Postscript. The postscript here functions as an epilogue. Prospero's

epilogue, a direct address to the audience, is one of Shakespeare's most influential moments of metatheatre –

> Now my charms are all o'erthrown,
> And what strength I have's mine own,
> Which is most faint. Now 'tis true
> I must be here confined by you
> Or sent to Naples.
>
> (Epilogue, ll. 1–5)

– and the subtitle of Arrowby's postscript plays wittily on the dramatic epilogue's own ability to hint at a life beyond the play, after the final act: 'Life Goes On'. It is Charles's account of things and people that we are resolutely given. Hartley's perspectives on the events described here might seem rather different.

This controlling and manipulating of history and the past is a central element in Act 1 Scene 2, the scene in *The Tempest* when we first see Shakespeare's magus-ruler, in a revealing exchange with his daughter Miranda. Arrowby has, of course, been quick to tell us at the start of the novel that he is 'wifeless, childless, brotherless, sisterless' (3): this is misleading, since his brother James will prove a crucial player in the narrative (and their rivalry is a further parallel with that between Prospero and Antonio in *The Tempest*), but there are also important ways in which Murdoch recasts the father–daughter relationship of Prospero and Miranda into the power games Charles indulges in with regard to Hartley. As with Miranda's life on the island, this involves confinement and control; at various stages, Charles abducts both Hartley and her son Titus.

When we first see Prospero onstage, the tempest has already been raised and Miranda, having witnessed the resulting trauma from onshore (sharing the audience's perspective on the first scene – an interesting moment of the initiation of empathy by Shakespeare, since we therefore share Miranda's concern here), begs her father to allay the 'wild waters' (1.2.2). Prospero – agreeing to this, and saying he did all in care of his daughter – decides she should 'know farther' (1.2.33), and proceeds to fill Miranda in on the details of her until-now-obscured personal history. The stage dynamic is telling here: Prospero dominates the dialogue, Miranda merely chipping in with one- or two-line reactions or questions. At the close of the discussion, Prospero hypnotises her into sleep so that he may engage in discussion with his spirit Ariel (the audience is invited by this juxtaposition to read this parent–child-like relationship as an equally controlling and manipulative one).

We will see in later chapters how Warner's *Indigo* and Forbes's *Bombay Ice*, both novelistic adaptations of *The Tempest*, are deeply influenced by the literary criticism of that play which was current in the 1980s and 1990s – that is to say, postcolonial and feminist readings. Murdoch's novel provides a kind of prehistory to those narratives, published as it was in 1978, before the strongest wave of postcolonial critiques of Shakespeare appeared. Feminist theory is rarely something Murdoch pays deep regard to in her novels, but her explorations of power do enable her to draw on readings of Prospero as a tyrant-patriarch, and to feed these into her portrayal of Charles. The benign white wizard of earlier twentieth-century readings and stage interpretations of Prospero began, in the 1960s and 1970s, to give way to darker, more ambivalent accounts of his role in the events of the play. These were in part influenced by feminist and Foucauldian theories (there was a parallel shift in readings of Duke Vincentio in *Measure for Measure*), and Murdoch's protagonist in *The Sea, The Sea* is clearly shaped, at least in part, by this paradigm shift.[17]

Magic, though, has always possessed a negative and confusing power in Murdoch's novels. Critics frequently remark on her interest in magus- or enchanter-figures, from Julius King in *A Fairly Honourable Defeat* to Thomas McCaskerville and Jess Baltram in *The Good Apprentice* (1985) and Lucas in *The Green Knight* (1993). Dipple remarks: 'One of the most frequently used, dangerous words in Murdoch is magic; she associates it not only with human misuse of theories, ideology and religious materials, but also with chimerical delights of the surfaces of art' (1982: 5). These views accord with Platonic warnings against the use of art as magic expounded in the *Timaeus*, and link Murdoch to contemporary writers like John Fowles and Muriel Spark, who deployed similar themes (Dipple, 1982: 99).[18] Fowles did so most overtly in his own *Tempest* appropriation, *The Magus*.[19] That text – first written in 1966 but revised in 1977 and therefore directly contemporaneous with *The Sea, The Sea* – has clear links with Murdoch's *Tempest* novel. It involves an equally self-conscious and self-deluded first-person narration, full of shifting tenses and artificial endings (the name of the narrator, Nicholas D'Urfe, advertises its own Platonic associations: D'Urfé was a 1620s French Platonic author) and, like Murdoch's writing, self-consciously deploys the medieval and Shakespearean romance structures of spirals and circularity (Alexander, 1990: 64). T. S. Eliot's *Four Quartets* serves as a talismanic object in this novel, placed as it is on the beach, with the quote 'The end is in the beginning' drawn to the finder's attention. Simon Loveday has described the 'sea-girt isolation' of *The Magus*, which would be an equally accurate description of Arrowby's residence at Shruff End (1985: 4). If *The Sea, The Sea* in some sense has Shruff End as its centre, and Charles's former life in the theatre and his undefined future as a frame, Fowles's novel moves from London to the Greek island of Phraxos and back to London. Loveday fruitfully compares this to the tripartite structure applied to Shakespearean festive comedy and late plays such as *The Winter's Tale* by Structuralist critics, which has already proved instructive in reading other appropriations here. Murdoch's novels lend themselves to such readings – her tightly knit, anti-comic societies and communities are frequently thrust into 'greenworlds' that test their class-ridden and education-led assumptions.

Magic is never an entirely ironic topic in either Murdoch's or Fowles's writings, but a distinction is drawn between the simply magical (which is associated with trickery) and the truly mystical. Shakespeare's late plays with their own ambiguous play of oracles and apparitions, are fertile ground in this respect. The sea, of course, in these plays is a potent agent of this mystical force (what Murdoch elsewhere refers to as 'contingency'), and provides both nurturing and destructive metaphors in *The Tempest*, *Pericles* and *The Winter's Tale*. An equally potent point of reference, though, is Plato and the theory of the cave from which the Good (and the concept of the 'good' is a recurring Murdoch concern) must emerge to look at the sun. In *The Black Prince*, Bradley Pearson is frequently described as being shocked by the sunlight as he emerges from the gloom of different locations (apartments, phone boxes) as well as moods. In *The Sea, The Sea*, Shruff End is a version of Plato's cave from which Charles, too, must emerge a changed and tested individual:[20]

> Since I started writing this 'book' or whatever it is I have felt as if I
> were walking about in a dark cavern where there are various 'lights',
> made perhaps by shafts or apertures which reach the outside world ...
> There is among those lights one great light towards which I have been
> half consciously wending my way. (77)

Both Pearson and Arrowby are post-Freudian studies in ob-
sessional love. It is intriguing that both find points of reference for
that love in Shakespearean characters, and in the peculiarly poignant and vulnerable figure of the boy-actor. The theatrical aspect to
passion has not escaped Murdoch: 'The theatre is a place of obsession. It is not a soft dreamland' (34). If Pearson's erotic attraction
to Julian Baffin depends on subconscious and conscious associations with both Hamlet and the figure of the Elizabethan boy-
actor in the guise of Ophelia, so Arrowby's relationship with the
actor Lizzie is a reworking of this relationship between the patriarch and the possessed or controlled child/spirit which found
numerous manifestations in Shakespeare – from Oberon and Puck
(and, by extension, the changeling child that has been the fascination of numerous appropriations of *Dream*) to Prospero and his
complex interchanges with Miranda, Caliban and Ariel in *The
Tempest*.

Fittingly, Arrowby and Lizzie's on–off relationship has Shakespearean as well as theatrical origins: Arrowby, no doubt, does not
register the irony of the professional résumé his account of their
affair constitutes:

> She fell in love with me during *Romeo and Juliet*, she revealed her love
> during *Twelfth Night*, we got to know each other during *A Midsummer
> Night's Dream*. Then (but that was later) I began to love her during
> *The Tempest*, and (but that was later still) I left her during *Measure for
> Measure* ... (49)

Noticeably, Charles falls for Lizzie only when he is in the dominant role of patriarch, and not in the context of equality provided
by *Romeo and Juliet*. The attraction to Lizzie is also bound up
with her cross-dressed performances:

> I somehow always picture Lizzie in breeches. She first won a little
> fame as principal boy in small provincial pantomimes. She was very
> slim in those days and rather boyish in appearance and used to stride
> around in boots and cut her hair very short. Her great ambition, never

realised, was to play Peter Pan. She was (briefly) quite serviceable as Shakespeare's transvestite girls. (49)

A case study could be made of Charles's controlling use of diminutives ('won a *little* fame' – emphasis added) and parentheses '(briefly)' to control Lizzie's achievements in this history. He claims a direct role in her successes ('She never prospered in the theatre after I went away' (52)) and, notably, places most value on her roles not as outspoken protagonists such as Viola but as the servile (and androgynous) Puck or Ariel: 'I made her into an adorable Viola, but her greatest success in that historic season was as Puck … I was touched by her love and by her superb obedience' (49–50).

The Sea, The Sea is a highly intertextual composition, referring and alluding outwards not only to Shakespeare but to other novels within the writer's own *œuvre* (similar tactics can be found in Atkinson, Trapido, Naylor, and the work of Margaret Drabble): here we find references to characters from *A Severed Head, Bruno's Dream* (the Shakespearean actor Will Boase) and *The Flight from the Enchanter* (Dipple, 1982: 84).

But the most obvious parallel with Shakespearean appropriations by other women writers considered here is Murdoch's interest in closure, and the false premiss of such a strategy in art and life. In a remarkable passage, Marguerite Alexander has written of the parallels she sees between postmodern fiction, and the implication of the reader in its self-conscious strategies and devices, and the metatheatrical contract with the audience to be found in Jacobean drama. In the plays of this era, she argues: 'when the meaning is stabilised before the final curtain it is in terms of such conventional piety as to suggest parody' (1990: 20). Alexander recognises a comparable drive in Murdoch's fiction: 'while her plots are always resolved, her novels nonetheless resist final closure' (1990: 182). Murdoch saw something quintessentially Shakespearean in this. Anne Barton's formulation of the 'non-endings' constituted by Shakespearean comic resolutions is helpful here; describing 'Artistic forms which dismiss their characters into happiness, often through the solemnization or promise of marriage' as 'problematic', she declares: 'Such endings are not real conclusions, even in the qualified sense that tragic obsequies are. They are a kind of arbitrary arrest. By means of art, the flux of life has been stilled' (Barton, 1994: 100–1). Barbara Trapido's self-conscious narrative balancing acts are also pertinent. As with Trapido's *Juggling*, even where Murdoch allows a constructed happy ending, such as in *The Nice and the Good*, she is not averse to a little Shakespearean destabilisation. Richard Todd has noted how the Jessica–Lorenzo exchange on the moon in *The Merchant of Venice* (which brings the concept of tragic love into the midst of their comic happiness) is recalled in *The Nice and the Good*'s closing pages (Todd, 1979: 86). The pleasing fiction of the happy ending is pointed up, and the possibility of failure (as in those loves recounted by Jessica and Lorenzo in their oddly melancholic duologue: 'The moon shines bright. In such a night as this' (5.1.1–19)) remains. In *The Nice and the Good*, the cracks and fissures in the relations between Pierce and Barbie and Kate and Octavian are clear to the reader, if not always to the interlocuters themselves. In the very midst of her happy ending, Murdoch, like Shakespeare, introduces a note of doubt.[21]

In *The Sea, The Sea*, Arrowby defines theatre as a form curiously susceptible to endings: 'It is do with endings, with partings, with packings up and dismantlings and the disbanding of family groups' (36); and certainly these are recurring themes in Murdoch's own quasi-dramatic narratives. Resolutions, though – on the stage as in life – are only ever temporary aesthetic achievements: Charles cannot resist evoking Shakespeare (Viola's soliloquy at 2.2.38–9 of *Twelfth Night* : 'O time, thou must untangle this, not I./ It is too hard a knot for me t'untie') in his epilogue in order to make this point: 'Time, like the sea, unties all knots ... Human arrangements are nothing but loose ends and hazy reckoning, whatever art may otherwise pretend in order to console us' (477). The fifth act of a Shakespearean late play – the reconciliations of Pericles, Thaisa and Marina or Leontes, Hermione and Perdita – are evoked only to be eventually eschewed. James (who has played both Caliban and Ariel at various points in this narrative) is dead at the close of *The Sea, The Sea*, and Lizzie proves too terrified to enslave herself to Charles again:

> That no doubt is how the story ought to end, with the seals and the stars, explanation, resignation, reconciliation, everything picked up into some radiant bland ambiguous higher significance, in calm of mind, all passion spent. However life, unlike art, has an irritating way of bumping and limping on, undoing conversions, casting doubt on solutions,

and generally illustrating the impossibility of living happily or virtu-
ously ever after ... (477)

Iris Murdoch's novels were an ongoing struggle with the relationship between art and life, reality and fantasy: in Shakespeare she
found the ultimate template for her philosophical and narrative
reasonings. In his memoir of his wife (then suffering from the
onset of Alzheimer's disease: Murdoch died in 1999), John Bayley
touchingly recalled the role that Shakespearean allusion played in
their conversations during forty-plus years of marriage. But the
function of Shakespeare in Murdoch's *œuvre* goes deeper than mere
allusion or quotation; it provides and sustains a rich seam of philosophical enquiry that was to endure, and to take ever more solid
shape throughout her writing life.

Notes

1 John Bayley is the author of *Shakespeare and Tragedy* (1981), and he
has written elsewhere of their joint interest in Shakespeare (Bayley,
1998). Murdoch credited Samuel Beckett with influencing *Under the
Net*: see Chevalier (1978: 93). This confirms the theatrical bias.
2 Spear (1995) describes Nick Boase as a 'Puck or Ariel', which twins
him with later characters such as Simon Foster in *A Fairly Honourable Defeat*. Nick is 'ubiquitous, all-knowing, all-seeing, all-hearing, a
voyeur, a creature of the night who peeps into windows and passes
through doors, himself unseen and unheard' (65).
3 Spear notes that Murdoch was an only child (1995: 2).
4 Again, *The Black Prince* and *The Sea, The Sea* are especially rich
examples of this strategy, although other novels such as *Under the
Net*, *A Severed Head*, and *The Italian Girl* also deploy first-person
narrative.
5 Bradbury claims:

> there was indeed something called Murdochland, as distinctive as
> Greeneland. It was largely a middle-class world, filled with recog-
> nizable types of character: the Near-Saint and the Failed Priest, the
> Strange Enchanter and the Love Prisoner, the Haunted Child and
> the Deathbed Contemplative, the Bookish Bureaucrat and the
> Radiant Woman ... a baroque and highly sexual world, where love
> relationships seemed to elicit certain quasi-symbolic themes: the
> nature of power and possession, the way we create or destroy reali-
> ties, the need for the beautiful, the good and the true. (1993: 370)

6 On enchanter-figures in Murdoch, see Byatt (1976). Julius as a figure

of sexual ambivalence akin to Oberon is discussed by Richard Todd (1979: 81).

7 See Hoskins (1972: 191–8).

8 Spear makes direct reference to the 'motiveless malignity' of Julius King (1995: 68).

9 Morgan's nomenclature carries residues of magical associations: the figure of Morgan le Fay from Arthurian romance (Dipple, 1982: 183). But she proves a weak enchantress in practice, suggesting another ironical Murdoch stance on the theme.

10 In this exchange, Julius appears to tower over Simon: the godlike position is intentional and disturbing (85–6).

11 Dipple (1982: 84) has observed the recurrence of talismanic objects – stones, boxes, paperweights, kites – in Murdoch's fiction. The Chinese bronze water buffalo whose destruction is read as – and proves – portentous in *The Black Prince* is a further example. Interestingly, Murdoch collected stones and objects throughout her life, an activity which proved one of the obsessions that manifested itself in her behaviour after the onset of Alzheimer's. In his account of her valuation of such objects, John Bayley offers a Platonic reading of their significance (1998: 157). The stones with which the children obsess themselves in *The Nice and the Good* are a fine example of the relevance of this to her fiction.

12 'If the Black Prince is the devil, he is also Hamlet procrastinating until it is too late to act, he is also the black Eros destructive in love' (Spear, 1995: 76).

13 There are obvious links between his sexually obsessed narration and that of Humbert Humbert in Nabokov's *Lolita*. Alexander discusses Nabokov's novel as a case study in the transforming power of imagination in love (1990: 65). The description is equally apposite for Bradley Pearson.

14 The character in *A Fairly Honourable Defeat* who is in some ways pitted against King is Morgan's husband Tallis. Since he is virtually ego-less, he has no obvious Shakespearean associations in the novel. I am deeply grateful to James McLaverty for his illuminating observations on this topic.

15 T. S. Eliot wrote his thesis on Bradley. The latter's notion of the dissociation of sensibility would seem to bear relevance to Pearson in the novel.

16 Bradley's work was in turn a huge influence on the Shakespearean criticism of John Bayley.

17 On the tyrannical potential of Prospero, see Greenblatt (1988). On Vincentio, see Dollimore (1985).

18 Alexander describes *The Magus* as an extended attack on literature as sympathetic magic (1990: 169).

19 Fowles had earlier played on *The Tempest* in his novel *The Collector* (1963), in which a character called Ferdinand 'collects' his Miranda,

and holds her hostage (she deems him a Caliban as a result). The links with Arrowby's taking Hartley and, to some extent, her son hostage are instructive.

20 A dark cave experience in which the threat of drowning is paramount is at the heart of *The Nice and the Good*; from this experience John Ducane emerges into the light of true love and friendship.

21 This strategy is not confined to *The Merchant of Venice*: one could equally invoke Malvolio's threat of revenge in *Twelfth Night*; the mythical future of Theseus and Hippolyta in *Dream* (they will bear the ill-fated Hippolytus, and themselves part); and, most notoriously, the figure of death that enters the stage in the fifth act of *Love's Labour's Lost* in the form of the messenger bringing news of the French King's demise.

SIX

'Finding a different sentence': Marina Warner's *Indigo; or, Mapping the Waters* as palimpsest of *The Tempest*

Marina Warner's *Indigo; or, Mapping the Waters* (1992) is a novel that contains within it the residual traces and marks of many other texts and types and genres of text. *Indigo*'s Shakespearean source-text, the 1611 late play *The Tempest*, is simply the most obvious of these, evident in the nomenclature of characters (Sycorax, Miranda, Ariel, Caliban) and in the island setting of many events. The novel deploys *The Tempest* in the context of a wider rumination on postcolonial inheritance, using a complex double (and sometimes overlapping) time-scheme of the seventeenth and twentieth centuries. The central agent of this exploration is the character of Miranda Everard, whose mixed ethnic origins realise the complicated generational history of her family which the events of the novel force her to confront and, in some respects, to come to terms with.

Like so many of the novels we are looking at here in the context of Shakespearean appropriation, *Indigo* signals its debt to a dramatic precursor by the provision of a *dramatis personae*, the list of 'Principal Characters' provided at the start.[1] Towards the end of the novel, the dramatic genre re-enters the narrative in the form of George Felix, a former agit-prop actor, who speaks Caliban's infamous speech on acquired language – 'You taught me language, and my profit on't/ Is I know how to curse. The red plague rid you/ For learning me your language!' (1.2.366–8) – in what Steven Connor has described as a self-consciously 'stagey' section (1996: 188).

Yet the *dramatis personae* of *Indigo* is preceded in the temporal structure of the text by the provision of a map, a strategy more familiar from the genres of printed novels or travel literature. This has obvious connections to postcolonial concerns. Cartography was one of the means by which European travellers sought to contain and control their 'discoveries'. For Connor, the map makes visible: 'The myth of the colonised land as a *tabula rasa*, an empty field of possibility, where men may start anew, like the sailors on Alonso's ship in the play, with their clothes freshened and not corrupted by the sea-water' (1996: 189–90). The map of the island proves anything but fixed in the context of the novel, where place-names alter and the name of the island itself undergoes several transmutations: Liamuiga becomes Everhope Island under Christopher Everard, and then Enfant-Béate under French occupation. Nomenclature acts as an unreliable signifier throughout – a process which confirms Caliban's assertion about the intimate relationship between colonial and linguistic power.

Repeating a trope we have identified in other focus texts, Warner's appropriation of Shakespeare is as much shaped by critical interpretations of *The Tempest* that were dominant at the moment of the novel's conception as by a personal, subjective reading. *Indigo* is strongly influenced by 1980s postcolonial readings of the playtext: the scholarship of Paul Brown (1985), Peter Hulme (1986) (whose *Colonial Encounters* Warner directly cites in her acknowledgements), and Stephen Greenblatt (1990) provides seminal critical intertexts. Warner closes the 'Now' sections of the novel quite deliberately in the political moment of the 1980s, as if to signal this aspect of *Indigo*'s textual and ethical inheritance.

Postcolonial readings frequently focused on Caliban and, to a lesser extent, Ariel as victims of colonial power in the text, and as figures of resistance and subversion. As a result, Prospero was constructed as an oppressive coloniser.[2] This replaced a previously dominant trend of regarding the play as a quasi-philosophical rumination on art and magic in which Prospero, as central magus, was represented as a more benevolent and positive character.[3] A tension can be noted between postcolonial appropriations of *The Tempest* by non-white authors such as George Lamming and Aimé Césaire and those which issued from an ostensibly white, and academic, subject position, such as Murdoch's *The Sea, The Sea* or Fowles's *The Magus*.

For Warner, however, as for many women critics, postcolonial readings of *The Tempest* themselves sat in an uncomfortable tension with feminist responses to the play. The latter inevitably recorded a female presence in the dramaturgic structure only in terms of absence.[4] Miranda is the only female character, apart from the masquers, and in early modern theatres all these roles would have been performed by male actors. Ferdinand's sister Claribel (married to the King of Tunis) and Sycorax, Caliban's sorceress-mother, are talked of but never seen, and the same is true of Miranda's nameless late mother. Warner responds to these challenges in a number of ways. First, by making Sycorax both visible and central to her novel, and displacing the colonising (if not magical) aspects of Prospero into the flawed adventurer 'Kit', she registers that present absence of the play proper. Secondly, by feminising Ariel (recognising in a material way the androgynous casting the part frequently receives), she expands the potential for female presence in the text.[5]

We are seeing, then – embodied in the map of the island included in the materiality of the novel as printed, and in these comparisons with the Shakespearean source-text – a series of conscious and inventive displacements by Warner. The relationship between a character in *Indigo* and its counterpart in *The Tempest* may not, therefore, be straightforward: Ariel is a woman but also, as an Arawak Indian, an ethnic outsider on the island. She later becomes known as Mme Verard in romanticised French histories of Enfant-Béate. Warner's 'Caliban' – more properly called Dulé in the narrative since the name Caliban is one ascribed him by the English invaders – is also from a world elsewhere, shipwrecked from the slave cargo-vessel while still inside his mother's womb. Names of characters, as well as their appearances, are constantly mutating and transmuting in the novel: Xanthe, Miranda's half-sister, is in addition 'Princess', 'Goldie' and 'Goldilocks', those nicknames evoking fairytale associations of the favoured blonde sister and emphasising, by contrast, Miranda's darkness. The trope of gold reminds us further of the Midas story recounted by Serafine to a young Miranda, the novel's opening sequence. On the map, place-names such as Belmont (with its sideways Shakespearean reference to Portia's home in *The Merchant of Venice*, a fantastic place intended to contrast with the 'realities' of mercantile Renaissance Venice) or Jamieston (an allusion to the Elizabethan, Jacobean and Caroline referents to be found on any contemporary map of the USA: Maryland, Virginia, Jamestown, Carolina) embody a series of writings and rewritings of the island of Liamuiga.

The printed map provided supposedly for the direction and guidance of the unfamiliar reader, although misleading for all the above reasons, is also resonant of specific subgenres such as fantasy – the reader might recall, for example, the maps of 'Middle Earth' provided in J. R. R. Tolkien's *Lord of the Rings* sequence – or children's literature – such as the geography of Kenneth Grahame's mammalian world in *The Wind in the Willows*. Once again, the 'authority' of Shakespeare is thrown into a curious mix with other forms of literature and literary inheritance. By the close of this novel, *The Tempest*, while it is a dominant text in our thinking and reading, is only one of many informing intertexts that we have identified and engaged with. Warner signifies this complicated textuality from the start, via her plethora of epigraphs: from Derek Walcott and William Empson, through Spanish proverbs and the letters of Vincent Van Gogh, to the poetry of Paul Celan, Emily Dickinson and Robert Lowell. Navigating these epigraphs, the reader begins to see how *The Tempest* and its themes have been much engaged with down the centuries by artists of various ethnic origins, who had interests in different genres and media. As well as bringing poetry, drama and criticism into the frame, the Van Gogh quotation reminds us of the painter's palette as an alternative site of appropriation and reinterpretation. Miranda's later profession as photographer further expands the aesthetic reference points.[6]

Other appropriations of *The Tempest* act as crucial intertexts in *Indigo*. In this way, Warner's novel interacts as much with the changing history of the play's reception as with any Shakespearean 'original' or Ur-text. Part 6 of the novel, 'Maroon/Black' (and the significance of these hybrid colours will be discussed later), has as its epigraph Auden's 'Tell Me the Truth About Love'. Any mention of Auden in a *Tempest* context brings to mind his own substantial poetic response to the play: *The Sea and the Mirror* (1938). This text is invoked in a more explicit fashion by Leslie Forbes in *Bombay Ice*, but it is an implicit influence here, too. In the voicing of Sycorax, Warner follows in the footsteps of other women writers who have attempted to articulate the silent women of Shakespeare's play, most notably the modernist poet H. D., whose *By Avon River* gives voice to Claribel.[7] Even Murdoch's *The Sea, The Sea*, whose philosophical stance might be something Warner could be felt to be rejecting in her politically and materially grounded approach, may be evoked in the title of the novel: the opening lines of *The Sea, The Sea* have Charles Arrowby, retired theatre director, reflecting on the 'indigo' blue of the sea surrounding his island retreat.

Shakespeare, as elsewhere in his canon, was employing a number of his own intertexts in *The Tempest*, from historically and socially informing accounts of New World 'adventurism' to the work of classical forebears such as Virgil and Ovid.[8] All these texts swim in and out of the reader's ken as they read and respond to *Indigo* and, in an inflected movement, to *The Tempest*. Like Ariel's songs, they thread themselves through Warner's narrative. What they all engage with, and what they help us as readers to recognise, are three central topics in Warner's adaptation: History, Voice and Time.

History and herstory

In the narrative of *Indigo*, different notions of text and artistic expression proliferate. The aforementioned map, as well as raising associations with fictional literatures, is redolent of the colonial project that provides the focus of the seventeenth-century portions of the split time-frame. Other texts contribute to the historical record of colonialism: we have Sir Christopher 'Kit' Everard's journal of his imperial quest to Liamuiga, his letters home to his fiancée Rebecca, and the marble tablet that records his exploits in the cemetery at the Church of St Blaise Figtree on the island. At first glance, these might seem fixed texts, records in stone (in the case of the epitaph, literally so) of a historical fact:

> First read then weep when thou art hereby taught
> That Everard lies interréd here, one that bought
> With a loss of Noble blood Illustrious Name
> Of a Commander Great in Acts of Fame:
> Trained from his youth in Arms, his courage bold

Attempted brave Exploits, and uncontrolled
By Fortune's fiercest Frowns, he still gave forth
Large Narratives of Military worth.
Unsluice your briny floods, what! Can ye keep
Your eyes from tears and see the marble weep?
Burst out for shame: or if ye find no vent
For tears, yet stay, and see the stones relent.
(Warner, 1992: 316–17)

But, as Kate Chedgzoy has shown, a hurricane on the island in the 1980s has cracked the tablet and 'rewritten' its message, fragmenting it into an indictment of the colonial project (a similar 'tempest' will uproot Sy Nebris's cash-crop of oyster beds) (1995: 94–5):

> In the last hurricane, the bell of St Blaise's had been torn from the belfry and dashed to the graveyard, where it smashed through the roof over the tomb and landed on the gravestone, cracking the sarcophagus, and breaking the inscription in two and scoring certain words, so that Miranda, reading it with Xanthe when they'd been taken to visit the monument on the second day of their stay, found a different sentence, 'Weep ... blood ... in Arms ... uncontrolled ... Narratives of ... shame' ... (317)

These 'narratives of ... shame' in part constitute Eurocentric post-colonial guilt over the past, but also a genuine sense of responsibility. In a very real way, they represent the personal history that Miranda is forced to confront in the course of the story. The availability of other kinds of texts, alternative histories and storytelling, help to challenge and destabilise superficial understandings of 'recorded history' in *Indigo*.[9]

History was traditionally regarded as a male domain in patriarchal societies; orality and storytelling, on the other hand, were defined as female. This dichotomy is something Warner's own academic publications might be felt to have endorsed. Critical works like *From the Beast to the Blonde* (1995) have a deep investment in the reclamation and revalorisation of female oral culture. Angela Carter's lifelong interest in fairytales was comparable in its aims and objectives, and the same tension between oral and written histories is played out on the pages of *Wise Children*. In *Indigo*, there is a pervasive presence of female storytelling throughout the narrative, provided most importantly by the framing tales of

Serafine, Miranda's Liamuigan-born nanny. The significance of these we will consider later, but to read *Indigo* in terms of these strict binaries would be to oversimplify the complicated and subtle operations of textuality in the novel. There is little 'pure' printed history in *Indigo*: rather, texts such as Kit's journal are the raw materials of the discipline, and the feminocentric stance of Warner's novel ensures that as patriarchal authorities they appear fragile and flawed. Nor is writing the sole domain of white male imperialists: Sycorax makes her mark on the island, recording her tracks with ciphers scratched into boundary trees. These scratchings prove indecipherable to the European invaders, but this does not devalue them as writing or historical record (122).[10] Ultimately, orality proves no more 'trustworthy', no more 'truthful', than the destabilised written male histories of *Indigo*. Serafine revises her stories with a youthful audience in mind: 'But this savage story isn't seemly for the little English girls, so Serafine has adapted it, as storytellers do' (224).

Warner seems to align herself with her character here, juxtaposing her alterations of Shakespeare with Serafine's 're-visions'. But as the passage continues, the 're-vision' can seem more insidious, less palatable, since the readers already have an alternative account fresh in their memory:

> There's another story with a happy ending they know, not just from Serafine; it's traditional in their family, and in the history books in which the Everards have a mention.
> How the first Kit Everard won the love of an islander and how she saved him and his brave band of pioneers.
> It's come down through the years, this story. From first-hand sources, authenticated. Serafine knows it; all her family, working on the Everard lands, knew it; they passed it on: (224–5)

This passage is significant not least for its implicit questioning of closure, something Connor identifies as a crucial factor in Warner's novel, and one which, for him, compensates in part for the sentimentalised 'happy ending' (1996: 197). The 'story' mentioned has been passed down from another Eurocentric source, a French missionary priest called Père Labat, who in 1724 wrote a travel book, *Nouveau Voyage aux Isles de l'Amérique*, on 'the new world of the islands' (225) – that phrase itself is deliberately disingenuous in this context – and recounted his meeting with 'a survivor from the heroic days': a wizened 'Indian hag', who is, of course, Ariel. Warner here merges Labat's genuine text with her fictional creations, blurring the boundary lines of 'fact' even further. Time has transmuted Ariel into 'Mme Verard' (225), saviour of the English. There may be an embedded pun in that apocryphal name on 'truth' (veracity, *vérité*).

The opening scene of *Indigo* is a conscious displacement of Act 1 Scene 2 of *The Tempest*, where we first encounter Prospero and Miranda and where, following the storm, Prospero attempts to uncover Miranda's personal history for her: 'Sit down,/ For now thou must know farther' (1.2.32–3). Jonathan Bate has noted the significance of this scene in the Shakespearean canon:

> The exposition of the past history of the characters is unusually laboured, which suggests that the matter was important to the dramatist. Typically, the mature Shakespeare will begin a play with a couple of courtiers – Gloucester and Kent in *Lear*, Philo and Demetrius in *Antony and Cleopatra*, Camillo and Archidamus in *The Winter's Tale* – sketching in the background to the story. But such opening scenes usually last no more than a few minutes; Shakespeare then gets on with the action of the play … In *The Tempest*, however, having grabbed his audience's attention with the storm, he proceeds with an expository scene of some 500 lines, easily the longest in the play. (1997: 244)

Warner's revisiting of this scene retains subtle echoes of its Shakespearean precedent, even though – in an action indicative of *Indigo*'s wider gender-based displacements – the scene is no longer between autocratic father and submissive daughter, but between a questioning Miranda and her surrogate mother/nanny Serafine. In this shift, alternative notions of status or hierarchy, and indeed power, are advanced:[11] 'Miranda was sitting on a rug Serafine had spread near the bench she usually chose, beside the huge marble log that lay athwart the lawn like a *shipwrecked spar*' (4; emphasis added). The shipwreck sequence that initiates the play is evoked here, but so too are Caliban's log-carrying duties, as well as Sycorax's tree, which Warner renders a central icon of ambivalent power in the narrative.

There is a tension throughout *Indigo* between what we might term personal history and so-called recorded public history. Warner's autobiography is pertinent here, since there are ways in which her family history intersects with the themes and anxieties

of the novel, which, as Caroline Cakebread has observed, is concerned with the 'legacy of colonialism in modern British life'
(1999: 217). St Kitts Warner is a real island in the Caribbean,
formerly known as Liamuiga, and renamed after one of Warner's
own forebears, Sir Thomas Warner, a figure translated into Sir
Christopher 'Kit' Everard in the novel. Elsewhere her cricket-
playing ancestor, Sir Pelham Warner, becomes Sir Anthony
Everard, author, in a manner akin to Sir Pelham, of books on his
favourite sport, in this case the fictional Flinders (a ball game
played by teams in an enclosure called a Stockade).[12] There is an
element of personal guilt and responsibility in Warner's choice of
focus for her novel:

> My family's Creole past, gainsaid, erased, became the inspiration for
> *Indigo* ... *The Tempest* gave me a structure to work with ... Because
> our family was involved in an enterprise that so resembles Prospero's
> theft, that foundation act of Empire, I felt compelled to examine the
> case, and imagine, in fiction, the life and culture of Sycorax, and of
> Ariel, and Caliban ... I wanted to hear their voices in the noises of the
> isle. (Warner, 1993: 203)

The 'mapping process' undertaken in *Indigo* is a very personal as
well as highly public task. Yet, like the circulating narratives and
circular structure of the novel, in the end it is also somewhat
impossible. The subtitle or alternative title of *Indigo* is 'Mapping
the Waters'. It might be suggested that cartographers map water
only in the sense that it circumscribes and defines land, in the
respect that it is ownable, possessable territory. Mapping the waters,
therefore, might seem a fantasy project, and that understanding
makes its own sly comment on the colonial enterprise of the Renaissance. Maritime charts are, however, concerned with the naviga-
bility of the seas. If we recall the notion that the experience of
reading this novel is an act of personal navigation, the image becomes a highly relevant and pertinent possibility.

Water is a feminised element, linked to the birth-waters of an
expectant mother (Bachelard, 1985). It is surely no coincidence
that, according to Prospero's narrative (and it is a fact of the play
that as a character she is almost entirely constructed by Prospero's
words), Sycorax makes her journey to the island of *The Tempest* in
a state of expectancy: 'This blue-eyed hag was hither brought with
child' (1.2.271). Prospero's journey across the water to the island

with his daughter and his books has been read in the context of a
rebirth (Lanier, 1996):

> Thou didst smile,
> Infusèd with a fortitude from heaven,
> When I have decked the sea with drops of salt,
> Under my burden groaned;
>
> (1.2.153–6)

As well as *The Tempest*, *Pericles*, *Cymbeline* and *The Winter's Tale*
all deploy water-based, life-changing events and journeys.[13] Helen
Hackett has directly associated the agency of the sea in the late
plays to this theme: 'Even the sea, which so persistently appears
in these plays either as a place of actual shipwreck or as a metaphor
for turbulent fortune, can be understood as a kind of amniotic
fluid from which characters supposed dead are reborn' (1999: 30).

Water has other symbolic qualities in *Indigo*, where it serves as
a major ingredient in the manufacture of indigo dye, Sycorax's
profession. Water is also an element in the constitution of ink,
that central property in the art of writing. Warner's narrative is
explicit in making these connections. Just as Sycorax's hands and
body are stained blue by the dyeing process, so Serafine's hands
seem to be marked or mapped out in similar ways. Warner's choice
of vocabulary is deliberate in this respect, carefully drawing together the threads of her narrative web. The oral storyteller is
thus explicitly linked with her seventeenth-century island prede-
cessor, but also, by extension, with the hidden writer, Warner herself: 'Serafine's palms were mapped with darker lines as if she had
steeped them in ink to bring out the pattern; the lines crisscrossed
and wandered, and Miranda would have liked to be able to puzzle
out the script' (4). This image is a potent one for the novel as a
whole, where we witness Miranda attempting to puzzle out the
mysteries and occlusions of her personal and genealogical history.

Serafine's story at the beginning of *Indigo* is one in which
'everything risked changing shape' (4). Its metamorphic qualities
associate it directly with the Ovidian texts that influenced Shakespeare (and not least *The Tempest*), and that we have seen reassert
themselves in female appropriations from Murdoch to Atkinson.
But the circular framework that her storytelling provides, both in
the text and in Miranda's life (Serafine tells Miranda's child a

story at the close of the novel), and its reliance on structures of
archetype and repetition, link it more widely to the structure of
myth that the poet Ted Hughes saw as central to the Shakespearean imagination (1992). Myth provides its own structural counterpart to linear progressive history in this novel, and is one of the
most significant means by which Warner questions our understandings of time in the narrative.

'Changing stories into another time'

Patricia Drechsel Tobin has written of narrative time in the following terms: 'Time exerts a double pressure on the realistic novel: as
form, it is largely silent and unobtrusive, but as process it is noisy
and ubiquitous' (Tobin, 1978: 4). For *Indigo* – where, as we shall
see in the next section, presence is often problematically associated with voice and noise – this is a pertinent statement. There
are several kinds of time operating in the novel. Connor (1996)
has spoken of 'private time' and 'public time', terms which have
obvious relation to the notions of personal and public history
explored in the preceding section. Tobin adds a further category
of 'family time', the genealogical form of history which we have
registered as central to Miranda's experiences in *Indigo*.[14] As with
other novelists examined here, however, there is an embedded
contrast in Warner's text between linear, progressive, or develop-
mental time and circular, or mythical, time. When Sycorax initially
describes the indigo dyeing process, it might seem to be a straightforward linear sequence:

> The blue I used to make, she thought to herself, was the culmination
> of a sequence. It marked the end of the long process of transformations
> – starting with the seething leaves of the plant, then the reeking green
> stage of the first steepings, and the sulphurous yellow stage of the
> liquor before it was exposed to the air, then binding with the air, it
> gradually turned to blue. (147)

The sequence of colours here, with its end process of indigo in
sight, appears to parallel the colour subtitles Warner gives the
different parts of her novel. As we saw in the image of Serafine's
palms, the dyeing process is linked to the act of writing and
authorship. But a closer inspection of the colour sequence

destabilises linear certainty: we commence with 'Lilac/Pink', progress through 'Indigo/Blue', 'Orange/Red', 'Gold/White' and 'Green/Khaki', to 'Maroon/Black'. What might have been pre- sumed the endpoint of our sequence in a linear reading – indigo – instead surprises us early in the sequence, presaging Sycorax's entrance on to the historical stage. No colour comes pure, either; each is alongside a near or close relative in the prism, offering an image of the hybridity of appearance and identity that character- ises many of the novel's protagonists: from Miranda, whose Afro hairstyle in 1960s Paris is an effort to assert one aspect of her ethnic identity, to her father Kit, bullied at school for his mixed Creole parentage.[15] Each of these colour pairings has a local sig- nificance as well: Lilac/Pink offers a more accurate rendering of the appearance of so-called 'white' skin, an asserted inheritance in this novel, yet notably never described as pure white. At different moments, the sunburned Sir Christopher on Liamuiga appears 'red' or 'pink' to the natives (and others) who encounter him (Sy Nebris repeats this effect in the modern era). Kit's illegitimate child with Ariel is called Roukoubé or Red Bear Cub, which simultaneously asserts his parentage and that of the boy's Arawak Indian mother. Indigo/Blue is legible enough but just as the dye 'turns blue' so readers might wish to recall that bodies turn blue in death. Sycorax's death and yet endurance shapes the sounds and events of this novel. Gold/White invokes Xanthe and her fairytale nicknames, but also the greed for gold that characterises the capitalistic enterprise of white settlers on Enfant-Béate, such as herself and Sy Nebris. Green/Khaki in Part 5 conjures up links with the military coup on the island and the army fatigues worn by Atala Seacole and her cohorts, but green also has links to nature and ecology, and to innocence and sickness. We end with the recon- ciliation of Miranda and George, which might be read as the reaching of accord by the modern protagonist with her black in- heritance, but the maroon remains there to nuance and shade the black, reminding us of the important history of maroons, escaped slaves and figures of opposition and resistance in the Caribbean, and therefore to destabilise closure or any sense of terminus in the narrative.[16]

Single readings and sequences are resisted in this anti-linear novel. For the same reason, the dyeing churn that Sycorax uses in manufacturing indigo becomes elsewhere an emblem of circularity and endurance, rather than linear endstopped experience: 'She cannot abjure, give up, control the force by which she is possessed. On her own, she cannot stop the churn from tumbling round' (213). In a subtle evocation of the language of her Shakespearean source-text, Warner here contrasts the powers of Sycorax with those of Prospero: unlike him, she cannot 'abjure' or eschew the 'rough magic' which has come to define her (*The Tempest*, 5.1.50–1).

One of the ways in which the reader registers the operations of time upon Sycorax, rather than her necessary control of time, is in the shifting tenses which characterise her sections of the narrative. Warner, as we shall see in the next section, has not opted for a focused first-person narrator but moves instead through several points of view in the course of a third-person narrative. The Sycorax sections, which we might expect to constitute the 'Then' or seventeenth-century portions of the novel, are in truth a confusing blend of present and past tenses. At the opening of Part 2, the reader is informed of the place and time in which the passage is supposedly located: 'Liamuiga, 1600–'. It seems clear that we are in the seventeenth century; and yet, as we read on, the world of the island described stands in opposition to our notion of early modern society: 'The isle is full of noises, so they say, and Sycorax is the source of many. Recent sound effects – the chattering of loose halyards against the masts on the fancy yachts riding at anchor in the bays, the gush and swoosh of water in the oyster pool at the luxury hotel – aren't of her making' (77). Gillian Beer's notion of 'limber echoes' is active here: Caliban's iconic poetry – 'The isle is full of noises,/ Sounds and sweet airs, that give delight and hurt not' (3.2.130–1) – is conjured up in the phrase which frames the 'Sycorax' portions of the novel, emphasising again the relevance of circular structures and motifs of repetition. But the luxury yachts and the five-star hotel are very much part of late-twentieth-century manifestations on the island; in this way we are made aware that Sycorax as a character is not bounded by linear time.

There is a pain in Sycorax's endurance, the 'living death' that her body undergoes. It is noticeable that she does not possess the power of eternal youth, finding her life never-ending only once her body is wracked and bent by age and experience. This mirrors the hooped shape Sycorax is described as being bent into in *The Tempest*: 'The foul witch Sycorax, who with age and envy/ Was grown into a hoop' (1.2.259–60); it becomes here the arthritic consequence of Sycorax's fall from her tree-house abode (Cakebread, 1999: 227). As elsewhere in the novel, Warner finds a material and secular counterpart for the magic and mystery of the play. Sycorax describes her death as commencing the day the dead slaves are washed up on the shores of Liamuiga: their fish-nibbled corpses offer a corporeal counterpart to the bodily transformations wrought by the sea in *The Tempest*: 'those are pearls that were his eyes' (1.2.402).

In *The Tempest*, Sycorax is said to have confined Ariel within a tree (a punishment Prospero also threatens him with, thus strengthening the kinship that many critics have noted between the banished Algerian witch and her white magus counterpart). In *Indigo*, this becomes Sycorax's own fate. A passage dated 'Enfant-Béate, 1700–' has her in a strange state of decomposition and yet survival:

> Her long death has barely begun, however, for she can still hear the prayers of those who come to bring garlands … They push a tack into the bark of the saman tree and make a wish, they whisper their pleas to the spirit inhering in the tree, as they imagine, rightly (though Sycorax has no power, nor ever had, except in dreaming). (210)

The statement in parenthesis here is indicative of the ambiguous treatment Warner accords Sycorax's 'witchcraft' in the novel: it is at times a social construct, a reading forced on her by fellow villagers intrigued by her herbal knowledge and ability to bring Dulé forth from a dead mother; at other points, however, she has powers of sorts, even if they are only those of a mythic resistance of mortal time. The tacks pushed into the bark of the tree for superstitious (and ultimately touristic) purposes carry their own burden of history and public time. The islanders have traded the tacks and nails for the island's cash-crop of sugar, an eighteenth-century counterpart to Sycorax's cash-crop industry of indigo, which moved from the Caribbean to India at this moment.[17]

In these ways, then, Warner offers secular and material reasons for the events of Shakespeare's play; in this respect, her approach mimics the moves of critical schools of thought such as postcolonialism and cultural materialism. But in recognising this 'secularizing of the mythical', as Connor describes it, we should not ignore the recurrent power of the mythical in the text (1996: 190). The material account of history would be a linear one, and we have already noted how important circularity is to Warner's narrative. For Connor, the linear is representative of all that is European and progressive in the novel, whereas: 'Sycorax's experience of time, like that of the natives of the island, is as a recurring plenitude, in which no loss can be permanent' (1996: 191). Just as Warner holds two ideas of Sycorax in a delicate balance, so these two understandings of time operate alongside each other (and frequently in opposition to each other) in her narrative.[18]

'I wanted to hear their voices in the noises of the isle'

Sycorax, like the text and textual reception of *The Tempest*, enters and permeates all the different sections of the novel. This challenges Gilbert and Tompkins's reductive account of the possibilities of narrative fiction for hybridity of character.[19] Sycorax's presence in the shape of Serafine has already been noted; there are also elements of Sycorax in characters as diverse as Astrid (Miranda's own semi-absent mother) and the island's radical politician Atala Seacole (the name plays with a phonetic proximity, as well as evoking the nineteenth-century Jamaican writer Mary Seacole).[20] Even in the 1960s Paris hotel room in which Miranda finds herself at one stage, the lemony scent of the maid's scouring powder (229) recalls the lemon tree of Sycorax on Liamuiga.

Here Warner is responding, as many directors of stage productions of the play have, to the felt presence of Sycorax, even though she is already dead by the time its events commence.[21] Ted Hughes noted how, in *The Tempest*, 'Sycorax, the ultimate Queen of Hell, is still everywhere, like the natural pressure of the island's atmosphere. Prospero's statement that she is dead is little more than a figure of speech: the island ... is hers' (1992: 382). Like H. D.'s voicing of Claribel in *By Avon River*, Warner gives Sycorax voice in the novel, reversing what she regards as Shakespeare's act of suppression.[22]

Like much of the representation of Sycorax, however, this according of voice is ambiguously handled by Warner. By 1700, and the tree-worshipping passage quoted earlier, her voice has proved as subject to decay as her corporeal frame: 'her mouth – what is left of her mouth – gapes open in the direction of the ground above' (210). Too often, Warner's novel is simplistically described as a feminist text that 'voices' the silenced women of Shakespeare's plays; but Warner often appears proactive in silencing – or, at least, holding in a kind of enforced silence – her reclaimed protagonist. The response to Atala Seacole's liberationist cries on the island are hopeful but not yet fully realised and their objective is, oddly, an achieved silence:

> – What shall we do if we are trapped, again? If we fail? –
> Sycorax would have liked to call back, 'You must not fail! You will not fail!' But there is earth in her throat. After you, she is thinking, everything that began all those years ago will be accomplished, and the noises of the isle will be still and I – I shall at last come to silence. (376)

A similar ambivalence, as we have noted, surrounds the extent of Sycorax's powers. Sycorax possesses the herbal skills that, Diane Purkiss has suggested, were traditionally associated with witchcraft accusations, and her delivery of Dulé increases her sense of isolation and marginalisation from her husband's community (1996: 250): 'It wasn't natural, some said. It was pure witchcraft. Sycorax had cast a spell and brought the dead to life' (85).[23] Some people in the community are pleased to make these associations – not least her husband, who uses it as an excuse to part from her (86). This is a further example of a pragmatic explanation for magic in the novel, and Chedgzoy has drawn attention to this, suggesting that Sycorax merely internalises the community's construction of her powers, and starts to believe they exist, taking on the stereotypical attributes of such a figure (her beast 'familiars', for example) (1995: 126). There is truth in this, recognising as it does the power of gossip to construct character (87), but to read the rest of the novel in these pragmatic terms is to ignore the multilayered nature of Warner's secular yet mythical narrative. For elsewhere, in her omnipresence throughout the 'modern' sections of the novel, in her implication in Xanthe's drowning or the island's political

upheavals, Sycorax would seem to have powers, albeit limited ones.
As Connor astutely notes, the novel seems deliberately contradictory in its treatment of Sycorax: 'If the early part of *Indigo* is an
exercise in rehabilitation, rescuing Sycorax from the discredit of
Prospero's account of her, in these later portions she becomes a
more ambivalent and even sinister figure' (1996: 193). The conjure-
woman, an archetype that proves important to Gloria Naylor in
her adaptation of *The Tempest*, *Mama Day*, asserts itself in *Indigo*
through Serafine Killabree: 'Serafine could still conjure Enfant-
Béate when she wanted, even for those who had never been there,
like Miranda' (51). The 'voice' and 'noises' of Sycorax which
Warner has sounded so distinctively in the novel are still present
in the mythic and metamorphic imagination of Serafine at the
end:

> There are many noises in her head these befuddled days of her old age;
> they whisper news to her of this island and that, of people scattered
> here and there, from the past and from the present. Some are on the
> run still; but some have settled, they have ceased wandering, their
> maroon state is changing sound and shape. She's often too tired nowa-
> days to unscramble the noises, but she's happy hearing them, to change
> into stories another time. (402)

Notes

1 Carter's *Wise Children* has the same device, but located at the back of
the novel as printed.
2 An interesting dramatic variation on this theme, which offers parallels
with Warner's Creolised project, is Australian writer David Malouf's
play *Blood Relations* (1987), which recasts Caliban as the post-Abo-
riginal character of Dinny. Gilbert and Tompkins describe the play
thus:

> Hybridizing Shakespeare's *dramatis personae* to produce slightly
> different kinds of counter-discourse, Malouf focuses on the racial
> and territorial consequences of two centuries of European settle-
> ment ... The subversiveness of his characters lies not only in their
> imperfect imitations – their contaminations – of the canonical
> models, but also in the complex genealogical relationships which
> connect the various 'family' members. (1996: 33).

There are obvious links here to the complicated family tree in *Indigo*.
3 That critical history has already been traced in terms of its influence
on Murdoch's *The Sea, The Sea* (see Chapter 5). Bate recounts this

dramatic shift in critical thinking (1997: 240). He makes the crucial point that readings of the play by non-white authors had traversed this territory earlier – texts such as George Lamming's *The Pleasures of Exile* (1960) and his 1971 novel *Water with Berries*; and Aimé Césaire's play *Une tempête* (1968) – but it is true to say that these texts, such as they are present in Warner's novel, are mediated through these white-dominated forms of literary criticism.

4 See A. Thompson (1995), which details how William Davenant's Restoration adaptation of *The Tempest* created a number of new female characters, including Miranda's sister Dorinda, Caliban's sister Sycorax, and Ariel's consort, Milcha. Thompson observes: 'This proliferation of female roles can presumably be attributed in part to the need to provide employment for actresses on the Restoration stage' (168).

5 In 2000, Shakespeare's Globe had not only a female Ariel but a female Prospero (played by Vanessa Redgrave) in its production.

6 For a vivid and varied exploration of these multifaceted and multimedia appropriations of *The Tempest*, see Hulme and Sherman (2000).

7 For recent readings of that poem, see Chedgzoy (1995: 100–14); Friedman (1989); and M. N. Smith (2000).

8 Warner has reflected on these associations in a critical essay (Warner, 2000); see also Purkiss (1996); and Tudeau-Clayton (1998). On the classical and historical context of the play, see also Wilson (1997); and Brotton (1998).

9 It has been suggested in some circles that the postmodern recognition of truths and 'multiple histories' is at odds with the postcolonial project of revealing the truth behind the fictions. This seems to underestimate the complexities and aims of postcolonialism. I am grateful to Aidan Day for discussions on this topic.

The central theorist in the textualisation of history is, of course, Hayden White (1995). Connor has commented on the relevance of this to the genre of historical fiction in the twentieth century, which, he claims, is 'not just … passively marked with the imprint of history, but also … the ways in which history is made, and remade' (1996: 1).

10 See Mignolo (1995) on indigenous forms of history-writing in Latin America. I am grateful to Kate Chedgzoy for this reference.

11 This relationship between Miranda and Serafine recalls the one between Juliet and her nurse in *Romeo and Juliet*, where, famously, the Nurse (who, in an aristocratic family of this kind, would have served as wet-nurse to the child) knows Juliet far better than her own mother.

12 For a brilliant postcolonial account of cricket, see James (1963).

13 Earlier plays, such as *The Comedy of Errors* and *Twelfth Night*, make manifest an ongoing interest in this theme, but the late plays effect a curiously concentrated exploration of the significance of the sea.

14 Tobin (1978) credits Gabriel García Márquez's *One Hundred Years of Solitude*, a novel whose influence on *Wise Children* has already been noted (see Chapter 2), as influential in the challenge it offers to linear,

patrilineal notions of time: 'Nor does the family in its generations survive this assault on linearity. Patrilineal authority gives way to matrilateral accommodation, relations of descent to those of affiliation, the socialised family to the biological community or mythical alienation' (26).

15 The Paris sections of the novel assert the French Creole elements of Miranda's inheritance, recalling Estelle Desjours, the second Kit's own 'absent mother' who drowned on the island, a prefiguring of Xanthe's demise towards the end of *Indigo*.

16 See Price (1975). I am grateful to Diana Paton for this reference.

17 See Chedgzoy (1995: 125–6); Rowe (1991).

18 Warner has noted how Sycorax's life appears to operate on a time-scheme distinct from that of the Europeans of the play: 'The chronology of Sycorax's life warps against the chronology of the play ... Her ageing is somehow accelerated, moving faster than the pace of other characters' stories' (2000: 97).

19 Gilbert and Tompkins argue that postcolonial drama has a specific claim on this form of hybridity: 'Role-doubling, a specifically performative technique, harnesses the idea of the hybridity, in ways which fictional rewritings of *The Tempest* cannot approximate' (1996: 33). Elsewhere, this book is a subtle and engaging account of postcolonial drama; nevertheless, this reduction of narrative possibility is implicitly queried in work by novelists such as Warner, Naylor and Forbes.

20 On Mary Seacole, see Sage (1999). Damp seems to rise from Astrid, who conjures up notions of 'a dark hybrid that lives on water, half-mermaid, half-stormy petrel' (57).

21 Peter Brook, among other directors, has made Sycorax visible on the stage. This is a theatrical counterpart to those narrative appropriations which accord her a central role. In Naylor's *Mama Day* (the subject of Chapter 8), Sycorax is clearly invoked in the magical properties and powers of Miranda Day. In Frederick Buechner's *The Storm* (1998), she becomes, in an intriguing reversion, Miss Violet Sickert, colonial controller of the Florida quay of Plantation Island. In that same novel, Caliban is reworked as her supposed illegitimate son, Calvert, hired hand at Kenzie Maxwell's property. Kenzie (Prospero) also has a New Age windsurfing stepson, Averill, who is a very 1990s version of Shakespeare's 'watery sprite'.

22 'Among the noises of the isle, the voice of Sycorax is silenced' (Warner, 2000: 97).

23 In the play, of course, it is Prospero who is associated with these skills, in his fifth-act speech which directly reworks one of Medea's, the herbal sorceress in Ovid's *Metamorphoses*: 'graves at my command/ Have waked their sleepers, oped, and let 'em forth/ By my so potent art' (5.1.50–2).

SEVEN

Reclaimed from the sea: Leslie Forbes's *Bombay Ice*

Before any narrative is offered to the reader, Leslie Forbes's *Bombay Ice* (1998) provides a 'Cast-List'. This equivalent to a *dramatis personae*, akin to print strategies in *Indigo* and *Wise Children*, ensures that her novel retains a sense of its dramatic origins in *The Tempest*. That play provides plotlines, misleading clues, and characterology for Forbes's complex novel–thriller. The book, like *Wise Children* and *Juggling*, is divided into five acts and an epilogue. But, in precise terms, it is not a *dramatis personae per se* that *Bombay Ice* offers readers but, rather, a cast list. That choice of vocabulary informs the reader of the novel's alternative provenance in cinema and the related Indian film industry, which provide much of the text's foreground and background, as well as alternative subtexts to Shakespearean ones.

Bombay Ice is narrated by Rosalind Benegal, a BBC employee, who finds herself on a trip to India in search of the answer to a mystery: the death of her brother-in-law's first wife, the film star Maya Sharma. Since Ros's sister is called Miranda, and her husband – whom Ros clearly suspects of causing the death of Maya – is the Bollywood film director Prosper Sharma, who is himself engaged on an all-consuming project of adapting *The Tempest* for the cinema, the Shakespearean allusions are clear from early on. But Forbes's narrative is equally conscious of a parallel cinematic inheritance: the entire story is prefixed by a section entitled 'Flashback: Bengal Light'. This carries cinematic technique into the heart of the novel's structure and style.

Ros's quest to solve the mystery of Maya's demise (and, in many respects, to prove her brother-in-law's guilt) draws her into further related efforts to solve a series of murders of members of India's sexually ambiguous *hijra* community, in which she suspects both Sharma and his former protégé and now directorial rival, Caleb Mistry, of involvement. *Bombay Ice*'s narrative consciously invests itself with the generic conventions of the detective story and its cinematic corollary, the thriller. Yet it also resists and subverts those conventions. At various points in the narrative, Ros willingly assumes the role of detective, the person attempting to solve crimes. Indeed, it is the assumption of that role which she uses to justify her written memoir: 'I write this down to try to find some overall pattern to the deaths of that summer' (Forbes, 1998: 4).

The classic structure of detective fiction invariably includes a crime to be solved, a series of clues along the way (some helpful, some misleading), and an eventual resolution: the act of detection and revelation. Ros speaks of a desire to identify patterns, and the novel seems to be leading towards a climax which would identify Prosper Sharma (his name providing its own associations with the protagonist of *The Tempest*) as a murderer. Ros is fascinated throughout by patterns: from ritual religious calendars (Christian and Hindi) to those advanced in scientific versions of chaos theory or Mandelbrot's theory of patterns, and the cycles of the monsoon in Indian meteorology and culture. But in the true sense of the detective genre, no clear pattern or resolution is ever identified in *Bombay Ice*. In the epilogue, Ros concedes: 'So I am left with all these stories. And who is to say which one is true?' (399).

By such means, readers are alerted to several of the red herrings or false paths to enlightenment they themselves have pursued. The opening to the novel informs us that the epigraphs to Ros's memoirs (as we have noted, she tells us she is writing them down: there is a movement away from the oral, as if the written were somehow more trustworthy) are gleaned from Basil Chopra's posthumous biography of Prosper, entitled *The Sea in the Mirror*. That throwaway phrase 'posthumous' encourages us to expect Prosper's death as well as his identification as villain in the course of the novel, but neither event occurs. It is as if the narrative teases our need, as well as Ros's, to locate villains and find closure.

Thrillers are equally fond of red herrings: Alfred Hitchcock was famous for his 'MacGuffins'. Hitchcock's work is persistently invoked in *Bombay Ice* – from specific films such as *Strangers on a Train* and *North by Northwest* (the latter with its own embedded titular reference to Shakespeare (Morris, 1997)) to the acknowledgement of its influence on Sharma's directorial style. *Bombay Ice* both invites us to read in connections and persistently deconstructs those efforts.

The novel is structured, somewhat like the Bombay in which it takes place, via a series of intertexts and layers. By its close, readers are forced to ask themselves whether the entire narrative has been a (potentially self-deluding) web of fictions and fabrications. *The Tempest* provides the most obvious and deep-rooted intertext throughout, since it is the play on which Sharma's life-project is based. Prosper's name echoes Shakespeare's director-protagonist, and these associations are further reinforced by his interest in one of Shakespeare's mooted sources for that character: the Elizabethan magus and alchemist John Dee (Sherman, 1995). That this Prosper(o) is married to a Miranda starts, however, to skew the picture. Unlike Warner's *Indigo*, or other appropriations of *The Tempest* by women, Miranda is not the central character in Forbes's re-vision. In *Bombay Ice* she is displaced to the role of half-sister and second wife, while Rosalind (her nomenclature linking her to a very different Shakespearean heroine and another play, *As You Like It*) takes centre stage. Forbes has no doubt alighted on the fact that Rosalind is Shakespeare's most vocal female heroine, although, as we shall see, her cross-dressing trajectory in that play also holds important resonances for the narrator of *Bombay Ice*.

Other characters from Shakespeare's late play slip in and out of the narrative, this fluidity mirroring the permeable boundaries of Bombay/Mumbai city, but also the complex (and misleading) web of allusions the novel engages with. Prosper's filmmaking protégé was Caleb Mistry. He has since turned his back on Sharma's Westernised elitist art in favour of indigenous Hindi filmmaking. The postcolonial debate so prevalent in literary critical readings of *The Tempest* of recent decades is therefore made manifest in this fraught relationship. Mistry's first name invokes Prospero's surrogate son in the play, Caliban. But Caliban's echoes are also to be heard elsewhere in the novel: Sami the murdered *hijra* proves to be Caleb's lost son ('This thing of darkness I/ Acknowledge mine' (5.1.278–9)) as well as being Prosper's sometime lover and the intended Ariel of his film.

By marrying this Prosper(o) to his Miranda, Forbes brings into play the incestuous subtexts that are occasionally read into this father–daughter relationship as well as that of Lear and Cordelia. Incest and sexual abuse undoubtedly provide a series of informing subtexts in the novel. Ros's mother is, like Miranda's in the play, a shadowy absence. We know she has died, as have Ros's father and grandparents. This links Ros to numerous orphaned or motherless Shakespearean heroines, from Viola to Perdita. Very gradually we learn some details of Ros's mother's life and death. Only on page 358 of the novel is she accorded a name. This, too, proves to have Shakespearean resonance. Called Jessica, she is linked to Shylock's daughter, who escapes dressed as a pageboy in the midst of Carnival in *The Merchant of Venice*. This Jessica has mixed cultural references akin to the Jewish–Christian bind in which Shakespeare's heroine finds herself.

But *The Tempest* has not one but two absent mothers: the other is Sycorax, Caliban's witch-mother. Forbes makes this connection overt in *Bombay Ice*; describing her mother's seduction by her father, Ros records: 'My mother was a blue-eyed hag seduced by a British gentleman' (165). Sycorax is the 'blue-eyed hag' of the play (1.2.271), and this connects Ros to Caliban as well. We have already explored the use made by Warner of Sycorax's associations with herbalism and witchcraft; Forbes continues this train of thought, linking seventeenth-century alchemy with magic and, by association, with Jessica's profession as a gilder in the twentieth century. Her trade is implicitly linked with a knowledge of chemicals and poisons, and her notebooks contain herbal recipes, including those for abortifacients, a cause of obvious distress to her daughter when she reads them. Elsewhere in the novel it is implied that Jessica dies from drowning in a bath, her failure to struggle induced by the swallowing of strychnine. Like much else in the narrative, however, this is subject to interpretation – not least the reader's perception of Ros's reliability as a narrator and recorder of such complicated personal histories.

In addition, readers are informed that Jessica suffered from Münchhausen's syndrome. This can manifest itself in a number of

ways, not least in self-harm. In its 'by proxy' manifestation, however, it realises itself in harm meted out to children (Allison and
Roberts, 1998; Levin and Sheridan, 1995). In this way we might
wish to read Ros as a victim of abuse. Münchhausen's sufferers
have often themselves suffered parental abuse (once again, the
incestuous subtext is introduced to our minds), but the name for
the disease derives from its victims' tendency to lie and cover up
their actions. Baron Münchhausen was a famous storyteller, and
Ros's mother is persistently associated with storytelling in the
narrative. But so, too, is Ros, and when the reader, in a chilling
moment, realises there is at least a possibility that Ros murdered
her own mother by assisting her drowning, or even poisoning her,
we realise that the storytelling capacity – and potentially the
syndrome itself – may have been handed down genetically.

A crucial intertext for *The Tempest* was Ovid's *Metamorphoses*:
in particular the story of Medea, the skilful herbalist/witch, infamous for poisoning her children as revenge against her unfaith-
ful husband, Jason, as recounted in Book 15. Commentators on
the play have noted a link between Sycorax and Medea, but also
the troubling connection that Shakespeare encouraged informed
audiences to make between Prospero, the white magus, and the
black magic of his Algerian counterpart (Orgel, 1994: 19). As noted
in previous chapters, Act 5 Scene 1 of the play, Prospero's 'Ye
elves of hills, brooks, standing lakes' soliloquy, where he talks of
raising the dead, is a direct reworking of one of Medea's speeches,
and so implicitly parallels him with, rather than distinguishing
him from, Sycorax. This reinforces the parental instincts Prospero
appears to feel for Caliban.

> I have bedimmed
> The noontide sun, called forth the mutinous winds,
> And 'twixt the green sea and the azured vault
> Set roaring war – to the dread rattling thunder
> Have I given fire, and rifted Jove's stout oak
> With his own bolt; the strong-based promontory
> Have I made shake, and by the spurs plucked up
> The pine and cedar; graves at my command
> Have waked their sleepers, oped, and let 'em forth
> By my so potent art.
>   (5.1.41–50)

The same speech forms an epigraph to a later section of *Bombay Ice*, and the Mary Innes 1955 translation of the *Metamorphoses* is directly quoted (217). The Medean frame of reference is clearly intended as a further clue for readers to interpret. At the beginning of *Bombay Ice*, Ros declares: 'I have some knowledge of poisons' (3). The Sycorax/Medea analogy thereby proves as fluid as the Caliban one.

The Ovidian references in the narrative are not restricted solely to Medea's story. The Bombay *mise en scène* of the novel forms links with the chaotic, unstable, and perpetually changing world of the *Metamorphoses*. That narrative simmers with the subjects of rape, incest and violence just beneath the surface of its beautiful transformations, and therefore offers a potent analogy both to the events of Shakespeare's play and to those of Ros Benegal's unwieldy memoir. Ovidian references find their way, like so much else, into Sharma's *Tempest* film (one of the reasons the film is never completed is that the director endlessly seeks to incorporate new discoveries and the latest fashions). One description of the film offered to Ros is that it depicts: 'men turning into women and then into snakes and fish, storms brewing in mirrors, Jacobean magic sequences that turn into computer magic' (278).

Chopra's aforementioned biography of Sharma provides further intertexts. Entitled *The Sea in the Mirror*, it evokes the working title of Sharma's epic film, but that itself is an allusion to W. H. Auden's poetic appropriation of *The Tempest*, *The Sea and the Mirror*. That connection, which the reader is initially left to make alone, is later confirmed by the narrative (114). This is part of the teasing effect of Forbes's writing: like a classic detective-story writer, she encourages readers to feel good about finding clues and identifying connections, only to deconstruct them or reveal them anyway.[1] Just as the reader might begin to feel smug at recognising the potential plagiarism of Sharma's digitally enhanced *Tempest*, so Thomas Jacobs, Ros's Anglophile taxi-driver, makes that same point:

> 'Have you heard of a film called *Prospero's Books* by a Mr Peter Greenaway?' he asked, and carried on without waiting for an answer. 'I am hoping that it will come to a cinema near me so I may observe *The Tempest* given new lease of life with latest in computer technology. Wouldn't this be something, Miss Benegal?' (378)

Thomas is, of course, a version of the cliché of the taxi-driver who quotes Shakespeare (a trope of which *Shakespeare in Love* made comic capital), but he also raises important questions about class and identity in the novel. This P. G. Wodehouse-reading Christian is a product of the British Empire; in that respect he is another Caliban, although the character he cites directly from *The Tempest* is, intriguingly, the Boatswain of the opening scene (23). David Norbrook has brilliantly explored the class connotations of this scene (1992), and in the monsoon-drenched pages of Forbes's novel, water acts as a leveller much as it does in Shakespeare's play. For class in India, one might read caste, and the hierarchies of Indian communities – Hindi, Muslim, Christian, and *hijra* – play a major role in the narrative's events and outcome. The rank-driven explorations of Shakespeare's 1611 play prove curiously pertinent in this late-twentieth-century context.

The film industry has its own considerable hierarchies, embodied most clearly in the role of director and, as we have noted, film is as dominant, if not more prominent, an intertext and intersecting genre as drama throughout *Bombay Ice*. This says something about the most popular form of Shakespearean dissemination in the current age. Bombay is the centre of the Hindi filmmaking industry (now affectionately known as 'Bollywood'), and several of the sequences described in Ros's narrative – recounted, as it were, in textual form – are filmed: from Maya's fall from the balcony – the central puzzle of the novel: did she fall or was she pushed? – to the amateur cameraman's recording of the first *hijra* murder victim's corpse washing up on Chowpatty Beach. Ros watches the latter sequence on CNN in her Mumbai hotel room, one of the novel's many instances of cultural intersection between East and West (12). Film functions as a recorder, but also as a distancing effect, and can be the potential cause of misreadings, subject as it is to manipulation in both the technical and interpretative processes that are applied to it. Tellingly, Ros views the masochistic sex scene she engages in with Bollywood director Mistry at his ice-house studios as a sequence, viewed, directed and edited (166).[2]

Ros's tendency, as in the latter example, to aestheticise events, to read everything through the prism of art, infects her unreliable narrative. If one of the fundamental debates in *The Tempest* as Iris Murdoch recognised it was between life and art (with Prospero as the play's central artist-magician), then Ros's narrative frequently displays a tendency to turn life into art. Even murder, or the procedure of autopsy, falls prey to this tendency. The use of wax in the autopsy process is compared to the traditional arts of Indian jewellers, and Ros describes killing as 'the twentieth century's ultimate art form' (14), reflecting that with 'Judicious editing, a little pacey music ... the most banal murder can be given drama' (14). At times Ros tries to remind herself of the difference between life and art: 'It's rare for a real murder to have the drama of fiction. Fictional death has victims with sympathetic haircuts, good lighting, suspense. Movie heroes never wear grey shoes' (14); nevertheless, her aestheticising tendency affects any objective judgement she might make of her situation. Objectivity may always have been an impossible aim, since Ros is, like other first-person fictional narrators, a biased recorder of events. Forbes utilises the now familiar strategy of having Ros recording her memoirs (Romberg, 1962).[3] Those memoirs – like Dora Chance's in *Wise Children* or Ginny Cook's recollections of her father in Smiley's *A Thousand Acres* – are necessarily partisan, subjective, and tinged with bias.

'Louder than the weather': identity and family

Family is once again a central theme in Forbes's novel, and Shakespearean archetypes help to inform the complex networks of kinship and affection within which her characters find themselves. As we have seen, Ros is an ostensible orphan. Her trip to India is in part a search for a lost family map and an effort at reconciliation with her half-sister, Miranda. So considerable is this emotional and psychological drive that at one point Rosalind (like her cross-dressed Shakespearean namesake) finds herself attired in her sister's clothes: 'In my sister's clothes I had acquired a new identity: mother of a rich man's son' (332). Dressed as Miranda, Ros also finds a link with her Indian cultural roots and, by extension, her late father, whose act of abandonment she clearly still feels deeply.

In another filmic moment in the narrative, Ros flashes back to her sister's companionship in childhood, suggesting that they were 'twins' of a sort (16). This provides a further Shakespearean connection with plays involving twinned characters or siblings – not least *The Tempest*, where links have been traced between Miranda and Caliban, and Prospero and Sycorax, as well as the more obvious blood-brother relationship of Prospero and Antonio. Ros recalls an image of Miranda and herself underwater – 'amphibious Siamese twins with pipes of bamboo for snorkels' (16). The metaphor of the amphibious, the permeability of land and water, most obviously embodied in the cartography of Bombay/Mumbai, pervades the novel and echoes Caliban's half-man, half-fish status in Shakespeare's playtext. The notion of being underwater also carries with it more troubling implications of drowning which find their counterpart in various murders, achieved and attempted, in *Bombay Ice*.

By travelling to India, Ros is forced to face up to her own past – this is why the flashback structure to the novel is so vital. She compares the process of memory retrieval to the act of forming the city of Bombay: 'To reclaim lost land you need to dredge up the past, the drowned' (17). The past is compared to a drowned thing, and in Ros's case it will certainly reveal drownings and suppressions. In the course of the narrative, Ros undergoes her own 'personal monsoon' as she tries to rethink the 'map of a family' (17). Bombay's particular past is that of empire: this is a novel stamped with the awareness and heightened self-reflectiveness of postcolonialism. The legacy of the British Empire is read in explicitly sexual terms in the novel: 'Consider Britain and India: empire as incest' (182). But Bombay's 'detritus of old empires' (18) is not solely British in identity: the Moghul period is also a defining one in Indian history. This is the period in which Prosper Sharma has chosen to locate his Indianised version of *The Tempest*. Bombay, like the novel's protagonist/narrator, has a distinctly hybrid sense of identity. Ros is a blend of Indian, Scottish and English inheritances; as she states, once again fashioning a real condition into an aesthetic technique: 'The gesso I was made of was too liquid a blend' (50). Her mother's grandfather, a Glaswegian army clerk, had seduced and married a Chitral woman in the Hindu Kush. They eventually left Kerala for Scotland, where Ros describes the sub-Ovidian metamorphosis her grandmother underwent: 'Gran had shed her half-Chitrali skin like a snake in spring, and emerged as a respectable working-class Scotswoman' (50). Snakes provide a leitmotiv in the novel, ranging from the reality of the cobra nests which thrive in the damp monsoon con-

ditions (Singh, 1987: 37), and prove crucial to Ros in her run-in
with Anthony Unmann, to the literary archetype of sexual tempt-
ation. Describing the pressure placed on her during childhood to
conform to the different cultural identities provided by her mixed
parentage and grandparentage, Ros recalls her mother's contradictory demands: 'First she wanted me to be British; then she
wanted me to be Indian' (49). Like that of Miranda in *Indigo*,
Ros's hybrid identity is both a strength and a weakness. As with
Warner's protagonist, we witness Ros trying on different identities: as well as borrowing her sister's wardrobe, she tries on Sunila's
clothes in an attempt to understand what it might feel like to be
a *hijra* (290–1). The moment is deliberately reminiscent of Ros's
Shakespearean namesake's layering of identity in *As You Like It*:
there, Rosalind, a boy actor dressed for the part of Shakespeare's
heroine, dresses as a boy, Ganymede, in order to escape to the
Forest of Arden, and then as 'Rosalind' in order to educate Orlando
in the ways of wooing.

The implicit connection Forbes's novel makes between contemporary Indian family structures and those of Shakespeare's seventeenth-century England have been recognised in numerous recent
stage productions of plays such as *Romeo and Juliet*, which directly
engage with topics including kinship networks and arranged
marriage.[4] Ros is only too aware of the rebellion her accusation
against her eminent brother-in-law represents: 'In the script for a
good Hindu girl the first lines read "Loyalty to family". Which
includes brother-in-laws.' (187). But the point is that she is not 'a
good Hindu girl' in the sense that her more conformist half-sister
is, but, rather, a dangerous mix, a hybrid.

Identity and costume are closely allied in the text of *Bombay
Ice*, as they would have been in any original production of *The
Tempest* – a point beautifully acknowledged towards the end of the
novel, when Ros reflects on the disappearance of Robi's corpse: 'I
thought of Ariel in Shakespeare's time, who probably wore some
form of cloak labelled with the word "Invisible" to denote invisi-
bility. Poverty has the same effect' (400). But as well as the obvious
gender and class issues bound up in costumes and most explicitly
enacted in the *hijra* community's female attire, there is also an
implicit tension in India between traditional costume, such as the
shalwar kamiz, and Western dress. Ros moves in and out of these

sumptuary identities in the novel, and the 'Jurassic Park is coming' t-shirt worn by the murdered Robi becomes a grim talisman
of the battle between Western (embodied here by Hollywood, another form of empire in the novel and in Bombay society[5]) and
Indian values.

History as well as identity, as we saw in *Indigo*, is an explicitly
gendered concept. Ros acknowledges this in her account of her
parents' respective professions and personal proclivities: 'Dad had
dealt in histories, Mum in stories' (41). The word 'His-story'
embodies the notion of patriarchal truth, although followers of
Hayden White would argue that history is just another version of
storytelling (White, 1973, 1987). As Hutcheon has observed: 'History and fiction have always been notoriously porous genres' (1995:
73). But the binary Forbes brings so self-consciously into play
here returns us problematically to the association of women and
storytelling and, by extension, gossip and unreliability, in this
female-authored text.[6] Jessica, Ros's mother, was a gilder – a term
which, for all its magical properties, suggests a false surface, a
gilding of appearances and the truth. India, too, is associated with
the art of storytelling in the novel, as it has been in other novels
by Anglo-Indian writers, most notably by Salman Rushdie in *Mid-
night's Children* (1981). Orality as the state of the colonised may be
the implication: certainly, Caliban speaks the most beautiful poetry in *The Tempest* while being, in official terms, illiterate. But
the storytelling in both Ros's and her mother's case is troublingly
linked to Münchhausen's syndrome and mental disorder. In this
respect, the narrative cannot seem to extricate this connection of
orality and the female into anything more liberating.

Ros's parents met in the suitably textual confines of the British
Library. He was studying Renaissance hydraulic artists: men (for
they were men – another instance of 'his-story') who sought to
control the elements – in particular water – by means of mathematics and magic: men such as Salomon De Caus, whom the novel
describes as the 'Prospero of Heidelberg' (48) (Strong, 1984: 50–
7). The seventeenth century undoubtedly regarded the arts of
science and magic as more closely allied than the present age,
although Forbes suggests that this may simply be a Eurocentric
view, and that Hindi culture is still more embracing of ambivalences and permeable boundaries than Western empiricism. Ros's

mother was gilding a new edition of Sir Walter Ralegh's *The Discoverie of the large, rich and beautifull Empire of Guiana, with relation to the great and golden cities of Manoa (which the Spaniards call El Dorado)*. The mention of this text in *Bombay Ice* brings into focus the novel's aforementioned themes of colonialism and the related quest for gold. Ralegh's text influenced the genre of travel narratives which, as well as being an influence on *The Tempest*, have made their mark on *Bombay Ice*: in this way the seventeenth century, as well as Shakespeare, is made to speak to the modern age (Greenblatt, 1991).

For Ros Benegal, though, both Shakespeare and history are undoubtedly patriarchal texts. In this respect she is another Miranda after all, authored by her father's exile, written into being in that moment: 'We were always leaving places I loved in storms' (36). The echoes of Miranda's journey to the island with Prospero, described as a rebirth, are inescapable. The Prospero–Miranda relationship is therefore figured in a number of ways within *Bombay Ice*, present as it is in Ros's relationship with her father, but also with her brother-in-law. The Prospero–Caliban relationship finds analogues not only in the Sharma–Mistry father–son relationship, but in the story of Caleb's lost son. He is possibly the *hijra* Sami. That Sami also turns out to be a 'thing of darkness' in Prosper's life (we learn that she/he regarded him as a father (206)) complicates the picture further. Sami becomes jealous, and resorts to blackmail, when she/he realises that Prosper is still sleeping with his wife. This provides us with a further spin on the Prospero–Caliban–Miranda triad of the play, which also operates around a sexual jealousy of sorts, one which envelops Ferdinand when he joins the island community. We have, then, in kinship with other novels we have considered here, another series of families, both biological and affective, with all their attendant hierarchies and estrangements. Failed patriarchs are also once again the order of the day.

'Love, death and the middle bit': Bombay, Bollywood, *hijra*, hybridity

Perhaps the strongest kinship network proffered by the Bombay of the novel is not one based on blood ties at all, but the self-formed and self-sustaining 'family' of the *hijra* community – what Serena

Nanda has called the 'web of fictive kinship' (1990: 45). Sunila talks openly of the dead Sami as her 'sister', and for a time Ros seems tempted by the close bonds to be found among this communal group which has its matriarch figure in the *naik* or guru.

*Hijra*s are not necessarily homosexuals, nor are they hermaphrodites or eunuchs. They are not born as females, but grow up to act like women, to 'manifest themselves as women – mimetics' (Nanda, 1990: xii). Their world is one of convincing performance which connects them with the seventeenth-century boy-actor already conjured up in readers' minds by Ros's Shakespearean nomenclature. Their 'family' is a piece of convincing mimesis. One of the best-known means by which *hijras* earn a living is by going to houses with newly born sons and demanding payment for their celebratory performances. On the whole, this tradition is tolerated, although cases of tension and even violence have resulted. In an odd twist, this customary practice finds sons who have rejected their own sex in favour of a performed gender enacting the social potency of sons. In *Bombay Ice*, a novel where the talismanic power of sons is a felt quantity, the relevance of this seems obvious.

Ros, conscious of her status as an outsider in both her stated communities in the novel – Anglo-Scottish and Indian – identifies with the marginalisation of the *hijra* community:

> Not even the most cynical politician would claim that they could ever afford to house these people properly. They had to be marginalised to be affordable, pushed to the outskirts where they wouldn't upset the tourists as much. They were part of a long tradition of cartography where marginalised people belonged, quite literally, to the margins of maps, the borderlines, beyond which lived the edge monsters – centaurs, harpies, mermaids, hybrids of promiscuous unions between different species. (209–10)

Ros identifies Sami and herself as modern equivalents of these 'edge monsters': hybrids without a defined sense of space, home or belonging: 'I see myself this way, and Sami. Two hybrids, out on the edge of the map' (210).

Maps form a central trope in this novel, as in *Indigo*. They are suggestive of Bombay's problematic cartography and history, as well as the personal history of the family tree. Ros is fascinated by old maps of the city which depict it as a series of islands floating on water (10).[7] Elsewhere in the novel, she makes similarly liquid assessments of her personal 'gesso' or identity. Bombay is reclaimed land, and by travelling to India Ros is trying to reclaim something of her own sense of self, but as she notes: 'how do you reclaim something that was never yours in the first place?' (10).

Shakespeare and the specific text of *The Tempest* have a similar function in the novel, shoring up a traditional culture and yet proving liquid and permeable, changeable and even insubstantial. Indian culture both defines itself against and reinscribes itself within the British imperial past, for which Shakespeare has become a virtual synecdoche.[8] At certain points, Rosalind seems to resent these glib associations: 'I wish people would stop quoting Shakespeare at me. What d'you think – we spend all our time in Britain strolling around in bowler hats reciting iambic pentameters?' (164). But Shakespeare, as well as being a signifier of all things British in India, is part of India's own hybrid and intertextual culture: Ros sees an instructive analogy between herself and the 'bastardised versions' of Shakespeare produced in Bombay (4).

Bombay, like Ros, has a hybrid identity: the 'city of gold' has two names: Bombay and Mumbai – the former being inscribed with its imperial past, hence the desire to slough it off in favour of the latter. Like Ros, the city can converse in different languages. Like the *hijra*s, Bombay is of two essences, land and water; the city embodies the novel's informing subtext of transformation and metamorphosis, which has Shakespearean links with Ovidian-influenced plays like *Dream*, *Twelfth Night*, *As You Like It* and *The Tempest*, although – as travel writer Gillian Tindall notes – tradition can still prove stifling in this site of metamorphosis: 'Among such continual change, nothing, in essence, changes' (1982: 250).

The monsoon, which provides the novel's most obvious analogue to the tempest of Shakespeare's play, is an example of both change and stasis, wreaking as it does havoc on the city's landscape and inhabitants, but in an oddly predictable way. The seventeenth and eighteenth centuries, the era at the start of which *The Tempest* stands, was also, ironically, the era in which a scientific assessment of the monsoon was first carried out by Captain Henry Piddington (1797–1858), in *The Sailor's Hornbook for the Law of Storms* (Kutzbach, 1987: 176). Forbes's novel acknowledges that for all the collation of 'facts' about the monsoon, it remains, like Bombay itself, something capable of almost carnivalesque disorder.

In *Bombay Ice*, Forbes examines the effects and impacts of Indian religion, culture, tradition, weather and geography on its inhabitants, carrying out the kind of investigation often called 'cultural geography' by modern practitioners of interdisciplinary studies of this kind; what J. Hillis Miller described as 'topographies' or 'the mental mappings we make of our environments' (1995: 9). Part of Bombay's cultural geography is clearly the film industry, or 'Bollywood'. That nickname encapsulates the postcolonial problematic of defining an indigenous Indian film industry in a sphere dominated by Western capitalists, and in particular by the Hollywood filmmaking empire. Nevertheless, great emphasis is placed in the novel on the distinctive style of cinema developed by Bombay, even when a product of empire like Prosper Sharma seeks to film Shakespeare: 'But even Hindi copies of Hollywood are remade to fit an Indian frame – that archetypal concern for the value of an extended family' (136). Cinema provides a modern counterpart to the seventeenth-century world of magic and alchemy which proves so resonant in *The Tempest*.

The power of film as popular culture in modern India is hard to overestimate, and it provides a potent parallel to the commercial theatre that would have staged *The Tempest* in Shakespeare's day. The early modern theatre was frequently closed down due to outbreaks of plague epidemics in urban London, for fear that the close proximity of members of the audience would aid the spread of the disease (Barroll, 1991; Ross, 1999). When bubonic plague broke out in Bombay in the late 1980s, cinema houses were closed for the same reason. But when any form is popular, corruption becomes an inevitability, and Bollywood – like its southern Californian counterpart, or its Far Eastern equivalents – has its own mafia, represented in the novel by the henchmen who attack Ros in Mistry's studio following their violent sexual liaison.

Tindall describes Bollywood as 'an extraordinary insulated eastern Hollywood populated by stars still more legendary than those of California in the thirties and forties' (1982: 21). Sharma and his first wife Maya, along with Mistry himself, were and are clearly part of that star system. When, at the close of the novel, nothing has been proved about Sharma, gossip wreaks its own exile upon this second Prospero, as his career fails.

Kishore Valicha has identified two distinct strains of Indian filmmaking – the neo-realist, exemplified by the work of Satyajit Ray, and the fantastic, represented by Bollywood (1988: 4). Both Caleb Mistry's schlock populist films and Sharma's fantasy-driven *Tempest* belong to the latter category. Mistry's studio acts as a kind of microcosm of modern Bombay, its hybridity, artificiality, chaos and violence:

> Inside the ice house, four different seasons coexisted within fifty yards of each other. Doors were kicked down in a monsoon downpour, women were raped and beaten under a spring moon, men spilled stage blood into salt snow, and, to this muted drumbeat of head jabs and knee thrusts, a man had his eyes gouged out under the cobalt brilliance of a 10,000 watt summer. (53–4)

In the novel, Mistry is associated with a popular cultural, in-digenous form of filmmaking that Sharma's elitist arthouse work eschews. But what is striking about rereading the passage quoted above in the context of regarding *Bombay Ice* as a Shakespearean appropriation is the suggestion of Shakespearean plays that can be found here too: from the monsoon downpour which might imply *Lear* or *The Tempest*, which both have life-defining and life-altering storms, the gruesome rape of *Titus Andronicus*, the spilt blood of *Macbeth* and *Hamlet*, and the onstage gouging out of Gloucester's eyes in *Lear*. The fact that the plays evoked are all tragedies may add to our sense of premonition about the events occurring in Mistry's and Sharma's studios, but it also indicates that Forbes, like Carter, is interested in the popular cultural force of the Shake-spearean canon, and its archetypal plots and themes. When Mistry tries to define the stock plots of Hindi films, the connection be-comes explicit:

> We are reduced to three plots. One: a young couple has brief idyll of happiness, followed by death of one or both. Two: family breakup be-cause of nefarious doings of a villain. Climax, melodrama, followed by prompt reconciliation. Family reunited and villain forgiven and/or violently blown away. Three: the good and bad siblings – good one devoted to Mum, bad, sexy one … cruel and indifferent. After long separation and much gratuitous violence, a reunion. Even better if the siblings are twins, giving audience a childlike pleasure in seeing two images of the same person in a single frame – (136)[9]

Once again, the Shakespeare-aware reader will trace parallels and links: the doomed young lovers are suggestive of *Romeo and Juliet*;

the reconciled families could refer to plays from *Cymbeline* to *The Winter's Tale*; and twins feature in plays from *The Comedy of Errors* to *Twelfth Night*. As Ros herself wryly observes: 'Just like Shakespeare – all those separated twins. Three plots: love, death and the middle bit' (136).

The fifth-act climax of *Bombay Ice* sees the worlds of cinema and Shakespearean drama merge in the ultimate chaotic fusion: self-consciously, Ros notes: 'So now it begins, I thought. The last act' (381). Prosper is shooting the final scenes of his film in an unrealistic, deliberately stage-like way – the genres of narrative, film and drama merge in this fifth act, as they have throughout *Bombay Ice*.[10] Ros uses the moment to try to force Prosper into a revelation of his guilt: when Ariel speaks the lines 'Remember I have done thee worthy service' (1.2.248), images of Sami's corpse are projected on to a screen at the back of the stage. This scene is reminiscent of a number of early modern plays which used the device of the play-within-a-play to draw events to an (often bloody) climax – from Thomas Kyd's *The Spanish Tragedy* to Thomas Middleton's *Women Beware Women*. But most obviously it recalls not a Shakespearean fifth act, but a central one – Act 3 of *Hamlet, Prince of Denmark* where the Prince uses the staging of 'The Murder of Gonzago' by visiting players to determine his uncle's guilt:

> I have heard that guilty creatures sitting at a play
> Have by the very cunning of the scene
> Been struck so to the soul that presently
> They have proclaimed their malefactions;
> (2.2.566–9)

Here, as in *Hamlet*, we have ghosts and guilt. But the expectations of knowledgeable readers are deliberately thwarted: this is a detective story that resists the solving of the crime, a fifth act that resists resolution in the Shakespearean mode.

Whether Ros reaches a resolution in her own quest for identity is also open to debate. As the novel closes, so the monsoon that has provided the sense of build-up, suspense, threat and release in this carefully structured narrative retreats. It is late October/early November, and the moment is marked in the Hindi calendar by Diwali, or the festival of light. Ros, however, finds herself drawn back to another form of ritual demarcation:

Just before Diwali, I had an invitation to a Bonfire Night party from an old friend at the British Embassy in Bombay. The time seemed right to reclaim my British identity, what was left of it. (400)

Like Bombay, however, for Ros any act of reclamation must be ongoing. Like Shakespeare's texts, her sense of self will be constantly evolving, subject to the vicissitudes of time and place.

Notes

1 For a brilliant exposition of the role of Shakespeare in detective fiction, see Baker (1995). Her argument is that there is a moral imperative involved in detecting Shakespearean allusion that is comparable to the overall effects of the genre on the reader. Writers she discusses include Dorothy L. Sayers, Ngaio Marsh and Agatha Christie. She also identifies a novel in which Shakespeare himself features as a detective, Faye Kellerman's *The Quality of Mercy* (1989). In the title story of a recent short-story collection, 'A Good Hanging', Ian Rankin has his popular detective Inspector Rebus solving a crime at the Edinburgh Festival by identifying a quote from *Twelfth Night* (1998). Alison Joseph's *A Dark and Sinful Death* (1998), which involves a blinding out on lonely moorlands invokes *King Lear* in efforts to solve the crime.

2 The icehouse studios provide their own palimpsest of colonialism. Tindall (1982) records how the first cargo of ice arrived in Bombay in 1833, and that ice was subsequently regularly transported from North America in block form to feed the British expatriates' insatiable desire for ice cream and preserved foodstuffs (172). Forbes makes double use of the signification of ice in her novel, deploying Mistry's icehouse studios to embody an act of postcolonial Indian cultural redefinition, but also using the word 'ice' in her title to suggest an alternative sense of 'to ice' or murder.

3 One of the most brilliant recent examples is Isler's *The Prince of West End Avenue* (1994), where Otto Körner both relates and suppresses past experiences of the Holocaust from the vantage point of a New York Jewish retirement home. This novel is saturated with references to Eliot's 'Prufrock'.

4 For example, a Leicester Haymarket production of *Romeo and Juliet* in 2000 which was set in contemporary India.

5 And Indian cinema: Valicha discusses the quasi-imperial influence of Hollywood on postcolonial Indian filmmaking (1988:39).

6 Warner (1992), as we have seen, makes similar associations between women and orality, but with more positive outcomes.

7 For a study of these maps, see Tindall (1982).

8 It is almost a given of postcolonial critiques and revisions of *The Tempest* that the Prospero–Caliban, and at times the Prospero–Ariel, relationship stands for the colonial relationship of oppressor and oppressed: see Retamar (1989). Women writers in colonial and postcolonial subject positions have more frequently looked to Miranda as their template, but Showalter, among others, has challenged the political efficacy of such a position: (1991: esp. 41).

9 On these elements of Hindi popular films, see Valicha (1988: 35–8).

10 Once again, the alert reader will be aware that Sharma is caught in the trap of postcolonial referentiality, since Greenaway's *Prospero's Books* (1991) made similar recourse to the aesthetics of staged drama in its final moments – most famously when Sir John Gielgud as Prospero recites the 'Our revels now are ended' soliloquy in front of a red curtain direct to camera.

The novel seems to invite such connections when it states: 'Prosper is deliberately using a technique from the early days of Indian cinema ... when filmmakers here drew heavily on the kind of theatrical framing you get in Victorian melodrama' (382–3).

EIGHT

Including Shakespeare:
The novels of Gloria Naylor

In *Bailey's Cafe* (1992), Gloria Naylor's fourth novel, in a section entitled 'Miss Maple's Blues', the *Complete Works of Shakespeare* play a pivotal role in the life-story of Stanley. Like all Naylor's novels, *Bailey's Cafe* involves the deployment of multiple narrative voices. Stanley, or 'Miss Maple', wears women's clothing in summer and his story, one of a number told in the course of the novel, is in part an effort to explain the reasons for this. The café-owner, whose voice provides the framing narrative for the whole book, stresses that neither transvestism nor transsexuality offers the key to Stanley's identity: 'We're talking no wigs. We're talking no makeup. No padded falsies. No switching' (1992: 163).

Stanley's story is one of social aspiration. His father strives to have Stanley educated, to make available to his son opportunities denied to him, but Stanley is sceptical: 'Philosophy hadn't saved my father from the contempt we met in town' (174). When Stanley graduates from high school, and is about to take up a place at Stanford University, his father makes him the ostentatious gift of a complete set of Shakespeare. Stanley is not impressed by this either: 'I didn't call a complete set of Shakespeare a real gift – cream vellum or not, from England or wherever' (174).

Stanley, who would have much preferred the gift of condoms a friend had received on a comparable occasion – 'Now, that was a *real* gift. A man's gift' (175) – rejects the very idea of Shakespeare, as well as the significant object of the book. He articulates this in homophobic fashion, as if the present of the works of an effete English writer is somehow a denigrating comment on his own masculinity: 'the prevailing theory was that the old Bard had had some real dilemmas over his manhood' (174–5). The older Stanley, looking back with hindsight on this moment, is not immune to his adolescent paranoia: 'Manhood is a pervasive preoccupation when you're an adolescent boy, and you tend to see a fairy under every bush. I definitely saw one lurking under Iago, Brutus, that whining Hamlet' (175). There is something risible in Stanley's effrontery at the notion of owning books written by a homosexual, as if those objects could somehow 'infect' him and his much-emphasised heterosexuality. Yet there are also notes of relevance in his readings of characters like Iago, Brutus and Hamlet that contemporary queer theorists might attest to.[1] This is a typical example of Naylor's doubleness as a writer: events and expressions can often be read in entirely antithetical ways, without disrupting the narrative coherence.

The financial and emotional cost of the volumes to Stanley's father are embodied in the ritualistic unwrapping of these significant objects. There is an undoubted eroticism about the 'undressing' of the box:

> I could hear Papa grunting as he worked with the crowbar to remove the lid. The crate was packed with straw, and nested inside were oil-cloth envelopes. Each envelope closed with a hook and eye; and inside was a bundle wrapped with brown paper and taped firmly. After the brown paper was removed, there was still a wrapping of royal blue felt to be undone before you got to the single volume ... Peters nodded, and Papa handed him the book. Peters opened the cover like a man making love... (177)

The 'spell' of this moment is broken by the sound of the front door and the violent entry of the Gatlin family with whom Stanley's father has an ongoing dispute. A violent ritual humiliation of the three men in the shop – Stanley, his father, and Peters the bookseller – by the Gatlin gang ensues. They are pinned down and stripped naked, blades are brandished, and their manhood is mocked: 'And it ain't got a big wanger neither' (180). When they are subsequently locked in the storeroom, naked and ashamed, a touching scene of reconciliation occurs between Stanley and his father, in which the latter tries to explain his educational and intellectual ambitions for his son:

My flesh against his flesh: ... It hasn't been easy, Stanley, but I did it for you. From the day you were born I've been speaking to you in a language that I wanted you to master, knowing that once you did, there was nothing that could be done to make you feel less than what you are... (182)

The notion of mastering languages other than one's own recalls the speech of Caliban in *The Tempest* which has proved central to postcolonial appropriations of that play: 'You taught me language, and my profit on't/ Is I know how to curse' (1.2.366–7).

Stanley's father regards mastery of intellectual discourse as the key to social mobility in the USA, and it is Shakespeare's implicit association with the notion of a master-discourse that has encouraged critics such as Peter Erickson and Gary Storhoff to read what happens next in 'Miss Maple's Blues' as a decisive rejection of what the Shakespearean canon represents (Erickson, 1993a; Storhoff, 1997). In their readings, Stanley is depicted as the Caliban who rejects white imperial culture, discovering in his cross-dressing an alternative and potentially radical path in life.[2]

The Gatlin brothers systematically destroy the valuable Shakespearean volumes in the stockroom:

We smelled it before we saw it. They had gotten to the books. The silk cover was gouged with holes, the spine busted and bent over double. They'd torn out handfuls of pages, crushed what was left between their fists, and then urinated on the whole thing. The stench of *The Tempest* was quickly filling that close room. (183)

The mention of *The Tempest* in particular is critically and culturally loaded: Naylor's previous novel, *Mama Day*, is now widely recognised (and, indeed, taught – raising related questions of what achieves canonical status, and why) as an appropriation of *The Tempest*. Erickson suggests that the success of a novel so directly associated with the dead white male Shakespeare has led to a need on Naylor's part to move on (her previous two novels, as we shall see, also allude to and employ Shakespeare, albeit to a lesser extent), to disassociate herself from his influence. He describes this scene in *Bailey's Cafe* as Naylor's 'riddance ritual':

The entire network of Shakespearean allusions through the previous three novels is compressed into one image – the Shakespearean corpus represented in the most literal way possible as a set of books, physical objects shipped in a crate. (1993a: 34)

The implication is that Shakespeare as text no longer holds sway in Naylor's writing, merely Shakespeare as artefact, and that when his canon is reduced to this level of objectivity, its ultimate rejection is inevitable. Erickson goes on to describe the scene as a 'fitting conclusion to her long engagement with Shakespeare ... this farewell is a riddance ritual that announces the end of Naylor's artistic apprenticeship' (1993a: 34). As a critic I have the benefit – which Erickson did not when he made this claim – of knowing that Naylor's next novel, *The Men of Brewster Place* (1998), actually continues her engagement with Shakespeare (and *The Tempest*), as well as with the ability of his language and texts to touch critical communities other than those for which he might have initially composed drama and poetry. Nevertheless, an alternative reading seems possible from the passage in *Bailey's Cafe* alone. By urinating on the gorgeous bound volumes, and then setting fire to them, the Gatlins, rather than Stanley, come closer to enacting in the novel the desires of Caliban in the play to destroy Prospero's coveted library of books:

> Why, as I told thee, 'tis a custom with him
> I'th afternoon to sleep. There thou mayst brain him,
> Having first seized his books; or with a log
> Batter his skull, or paunch him with a stake,
> Or cut his weasand with a knife. Remember
> First to possess his books, for without them
> He's but a sot as I am...
>   Burn but his books.
>   (3.2.82–8, 90)[3]

In this way, Stanley witnesses an act of resistance, satisfying in some respect his own need for rebellion, while retaining the position of the good son. Book-burning must have a negative allusive role in a novel elsewhere concerned with the genocides of the twentieth century (the Holocaust and Hiroshima) and of previous centuries (represented most chillingly by the African slave trade). While there may be some truth in the claim that Naylor queries and questions the power invested in Shakespeare and the wider canon in passages such as these, it seems wrong to align her sympathetically with the Gatlins. In addition, the reconciliation between Stanley and his father that this violent moment enables is a striking adaptation of the themes of many of Shakespeare's late plays, including *The Tempest*. Elsewhere in his work on Naylor, Erickson rightly stresses her resistance to formal closure in her novels (1991a: 136). It would seem unlikely, therefore, that 'Miss Maple's Blues' would offer anything as formally rigid as a 'farewell to Shakespeare'.

In *The Men of Brewster Place*, Caliban's claim to have learned how to curse resurfaces in a revised context, and with a wholly positive outcome. Abshu's story, undoubtedly the most optimistic of the male life-stories contained here (he is also the character with whom Naylor opts to close her novel), recounts how he trains some young boys who are being bullied at the community centre where he is a volunteer to use Shakespearean language (and specifically curses) to get the better of the opposition:

> Abshu showed him how he could fight back with nothing but his mouth and his wits. And it didn't have to be a string of filth – fuck this; fuck that; and the infamous fuck you. Abshu spent three weeks with the boys teaching them to curse like Shakespeare did...
> 'You drudge, you clog,' Sammy went on. 'You unbaked and doughy youth.'
> 'Man, what language are you talking?' (1998: 141–2)

Here Shakespeare functions as empowering knowledge, and it is no coincidence that in Naylor's first novel, *The Women of Brewster Place* (1983), it is an all-black open-air production of *A Midsummer Night's Dream*, directed by Abshu, that provides a central cathartic moment in the midst of the despair charted elsewhere in the text.[4] Cora Lee, Naylor's subtle rewriting of the US cultural stereotype of the 'welfare mother', is persuaded by Kiswana Browne, middle-class resident of the urban nightmare that is the Brewster Place housing project, to attend the show with her children. Her initial sense of inferiority is clear: "'I don't know," Cora sighed ... "This stuff here – Shakespeare and all that. It'll be too deep for them and they'll start acting up and embarrassing me in front of all those people"' (1983: 119).

In reality, though, 'Shakespeare and all that' proves as much her children's birthright to enjoy as anybody's in the twentieth century: 'as the play gained momentum the evident slapstick quality in the situation drew its own humor. The fairy man had done something to the eyes of these people and everyone seemed to be chasing everyone else' (125). Shakespeare is undoubtedly bound up with ideas of education and aspiration in Cora's mind. She immediately worries about her children's futures in this context: 'That fairy queen looked just like Maybelline. Maybelline could be doing this some day' (125). There is also a moving sense of empowerment in her response to Sammy's question on the way home: '"Mama," Sammy pulled on her arm, "Shakespeare's black?" "Not yet," she said softly, remembering she had beaten him for writing the rhymes on her bathroom walls' (127).

In her next novel, *Linden Hills* (1986), Naylor appeared less positive about the possibilities of a 'black Shakespeare' than her Brewster Place protagonist. When Willie and Lester discuss the former's recent failure to write any new poetry, Lester responds:

> Are you kidding me? How'd you expect to find the time to do that? I'd get home and be too tired to even eat, some nights. Ya know, it even got to the point where my mom asked me if I was working too hard. I must have looked pretty bad for *her* to tell me to slack up. And yet people wonder why black folks ain't produced a Shakespeare. (1986: 282)

But one of the boys Abshu trains to fight back through Shakespeare in *The Men of Brewster Place* is called 'little Sammy', and Naylor is surely encouraging readers to see him as an older incarnation of Cora Lee's hopeful son. Naylor's intertextuality as a writer is much documented, and her novels connect not only outwards to other writers and cultures but – in an intricate, and sometimes destabilising, manner – with each other.

The 'Cora Lee' section of *The Women of Brewster Place* has been read as optimistic only in a qualified sense: Jill L. Matus notes: 'The visit to the play looks like a breakthrough, and in some ways it is … But one trip to the park to see Shakespeare is not going to resolve magically life's confusing demands' (1993: 133).[5] Cora is pregnant again by the end of the novel, but the lyrical beauty of her response to the Shakespearean moment surely remains with the reader, and allows her to transcend the constraining social stereotype:

> The long walk had tired them so there were few protests about going to bed. No one questioned it when she sponged them down and put them each into bed with a kiss – this had been a night of wonders. Cora Lee took their clothes, folded them, and put them away.

She then went through her apartment, turning off the lights and breathing in hopeful echoes of order and peace that lay in the clean house. She entered her bedroom in the dark and the shadow, who had let himself in with his key, moved in the bed. He didn't ask her where they had been and she didn't care to tell him. She went over and silently peeked in the crib at her sleeping daughter and let out a long sigh. Then she turned and firmly folded her evening like gold and lavender gauze deep within the creases of her dreams, and let her clothes drop to the floor. (127)

The power, and indeed necessity, of dreams is persistently referred to in the novel. The epigraph about a dream deferred derives from a poem by Langston Hughes, 'Harlem', which in itself constitutes a call to action on the part of its readers. To read the Cora Lee story in purely despairing terms is to deny the very spaces and opportunity for change that the novel seems so anxious to afford the women it describes.

'Shakespeare and all that': narrative intertextuality

Doublenesses and dualities are held in a remarkable intellectual tension in Naylor's work. In this respect Shakespeare can represent both a figure of cultural imperialism, to be resisted and contested, and an enabling and empowering literature. There is a comparable paradox in the work of women writers who struggle with the figure of Shakespearean male authority, yet find a space of access in the cultural familiarity which attends his work. There is a kinship here, too, with other African-American writers who have both invoked and reinterpreted Shakespeare with surprising frequency: John Edgar Wideman's *Philadelphia Fire* (1995 (1990)) is a strikingly individual take on *The Tempest*, as is Toni Morrison's *Tar Baby* (1997 (1981)); Maya Angelou and Rita Mae Dove have deployed Shakespeare in their poetry.[6] As Valerie Traub observes:

> Because Shakespearean drama holds pride of place within the dominant cultural field and is enlisted consistently by politicians, advertisers and academics for the promotion and defense of Anglo-European standards of aesthetic value, African-American writers' responses to Shakespeare would seem to be paradigmatic of the larger issue of the intertextuality of *cultures*. (1993: 150–1)

Intertextuality is an integral part of Naylor's novels. Drawing connections between the roles and functions of Shakespeare in Naylor's five novels is justified because she herself encourages – demands, even – the forging of those connections (Felton and Loris, 1997: 3). Erickson has remarked on the way in which Naylor's novels are linked by a series of 'internal cross-references to characters and places' (1991a: 125). For example, Kiswana Browne from *The Women of Brewster Place* re-emerges, in a more negative light, in *Linden Hills*. A central character in the latter text, Willa Prescott Nedeed, one of the victims of the fire that engulfs a Linden Hills property on Christmas Day in the dramatic close to the novel, is the grandchild of Miranda 'Mama' Day's sister Abigail in *Mama Day* (Cocoa refers directly to the Christmas fire when she first meets George in that latter novel). We move backwards in time to witness the quasi-biblical birth of George, Cocoa's tragically fated husband in *Mama Day*, at the millennially conscious close of *Bailey's Cafe*. And, in what is perhaps her most blatant act of self-intertextuality, *The Men of Brewster Place* offers the masculine flip-side to the women's stories recounted in Naylor's first novel: we hear Eugene's version of Lucelia's account of the death of their daughter Serena; Basil's account of how he tried to raise the money to repay his mother Mattie Michaels for the life savings she lost when he jumped bail; and we hear from Abshu, Kiswana Browne's director-boyfriend.[7] The spaces and places of her novels also intersect and overlap so that Linden Hills remains a touchstone of black middle-class aspirations in novels set in Brewster Place or the magical space of Willow Springs.

Naylor's narratives are also exemplary of African-American women writers' wider acts of intertextuality – what Karla Holloway has described as the 'diffusive voice' (1992: 60). Holloway relates this in part to a specifically African inheritance that values oral culture and recursive structures of storytelling. This mirrors the anti-linear narrative structures identified elsewhere in the work of white women writers such as Warner, Atkinson, and Carter: 'Complexity, multiple presences, and cyclic rather than linear principles are definitive aspects of the works of black women writers' (Holloway, 1992: 33). Naylor's work does lend itself to comparison with the work of fellow African-American writers such as Morrison and Alice Walker; the black diaspora, the power of ancestry and heritage, female genital mutilation, the notion of the 'sisterhood' and the figure of the conjure-woman are all shared themes and motifs. Naylor's work is significant, however, in its self-conscious and extended engagement with the European (and occasionally American) classical canon as well. The Shakespeare connection is obviously the most pertinent here, but there are other important reference points. *Linden Hills* invokes Dante's *Inferno* even at the level of narrative structure.[8] The structure of *Bailey's Cafe* links to that central text of the English medieval canon, Geoffrey Chaucer's *The Canterbury Tales.*[9] In that long poem, a group of pilgrims gather at the Tabard Inn, and under the aegis of the inn-host, Harry Bailly, are encouraged to tell tales, both personal and fabulous. The name of Naylor's café is obviously telling. It is equally significant that the name was already there when the Host-narrator of Naylor's sequence of tales (and, like Chaucer's Host, his statements top and tail the stories told by the pilgrims) arrived:

> I never changed the name of this place. When I found myself in here from that wharf in San Francisco, the name Bailey's Cafe was painted across the front window in those same red letters trimmed with gold and I saw no reason to remove it. Because of that, folks think my name is Bailey and I see no reason to tell them otherwise. (27–8)[10]

The novel's other major intertext is scriptural. The first customer at the café is Eve, and she has walked a thousand years (away from the authority figure of the 'Godfather') to get there. Other narratives tell of Esther, Mariam, and a possible second coming.

Elsewhere, in *Linden Hills*, the work of Walt Whitman is quoted at length (Berg, 1997: 98–111). The repressed name of the ancestor-slave in *Mama Day* is Sapphira, which is a biblical reference but may also in turn invoke Willa Cather's narrative treatment of slavery, *Sapphira and the Slave-Girl*, potently reassigning the white slave-mistress's name to the slave woman of Naylor's text. Traces of William Faulkner's *Go Down, Moses* in the same novel have been identified by Gary Storhoff (1997: 3), and Faulkner's lifelong interest in questions of ancestry, place, lineage and family history is obviously relevant, in a carefully reinflected way, to Naylor's work.

Nevertheless, Shakespeare is the most sustained intertextual presence in Naylor's writing, appearing – albeit to varying degrees – in all five of her published novels. We need to consider why she consistently evokes this reference point, as well as the manner in which she does so. Erickson has suggested, somewhat controversially, that in Naylor's use of Shakespeare, 'Shakespeare's cultural reach is diminished not extended' (1991a: 144). Whilst he is surely right to observe that Naylor 'appreciates Shakespeare while at the same time she is determined critically to rewrite him' (1991a: 126), to deduce from this that her project is somehow to reduce Shakespeare, and to close his textual circulation down, seems to miss the resonant music that his texts and language provide in her novels. In order to explore the motives and strategies of Naylor's Shakespearean echoes, the remainder of this chapter will focus on her most extended textual rumination on a Shakespeare play, examining and interrogating the role of *The Tempest* in *Mama Day*.[11]

'Voicing the voiceless': *Mama Day* (1988), *The Tempest* and the noises of the isle

Naylor has observed of her writing: 'I have tried throughout my career to give voice to the voiceless' (Felton and Loris, 1997: 253). In this respect, her project to reclaim the 'voiceless' characters of Shakespeare's *The Tempest* is one that shares a literary and feminist political commitment with H. D.'s voicing of the silent Claribel in *By Avon River*, and with Marina Warner's stylised reclamation of Sycorax in *Indigo*. Sycorax has a diffuse presence in *Mama Day*, implicit as she is in the goddess-like qualities of the Day family's powerful female ancestor Sapphira Wade, yet equally present in the magical properties and maternalistic powers of Miranda 'Mama' Day herself.[12] In one of the highly significant 'texts' that precede the narrative in the published version of the novel, the bill of sale that sold Sapphira to Bascombe Wade, her skills are described thus: 'Has served on occasion in the capacity of midwife and nurse, not without extreme mischief and suspicions of delving in witchcraft' (1). The traditional, stereotypical associations of witchcraft with midwifery are pertinent here, and certainly Mama Day is seen throughout the novel assisting with birth and questions of fertility, like her powerful forebear.[13] It might even be claimed that the negative constructions of Sycorax reside in the malevolent necromancy of the widow Ruby, Miranda's chief enemy in the narrative.

There can be little doubt that Naylor's novel seeks to displace the patriarchal centre of Shakespeare's 1611 play. Some critics have gone so far as to suggest that there is no Prospero in the novel – or, if there is, only to the extent that Mama Day subsumes and includes him.[14] Prospero's potential for the malign employment of his power may also be embodied in Ruby. But Naylor's comic skills should never be underestimated, and it is entirely feasible that in the feeble (and counterfeit) claims to medical knowledge of Dr Buzzard (real name Rainbow Simpson) a witty parody of Shakespeare's magus might be located.[15]

The decentring of both Caliban and Prospero has been a common element in female appropriations of *The Tempest*, and Naylor is no exception. Traub goes so far as to claim that there is no character based on Caliban in *Mama Day*, suggesting that this can be read in feminist terms: 'The deliberate erasure of Caliban may have to do, as well, with the decreasing attraction of the specifically *male* nationalism he has come to figure' (1993: 154), seeing instead an enactment of that character's desire in a diffuse way throughout the novel. Other critics have seen elements of Caliban in the figure of George, urban husband of Cocoa/Ophelia (Mama Day's grandchild) and newcomer to the island of Willow Springs. There is a recognition here of the maternal foundations of Caliban's own claims to the island in Shakespeare's play: 'This island's mine, by Sycorax my mother' (1.2.334). Sycorax was herself an Algerian incomer, and both Naylor's George and Warner's Dulé embody this subtlety in their characterisations. George is like Caliban in his deep-seated sense of inferiority and his capacity to worship false gods: he is quickly and easily impressed by the island's menfolk, including Dr Buzzard and Junior Lee. In the company of the latter pair, he regularly gets drunk in scenes which recall Caliban's encounters with alcohol in the company of Stephano and Trinculo (Storhoff, 1997: 170). Once again, it would seem that Naylor invokes the Shakespearean male characters, but in a largely comic and parodic context.

George will have a more tragic role to play in the later stages of the novel, but it is there that his associations with either Ferdinand or Caliban begin to fall away. Elsewhere, George fashions his own identifications with Shakespeare – but, tellingly, not with *The Tempest* and its reconciliatory possibilities, but with the tragic import of *King Lear*. Raised in the Wallace P. Andrews Shelter for Boys, George is a man without family in a novel where the power of home, family and ancestry is a palpable, living presence. He identifies – albeit in a misplaced sense (this character is a villain with whom Shakespeare sympathises little, ensuring that he meets a violent end) – with Edmund in *Lear*: 'I'd gone through *Lear* uncountable times. It had a special poignancy for me, reading about the rage of a bastard son, my own father having disappeared long before I was born' (106). George's efforts to enlist Shakespeare in his seduction of Cocoa are equally misplaced. The use of a tragedy for a seduction scene is a sad prefiguration of the tragic end to the relationship. That George measures his feelings for Cocoa in terms of her responses to and readings of Shakespeare is felt in the context of the narrative to be a further example of poor judgement: 'you came up to me, smelling like a stranded summer day, apologizing profusely for being late, but you'd been to the Coliseum book store, got turned around because it was a section you're rarely in, pulled out a copy of *King Lear* – and took my breath away' (101). Earlier in the narrative, George has scorned Cocoa's pulp-fiction reading habits. That he measures education and achievement via the reading of Shakespeare is a mark of George's middle-class aspirations – aspirations which, elsewhere in Naylor's canon, prove dangerous and destructive to the black community (in *Linden Hills*, for example, but also in Sadie's internalisation of those aspirations in *Bailey's Cafe*). It is this form of the cultural valuation and valorisation of Shakespeare that – Erickson is right to suggest (1991a: 139) – Naylor contends and contests. What is fascinating about her work, though, is that in effecting this radical critique, she does not eschew Shakespearean reference and allusion altogether; she merely harnesses it and reconfigures it to suit her own ethics, purposes and contexts.

The true relevance of *King Lear* to *Mama Day* is not its characterisations (which even George is concerned are misogynist) but its topography. Erickson has recorded the role of the pastoral location in both *Lear* and *The Tempest*: 'Both plays assume the salubrious value of pastoral space – the exposed heath in Lear's case, the magically controlled island in Prospero's. Both plays

employ the rhythm of the tempest followed by the restorative calm
after the storm' (1991a: 138). The pastoral is a literary genre which
is not usually associated with black literatures: the urban is more
regularly invoked as a setting.[16] *Mama Day* is clearly an important
exception to this perceived rule (there are of course others, including Walker's *The Color Purple*). Willow Springs as a location
evokes Edenic and paradisiacal associations in the novel. Connected
to the mainland only by a rickety wooden bridge, the temporary
nature of which is emphasised by the hurricanes which regularly
sweep through the region, it is a kind of black Utopia, quite literally Sir Thomas More's 'no-place', since it lies outside the law,
outside the political and geographical domain of the United States:
'And the way we saw it, America ain't entered the question at all
when it come to our land: Sapphira was African-born, Bascombe
Wade was from Norway' (5). One of the other prefatory texts to
Mama Day is, as with *Indigo*, a map, a visual realisation of the
significant spaces of the text (the other is a family tree, the importance of which, to this tale of ever-present ghosts and history, is
self-evident). The fertility and natural abundance of the island are
much emphasised in the novel, as is Miranda's ease with this world,
one of seed-raising, planting and leaf-mould compost:

> Usually, there ain't much happening here between Candle Walk and
> the first spring planting. Folks that keep gardens putter around, spread-
> ing a little manure, wood ash, and fish waste on their soil. They may
> sharpen some hoes, scrape the rust off the teeth of their rakes, or do a
> bit of pruning in their fruit trees. (131–2)

This quotidian pastoral idyll is juxtaposed in the novel with the
alternative urban island of modern Manhattan.[17] Naylor does not
effect this juxtaposition in any simplistic anti-urban way.[18] Each
space proves open to those who are prepared to understand it: just
as George fails to fully appreciate the 'noises of the isle' in Willow
Springs (when he and Cocoa enter the cemetery, he cannot hear
the spiritual voices of the past), so Cocoa misses the communal
possibilities of New York City:

> My city was a network of small towns, some even smaller than here in
> Willow Springs ... You'd never realize that because you went there and
> lived on our fringes. To live *in* New York you'd have to know about the
> florist in Jamaica Avenue who carried yellow roses even though they

didn't move well, but it was his dead wife's favourite color. The candy
store in Harlem that wouldn't sell cigarettes to twelve-year-olds without notes from their mothers. (61)

The vivid multiculturalism of George's New York is echoed in
Bailey's Cafe, where the café stands everywhere and nowhere in
strict geographical terms, thereby proving open to all.[19] The concept of the marginal depends on where you are standing. This is
yet another mark of Naylor's richness as an author: she does not
refigure Shakespeare simply by inverting or rejecting. The black
community her novels explore is a diverse and vibrant entity
affected by class, personal history, wealth and educational factors,
as much as by concepts of race (Christian, 1990: 348–73). The
world of Willow Springs is not the only answer, it is just one
thread in a complex geographical pattern.[20]

If topography and geography are both crucial and yet destabilised in the Naylor narrative, then time has a similar function;
once again this parallels tendencies and patterns we have encoun-
tered in other female appropriations. Miranda reflects on different
notions of time:

> Time is a funny thing. I was always puzzled with the way a single day
> could stretch itself out to the point of eternity in your mind, all the
> while years melted down into the fraction of a second. The clocks and
> calendars we had designed were incredibly crude attempts to order our
> reality – nearing the close of the twentieth century, and we were still
> slavishly tied to the cycles of the sun and the moon. (157–8)

As the family tree included at the start of the novel and the constant invocation of the past in the narrative indicate, personal
history is important to the inhabitants of Willow Springs. It is this
sense of personal history (which is invariably figured as female –
the family tree is a matrilineal one; all the tombstones in the cemetery lack surnames, since the surname Day is assumed) which
George feels the absence of (48). The year 1823 forms a historical
refrain of sorts in the novel; this date marks the deeding of Willow
Spring to his slaves by Bascombe Wade, and therefore the origins
of their community. In these respects, time seems clear, a matter
of historical record. However, as we saw in *Indigo*, historical record
is a fiction in its own way: 'It ain't about right or wrong, truth or
lies; it's about a slave woman who brought a whole new meaning

to both them words, soon as you cross over here from beyond the bridge' (3). Candle Walk – held annually on 22 December, thus linking it to pagan rituals of the Winter Solstice – is a festival that recurs through the generations, but it is also subject to change, partly owing to the penetration of the world beyond the bridge and its alternative commercial value-system. As Mama Day ruefully acknowledges:

> It's been going on since before they were born, and the ones born before them… Things took a little different turn with the young folks having more money, and working beyond the bridge. They started buying each other fancy gadgets from the catalogues, and you'd hear ignorant things like 'They ain't gave me nothing last Candle Walk, so they getting the same from me this year.' (110, 111)

Yet Miranda is movingly calm when she contemplates the eventual extinction of the ritual:

> It'll take generations, she says, for Willow Springs to stop doing it all. And more generations again to stop talking about the time 'when there used to be some kinda 18 & 23 going-on near December twenty-second.' By then, she figures, it wont be the world as we know it no way – and so no need for the memory. (111)

The value and importance of memory are crucial to an understanding of *Mama Day* and the community of Willow Springs. It is a world where ghosts speak and ancestors are a living presence. The reader realises by the close of the novel that they, too, have been subject to these voices in that George's section of the narrative, spoken in the first person, must have been articulated by his ghost. We are (and are not) very much part of the world of Willow Springs, as the prologue makes clear, describing us in the active moment as sitting listening to the story, the noises of the isle, having crossed the rickety bridge in our minds, and yet in physical reality placed in a 'world elsewhere'.:

> Think about it: ain't nobody really talking to you. We're sitting here in Willow Springs, and you're God-knows-where. It's August 1999 – ain't but a slim chance it's the same season where you are. Uh, huh, listen. Really listen this time: the only voice is your own. (10)

The millennial consciousness of the prologue, which sets us in 1999 and then talks of events some fourteen years earlier, is present elsewhere in *Mama Day*. Our central female protagonists, Sapphira and Miranda, have both lived lives that spanned centuries: Sapphira was born, according to that family tree, in 1799; Miranda was born in 1895. In her epilogue – a clever nod to Prospero's epilogue in *The Tempest*, which follows his morbid pronouncement: 'Every third thought shall be my grave' (5.1.314) – Miranda is also preparing for death. But in the mythical time of Willow Springs, Candle Walk will carry on, and her voice will continue to be heard:

> Some things stay the same. August is August. The hot wind blowing through the palmettos coulda been coming in 1899 when she remembers her first taste of … an icy slice of honeydew…
> Some things change…
> And some things are yet to be. She always finds her in the same place, sitting on the rise over The Sound. (312)

It remains unclear exactly who this woman is that Miranda joins in 'the other place'. It could be Sapphira, presiding presence of the island, but the novel has also in part been about Miranda's reconciliation with her own drowned mother, Ophelia. The Shakespearean reference in the latter's name seems a shackle, as with Cordelia in Margaret Atwood's *Cat's Eye* (see Chapter 10), predestining Ophelia to a watery grave. In a poignant moment, Mama Day cannot quilt a scrap of Ophelia's gingham into the Day quilt because of the dry rot that has set in. Nevertheless, when it is backed with Sapphira's homespun, this becomes possible. The power of spiritual life in Willow Springs enables an alternative form of reclamation of Shakespeare's drowned heroine and the text's absent mother. The women's lives and folkloric memories conjoin and strengthen each other. This is the power of the sisterhood in Naylor's novel, the female-centred world that George can neither comprehend nor hear, and which ultimately contributes to his death.

George's tragicomic task – to go to the chicken coop and bring back what he finds – has been read in terms of medieval quest romance and as a tragic scapegoating. If Prospero's power in *The Tempest* is associated with his library, Mama Day's is linked to her hens and their eggs, emblems of fertility and the female (Storhoff, 1997: 168). George does not believe in the project enough to understand it, to comprehend the simplicity of what is being asked of him: 'mumbo-jumbo' is what he terms it (295). In the shock of the red hen's attack, he suffers a cardiac arrest, and there is a strong implication in the novel that his death is a cathartic event that enables female reconciliation: the return of Cocoa, the second Ophelia, who has understandably shunned the inheritance of her name, to Willow Springs, and Mama Day's reconciliation with her past.

In order to achieve all this in the context of *The Tempest*, Shakespeare does not need to be diminished, but transformed and reconfigured into a new language, culture and context.[21] Prospero's reconciliation with the past, his dominion over land and his magical powers are rewritten in the powerful female colloquial idiom of Miranda Day. Part of Naylor's project must be registered as a formal one. Her deployment of the narrative voice in all her novels is polyphonic and diverse. In *The Women of Brewster Place*, separate women's life-stories are narrated by a third person; by the time of *The Men of Brewster Place*, there is an overarching narrator, as in *Bailey's Cafe*, Ben (the murdered janitor of the first novel; here we have another ghost, like George, which Naylor coyly confesses to as an act of artistic licence at the start of her narrative), but the men's stories are told largely in the first person. In *Mama Day* we move between an unidentified first-person narrator who addresses the reader directly (as does the café owner in *Bailey's Cafe*) and then alternating narrative perspectives, shifting from Cocoa to Miranda to George and back again in a series of concentric circles. Much of Naylor's writing is highly speech-based – this connects to the feminocentric oral tradition discussed above, and may offer another aspect of her formal interest in transferring the dramatic genre into narrative form – but it is also multiperspectival, empowering the reader to read, and indeed 'listen', for themselves.[22]

Shakespeare with soul?

Naylor cannot and perhaps should not be associated wholeheartedly with Cocoa's response to Shakespeare in *Mama Day*:

> Surely, he jests… that's the first thing that popped into my head when you asked me out again. I don't know where that phrase came from – had to be something from my high school Shakespeare and you had been going on and on about him earlier in the evening. Just proves that

Shakespeare didn't have a bit a soul – I don't care if he did write about Othello, Cleopatra, and some slave on a Caribbean island. If he had been in touch with our culture, he would have written somewhere, 'Nigger, are you out of your mind?' (64)

Cocoa's politicised use of discourse in this way will be praised by George later in the novel. It might seem that Shakespeare is being wholly rejected in this passage; nevertheless, important issues about the valency of his work for a black literary culture are raised. Cocoa may appear naive in making an association only with certain roles or plays with a direct relevance to contemporary African-American culture – those mentioned here, *Othello*, *Antony and Cleopatra*, and *The Tempest* – but likeness as the ground of relevance is immensely common in popular readings of high culture. Questions of access are being raised, which Naylor's engagement elsewhere in her novels with *Dream*, *Romeo and Juliet*, *The Taming of the Shrew*, and *Lear* helps to extend and nuance.

For a woman writer to engage with Shakespeare does not mean that she necessarily seeks the authentication of a master (or mastering) narrative. For a black writer to appropriate *The Tempest* is not necessarily to endorse its supposed proto-colonialist values. But neither should we assume that a political subject position is somehow invalidated by those who wish to assert a cultural value in the Shakespearean text (if not necessarily in the cultural agent that is 'Shakespeare') in their own communities. In the same way, it would be wrong to assume, as some critics have seemed to, that Naylor's deployment of Shakespeare has to be predicated on ultimate rejection.

In *The Men of Brewster Place*, Abshu (real name Cliff Jackson; but, as framing narrator Ben notes, 'it's what a man's done with his life that counts regardless of what name he's done it under' (133)) is undoubtedly held up as a beacon of hope for the future. Ben declares: 'I'm the past, and these young kids like Cliff Jackson are the future. And if there were more like him, I could rest a little easier about where we're gonna end up as a people' (134). It is Abshu who has believed in the power of art to offer openings and possibilities even to the most marginalised and disenfranchised members of his local community:

Abshu believed that there was something in Shakespeare for everyone, even the young of Brewster Place, and if he broadened their horizons

just a little bit, there might be enough room for some of them to slip
through and see what the world had waiting. No, it would not be a
perfect world, but definitely one with more room than they had now.
(135–6)

Shakespeare – for Naylor, as for Abshu – appears to be about
inclusion, about making space for everyone to have a voice; this is
why, in the end, Erickson's reductive trajectory for Naylor's engagement with Shakespeare, as one that necessarily requires a let-
ting-go, seems to miss the point. Our last vision of Abshu is on
the verge of the new millennium, as dawn breaks over his community, and in the millennial vocabulary of this (un-endstopped) final
paragraph, the political realities of black politics at the end of the
twentieth century are clearly sounded in the allusions to the Black
Power gesture of the clenched fist and the Million Man March on
Washington, D.C., in 1995:

> Abshu clenches his hands into fists that rest on his thighs. He thinks
> about the power of a million men; a million voices raised to a roar to
> say, No, this should not be. But even the voices of a million men, a
> million soldiers, cannot hold back the dawn.
>   And so he will leave this street to walk into a rising sun. One man
> against the dawning of the inevitable. One man who is determined to
> believe that this is the end of a battle, not the end of the war. And this
> one tired warrior is the best that Brewster Place has to offer the world.
> But one man standing is all that's needed – one manchild for the mil-
> lennium – as the music plays on ... and on... (172–3)

The overtones of Naylor's own religious beliefs are clearly sounded
here, as at the close of *Bailey's Cafe*, but so too are the rhythms of
the blues, and of black politics and history. What is most surprising, perhaps, is that Naylor incorporates Shakespearean texts quite
happily into this aesthetic framework and legacy. As Erickson has
stated: 'The debate is not about Shakespeare's elimination from
the canon but rather about the terms on which his work is to be
included' (1991a: 5).[23] Shakespeare is included in Gloria Naylor's
narrative, by her own choice and on her own terms.

Notes

1 See, for example, Goldberg (1992); Traub (1992); and B. Smith (1991).
2 See also Erickson (1996).
3 Caliban behaves in a similar way in Peter Greenaway's film version of the play, *Prospero's Books*, defecating on Prospero's prized books. This is also a film that makes great play of the power of Shakespeare as text and artefact (Lanier, 1996).
4 Naylor has spoken of the formative experience of seeing Joseph Papp's 'Shakespeare in the Park' free-access productions in Central Park, New York. She records how 'something about the way in which Shakespeare used language resonated with me' (Fowler, 1996: 149). Her emphasis on language is crucial to my argument here.
5 See also Erickson (1993b: 231–48); (1991a: 127).
6 See Andreas Sr (1999: 103–18). He notes that Morrison aligns Shakespeare with the African-American folktales of Uncle Remus (106). We have therefore a further instance of female authors destabilising Shakespearean authority via the juxtaposition with alternative textual categories such as children's literature (see Chapters 1 and 3). See also Walther (1993: 137–49).
7 *The Men of Brewster Place* is undoubtedly Naylor's response to critical charges of male stereotyping in *The Women of Brewster Place*: Celeste Fraser notes that 'Naylor risks perpetuating the erasure of the black male under the label "absent father"' (1993: 98). Interestingly, in the interview included in Felton and Loris, Naylor talked of a book which would explore the prehistory of *Mama Day* – dealing with Sapphira and the Bascombe Wade episode of 1823, but also projecting into the future with Cocoa in 2023. This novel may yet appear, but she abandoned it in the short term in favour of continuing the Brewster Place sequence (1997: 253).
8 Naylor has spoken of the deliberate mimetic patterning of the novel to resemble Dante's *terza rima*, calling it a 'conscious design feature' (Felton and Loris, 1997: 262).
9 See Wood (1997: 240–52); Rifkind (1993: 28–30). Wood reads the deployment of Chaucer in a way that is relevant for Naylor's 're-vision' of Shakespeare:

> While Naylor acknowledges the universal canonicity of Chaucer's work by using it as her structural foundation, such a use necessitates her mastery of Chaucer's text to the degree that she can rewrite it. Naylor must not only master *The Canterbury Tales* as a Western canonical text, but also contend with the strong connections to English themes and geography which mark *The Canterbury Tales* as an English nationalist text. Naylor accomplishes this by African-Americanizing *The Canterbury Tales* through her structural and narrative responses to Chaucer's work. (1997: 244)

10 Critics seem to ignore this moment in the narrative, and persist in calling the 'Host' Bailey, but the notion that the building, the narrative architecture, in which these stories take place was pre-existent is crucial.

11 Naylor was surely being deliberately playful when she claimed that the two primary intertexts for *Mama Day* were Faulkner's *As I Lay Dying* and Zora Neale Hurston's *Their Eyes Were Watching God*: cited in Andreas Sr (1999: 104–5).

12 Traub has spoken of how Sapphira 'newly configures' Sycorax (1993: 155).

13 On these traditional associations, see Purkiss (1996) and Sanders (1999).

14 See Christol (1994: 347–56). Erickson suggests that Mama Day's revenge against Ruby allows her a Prospero-like spectacular punitive display (1991a: 142).

15 A comparable reverse strategy would be the tragic inversion of the comic wall of *Dream* in the context of the magic realist conclusion to *The Women of Brewster Place*.

16 The urban nature of much African-American writing is discussed by Hokutani and Butler (1995). See also Lynch (1995: 181–95).

17 The quotidian nature of magic in the novel is discussed by Hayes (1997: 177).

18 Andreas Sr describes the novel's ethics as 'ideologically separatist and utopian' (1999: 118). I read this more ambivalently.

19 Wood describes the café and the street in which it is located, including Gabriel's pawnshop, as 'a liminal zone in which time stands still and place loses its permanence. This temporal and geographical destabilization mirrors the dislocation Naylor's characters experience and the instability of the universalist and nationalist positions these characters exemplify' (1997: 242).

20 The quilt motif is important here, as in much writing by North American – and often specifically African-American – women writers. See Meisenhelder (1997); Wagner-Martin (1988).

21 On the significance of folkloric memories in black women's writing, see Holloway (1992: 20).

22 This is a direct form of the 'talking back' Henry Louis Gates Jr has identified with black narrative (1988).

23 In more recent publications, Erickson makes contestable claims about the diminishing importance of Shakespeare, while at the same time his own critical career signifies the very opposite (1996: 347).

NINE

'Rainy days mean difficult choices': Jane Smiley's appropriation of *King Lear* in *A Thousand Acres*

> There was once a girl, as average-looking as she was well-adjusted,
> who lived with her stepmother who was not a very open and loving
> person because she herself had been abused in childhood.
>
> Margaret Atwood, 'There was once'

Jane Smiley has been very clear in print that her decision to write
narrative was not only instinctual but necessary. Recalling her
student encounters with the Bard, Smiley describes herself as 'possessed' by Dickens, but left cold by the reading (and even watching) of Shakespeare. His plays, and in some respects the entire
dramatic genre, involved 'too much talk … Drama was not going
to be my natural form … I grew up in a family of story-tellers,
gossipers, natural narrators' (Smiley, 1999: 162). The praise of
gossip alongside the criticism of dramatic dialogue might seem
self-contradictory, but what Smiley seems to confirm here is a
preference for a controlled vision, a story told from a point of
view and by a narrator: 'Drama privileges action over point-of-
view,' she states, saying of Shakespeare: 'I could not allow his
universality … My tool, the ace in my deck, was narrative form
itself' (1999: 172).

Smiley's particular frustrations with *King Lear*, the Shakespeare
play she so profitably appropriates in her Pulitzer-Prize-winning
novel *A Thousand Acres* (1992), derive in part from her dissatisfaction with the dialogue-heavy genre of drama:

> Perhaps what I blamed Lear for was actually a feature of dramatic
> form that I was uncomfortable with – all the talk, especially talk about

191

emotions, that seemed simultaneously to trivialise and make self-indulgent and shrill the passions being expressed. (1999: 162)

In truth, *A Thousand Acres*, narrated in the first person by Ginny Cook Smith, eldest daughter of Larry Cook, Midwestern farmer-patriarch and 'Lear' equivalent in the novel, is heavy with expressed emotions.[1] Smiley's need to effect the transition from performative flexibility to narrative fixity goes deeper than a rejection of emotionality:

> That Smiley chooses narrative as the method and the novel as the instrument to articulate her transformed, female-centered version of the Shakespearean original makes available, indeed insists upon, modes of storytelling that manage the problems of causality, chronology, and character in ways markedly different from the ways in which dramatic representation functions. (Alter, 1999: 145)

In her leaning towards essentially realist forms of narrative, Smiley endeavours to offer motive where Shakespeare keeps things open, and to 'fill the interstices of events' where the play allows issues to remain enigmatic (Alter, 1999: 146).

Smiley's frustrations with *Lear*, and her positive desire to reconfigure its arguments, also derive from what she has referred to as the inbuilt misogyny of the play: 'I wanted to communicate the ways in which I found the conventional readings of *King Lear* frustrating and wrong' (Smiley, 1999: 159). Those 'conventional readings' are readings which identify Goneril and Regan as the chief perpetrators of evil, and Lear as the sympathetic heart. By opting for the singularity of first-person narration, and according that role to her fictional Goneril, Ginny, Smiley opened up the possibility of explaining the sisters' actions, offering them an experiential history which the play suppresses. That history becomes one of incest and abuse within the family.

Like other authors we have looked at, Smiley is highly conscious of the shift from drama into the narrative mode, and signals this in the material structure of her book. As in *Juggling* or *Wise Children*, Smiley invokes the five acts of Shakespeare's play in the organisation of her novel, ensuring that the carefully sited third-act storm of *Lear*, the play's central plateau, occurs in her own middle section. But she also allows the narrative to travel beyond the closing moments of the playtext, moving not only into a sixth section but into an epilogue.

The tapestry of allusions to *Lear* is rich and suggestive. Many of the play's central images and metaphors are carefully reworked into a twentieth-century American farming context, from animal references to the significance of particular terms like 'nature', 'blindness' or 'nothing'. At times, these revisions can seem a little forced, even trite. Towards the novel's close, Pam and Linda – Ginny's nieces – are found watching 'The Wheel of Fortune' quiz show on television. While this twentieth-century reworking may say something about the commodification of culture, this still seems too pat an inclusion of one of the play's central concepts. Elsewhere the web of allusion operates more subtly. Smiley retains the central idea of the storm. Barbara Mathieson, however, has argued that this event, too, is reduced in significance – its only genuine impact is to disturb television reception: 'Smiley does not allow the reader to enter the elemental force of the storm, to feel its power or its violence firsthand' (1999: 133). This underestimates the fact that Ginny's sister Rose's shocking revelation of Larry's incestuous relationships with his daughters – something Ginny seems to have repressed in terms of her own personal history – comes in the midst of the storm. As in *Lear*, the inner storm proves as significant as its outer manifestations in the natural world.

Not all the play's events or images find immediate modern parallels or counterparts. Smiley doubted the efficacy of retaining Shakespeare's battle scenes. Her battles take place behind closed doors, in the troubled domestic space of the household. Instead of warfare, she has the Cook family test its private affections and rivalries in the highly public location of a legal hearing: Ginny and Rose win the case (ensuring that in a legal sense the sisters' actions are vindicated), but the impact upon all their relationships is irreparable. The victory is a hollow one: the halted building structures on the farm will go ahead, but now with built-in flaws; Ginny and Ty separate almost immediately. This is just one example in the novel where Smiley's recuperation of the sisters proves more ambivalent than even the author has claimed in interviews. But the legal hearing is not merely an alternative to battle scenes: it makes a further allusion to an earlier point in the drama when

Lear, sheltering from the storm, conducts a mock trial of a joint-stool, believing it, momentarily, to represent his vengeful elder daughters (3.6.49–51).

Smiley is equally effective in her reworking of character. Edmund and Edgar become Jess and Loren Clark – the former a Vietnam draft-dodger and exponent of organic farming techniques; the latter a hard-working conservative farmer easily pushed into the shadows by the return of his glamorous and controversial sibling. Their father, Harold, is an intriguing reworking of the Earl of Gloucester. In *Lear*, Gloucester is a flawed and problematic figure, although also one of great pathos in the scenes immediately following his blinding. At the play's start, he boasts of an adulterous liaison, grudgingly acknowledging Edmund as his illegitimate son: 'though this knave came somewhat saucily to the world before he was sent for, yet was his mother fair; there was good sport at his making, and the whoreson must be acknowledged' (1.1.20–2). Harold is a character of comparable ambivalence; boastful about his new tractor, he is quick to reject Loren in favour of Jess, and equally hasty in accusing Ginny and Rose of responsibility for the Cook family's break-up. Although he is an object of our pity in the aftermath of his blinding, Smiley is careful never to have her readers encounter this image of Harold direct, in stark contrast to the play, accordingly reducing the space for sympathy.

In the novel, King Lear becomes Larry Cook, farmer-patriarch of a thousand acres of Midwest agricultural land. Critics have questioned this domestication of Lear: Alter writes that 'Cook's diminished majesty is … acknowledged in the novel's title – "a thousand acres". This and no more is the extent of his kingdom', and suggests that this has a reductive effect on the play's monarch-protagonist (1999: 153). R. A. Foakes has criticised the tenor of recent stage productions on similar grounds (1996). Smiley appears to have been influenced by recent work on *Lear*, both critical and performative, in constructing her 'rewriting'. But in truth, even in the play, we never get more than a highly circumscribed view of Lear's kingdom.

Characterology undergoes some shifts from the source-play. Audiences and readers are asked to question where their sympathies lie. Presented to us only through the medium of Ginny's narrative, Larry is a less multifaceted or sympathetic figure than

Lear. Jess Clark, however, remains an ambivalent and problematic character like Edmund, linked to nature in his organic politics just as Edmund's Act 1 Scene 2 soliloquy asserts his worship of the goddess Nature. One of the more intriguing changes Smiley makes is to the character of Cornwall. In the novel he equates – albeit loosely – to Regan/Rose's husband, Pete. At times it might seem that Pete is guilty, or at least capable, of the same acts of random violence associated with the Duke. We learn that he once broke Rose's arm and, following his death, we hear how he taunted the blinded Harold. There is even the implication that Pete might have contributed to Harold's blindness by draining off the water in the tractor tank; that water could have halted the corrosion of Harold's corneas when he was accidentally sprayed with anhydrous ammonia. But Pete is a more three-dimensional figure than Cornwall. His complexity is demonstrated in his indecision over which *Monopoly* piece to play with. He is torn between the wheelbarrow – with which he has won before, and which could be taken to symbolise the steadiness of his life as an Iowan farmer – and the mounted horseman, a more heroic image perhaps allied to his former life in a rock band.[2] Ginny persistently compares Pete to film rebel James Dean. These allusions are part of a wider understanding in the narrative of Ginny's sexual attraction to Pete, which in turn tells us something about her dissatisfaction with married life to Ty.

Ty is *A Thousand Acres*'s equivalent to the Duke of Albany: steady in his manner, if questioning of his wife's response to her father: 'How far your eyes may pierce I cannot tell:/ Striving to better, oft we mar what's well' (1.4.344–5). He discusses his concerns with Caroline (the Cordelia counterpart), and inadvertently provides the means for the legal hearing that leads to the eventual loss of the farm. The farm is clearly Ty's driving concern, and his reason for acquiescing in Larry's questionable treatment of Caroline (cutting her out of any inheritance): property and acres are all-controlling entities in this community. Like Albany, Ty is not an unsympathetic character, albeit questionably passive. But he is denied here the closing presence accorded to Albany in the play. Other characters are similarly reduced or undermined: after Harold's blinding, Loren, Edgar's most obvious counterpart, virtually disappears from the text. Throughout he is sketchily drawn, like Caroline and Larry remaining largely offstage, in the shadows, and defined only by Ginny.

Cordelia is associated with voice in *Lear*, not least in her refusal to use hers in the opening scene in order to flatter her father: 'What shall Cordelia speak? Love, and be silent' (1.1.60). It is to the subject of her voice that Lear returns in his grief at her death: 'Her voice was ever soft,/ Gentle and low, an excellent thing in a woman' (5.3.271–2). That 'excellent thing in a woman' is a perennial problem for feminists who wish to argue for something other than implicit misogyny in *Lear*, and Smiley is all too aware of this. She elects to continue the focus on Caroline's voice, but transforms her into a practising lawyer for whom speech is all-important and powerful. In the play, Cordelia, rejected by her father and denied a dowry, is accepted by the King of France as a wife: Caroline has Frank, the fellow lawyer she marries in private following the rift with her family. The punning and slightly reductive reference is clear: in contrast to Cordelia's winning and persuasive asides to the audience, Smiley ensures that we as readers keep our distance from the 'perennially innocent' Caroline.

The shadowy portrayal of Caroline is just one element of Smiley's rewriting of the emphases of Shakespeare's plot in order to refocus attention on the much-berated older sisters. Other central characters are sidelined, or rendered marginal through comedy. The character who disappears without explanation halfway through *Lear* is his 'shadow' (1.4.228): the Fool. Some productions of the play have imaginatively doubled the Fool and Cordelia – the former expresses sympathy for the latter, and noticeably disappears from the play when she returns. A double referent has also been heard in Lear's line 'And my poor fool is hanged!' (5.3.304). Loren Clark – who, as we have already seen, disappears partway through *A Thousand Acres* – could potentially be both Edgar and Fool.[3] But Smiley herself has recently hinted that the Fool is actually present in the shape of Marv Carson.[4] What is clear is that the centrality and damning clarity of Lear's advisers are displaced here. The Larry of the novel has only the hot-headed Harold for support; in the play Lear has Gloucester, Edgar, the Fool, and, of course, his loyal adviser Kent. Ken[t?] La Salle, the family lawyer who initially supports the formation of the family corporation to run the farm and avoid crippling inheritance taxes, but later finds himself serving legal papers on Ginny and Rose, may be a residual trace of Kent, but on the whole these figures of counsel and support are avoided or reduced. The focus is on recuperating the women, and in order to achieve this, certain shifts of focus and strategy prove necessary.

If Smiley's initial frustration with *Lear* was with the play's implicit condemnation of Goneril and Regan, and if her attempt was to offer through narrative a kind of closure to actions and events which Shakespeare leaves tantalisingly open, then ultimately *A Thousand Acres* achieves something rather different. Ginny proves an 'unreliable narrator' in true late-twentieth-century style, and even the certainty of the incest motif, the chief peg in Smiley's construction of motive, is unstable by the close (Lodge, 1992: 155). Undoubtedly Smiley's novel 'takes the woman's part' in revising and appropriating *Lear*, but in the end the narrative, for all its mechanical precision (and Smiley has suggested that it is too mechanical (1999: 178)) unfolds and unravels itself into the areas of shadow and ambiguity that are, ironically, the real strength of the play in performance.

'She had a history': taking the woman's part

The most obvious means by which Smiley revises *Lear* in *A Thousand Acres* are via her changes to the representation of Goneril and Regan. In the play there is little that is redeeming about these characters. The speed with which they exploit their monarch-father's handover of power is too rapid to be sympathetic, and their complete failure to challenge their younger sister's banishment is troubling. Before the first scene has drawn to a close, they are conspiring. Goneril notes: 'You see how full of changes his age is; the observation we have made of it hath not been little: he always lov'd our sister most; and with what poor judgement he hath now cast her off appears too grossly' (1.1.287–90). The preferential treatment of Cordelia suggested here may offer some cause for sympathy, but Goneril's failure to speak openly against her younger sister's banishment dampens any stirrings of this an audience might feel. Regan appears equally self-serving: 'We must do something, and i'th'heat' (1.1.307). Unlike Edmund, who opens the next scene

with a witty and partly persuasive soliloquy winning at least a
modicum of audience understanding; or Cordelia, whose concerned
asides we have been party to throughout that tense first scene, we
are denied access to these sisters' motivations and worries. Only in
Act 5 is Goneril given asides, but these merely provide the audience
with knowledge of her growing sexual jealousy, and ultimately of
her efforts to murder her sister in an attempt to prevent her sexual
liaison with Edmund. By this stage she has been party to acts of
unacceptable brutality; this radically limits any sympathetic potential. In fact, in their suddenness and extremity of position, these
asides verge on a comic tone closer to the farcical portrayal of the
sisters in Shakespeare's folkloric source-text, *The True Chronicle
Historie of King Leir and his Daughters* (McLuskie, 1985: 98).
     Smiley clearly felt uncomfortable with the apparent lack of
motive for Goneril's and Regan's actions:

> I always felt that something else was going on in the family life of
> these people and that presenting the same events from a different point
> of view would result in a different story. I also felt that Regan and
> Goneril could not have been as bad as they're portrayed. I saw that the
> play had the organizational principles for a novel and that I could use
> one of the older sisters' points of view to show some things that I felt
> were implied in the play but not explicit. (1998: 69)

That latter statement is revealing. Smiley believes that Larry's abuse
of Ginny and Rose (sexual, emotional and psychological as it is
explored in the novel) is implicit in the play's depiction of Lear's
relationship to Goneril and Regan. Her argument would be that
her novel is not simply a feminist rewriting of Shakespeare, but a
response to matters implicit within the original text. That view
would seem to be upheld by the tenor of a number of recent stage
productions of *Lear*. Both Deborah Warner's direction of the play
at the Royal National Theatre in 1990 and Richard Eyre's in 1996, at
the same venue, played heavily with the concept of Lear's abuse of
his older daughters (Bennett, 1996: 39–78; Holland, 1997: 37–49).
     Smiley's claim is that she is rewriting not the play so much as
the critical interpretations of it, those 'conventional readings' which
would locate sympathy with Lear and Cordelia:

> Smiley has made it clear that ... *A Thousand Acres* was conceived not
> only as a response to the masculine distortions of perspective that she
> finds in Shakespeare's most apocalyptic play, one that theatrically em-

bodies and linguistically generates femaleness as the cause of the fallen world, but also as a response to that interpretation of *King Lear* 'which privileged the father's needs over the daughters'. (Alter, 1999: 145)

That said, it is not difficult to find what Alter describes as 'various forms of feminine silencing' in the play (1999: 145). Regan and Goneril have very little stage time in which to explain themselves. It has been calculated that their lines combined add up to only 12 per cent of the whole (Alter, 1999: 147).[5] In her desire to allow these sisters a point of view, Smiley insists on first-person narration by Ginny. This is certainly a sympathy-inducing move. From Ginny's perspective, we can identify the demands (many of them unreasonable) placed on herself and Rose by their father. We sense the oppression they have suffered over decades:

> My earliest memories of him are of being afraid to look him in the eye, to look at him at all. He was too big and his voice was too deep. If I had to speak to him, I addressed his overalls, his shirt, his boots. If he lifted me near his face, I shrank away from him. (Smiley, 1992: 19)

The metonymic power of Larry's boots is recalled at various points in the novel, but even more telling, in the light of the sexual abuse plotline that emerges, is the way Ginny shrinks from Larry's physical attentions. This sense of fear is Smiley's means of offering an explanation for the flattering of Larry that forms the opening of the novel, and is implicit in the sisters' grateful acceptance of the farm handover at Harold Clark's pig-roast. Larry makes Ginny feel invisible – always a suspect thing in this novel of subtexts and subterranean poisons. As Ginny will later declare: 'I feel like there's treacherous undercurrents all the time. I think I'm standing on solid ground, but then I discover that there's something moving underneath it, shifting from place to place' (104).

Seeing things from Ginny's point of view can render even darker in tone episodes that are direct appropriations of events in the play. In *Lear*, the king curses his older daughters for their refusal to obey his orders once he has ceded power to them. He curses Goneril with infertility:

> Hear, Nature, hear! dear Goddess, hear!
> Suspend thy purpose, if thou didst intend
> To make thy creature fruitful!
> Into her womb convey sterility!

> Dry up in her the organs of increase,
> And from her derogate body never spring
> A babe to honour her! If she must teem
> Create her child of spleen, that it may live
> And be a thwart disnatur'd torment to her!
> ...that she may feel
> How sharper than a serpent's tooth it is
> To have a thankless child!
>
> (1.4.273–82, 285–7)

This concept is shocking enough, a cruel inversion of Nature's ability to confer abundance, but in the novel it seems all the more so, since we have the detailed history of Ginny's miscarriages. Their root cause in the poisoning of the well-water by nitrates from fertiliser run-off makes that infertility, in material terms, Larry's fault. The contemporary language also has a less abstract register: 'I don't know what you are, just a bitch, is all, just a dried-up whore bitch' (181).[6]

Ginny's perspective is crucial to Smiley's intentions of recuperating Goneril and Regan, but the usual questions of bias that accrue around first-person fictional narrators remain an issue here. Ginny's view is at times confused, and at others highly prejudiced. As she herself acknowledges: 'The fact is that the same sequence of days can arrange themselves into a number of different stories' (155). Despite Smiley's professed aim of winning sympathy for her protagonist, Ginny plots her sister's murder, albeit in the grotesquely comic form of poisoned sausages. Alter notes that 'Smiley deliberately has constructed Ginny as an insecure and therefore potentially untrustworthy or unreliable observer' (1999: 148).

Ginny's miscarriages make her, in deeply poignant ways, one of the 'absent mothers' by now so familiar from Shakespearean plays and their appropriations. But her own mother is also a tangible absent presence in the novel. Ginny even suggests that her relationship with her father might have been different were her mother still around (20). The Clark brothers are also motherless, and readers are consequently forced to question the high incidence of cancer and personal illness that has decimated this Iowan community. Coppélia Kahn observed some years ago that there is 'no literal mother' in *Lear* (1986: 35). By contrast, in *A Thousand Acres*, Ginny stresses of her mother: 'She had a history' (224). Like *The Tempest*, Kahn argues, *Lear* articulates a 'patriarchal conception of

the family in which children owe their existence to their fathers
alone' (1986: 35). Incestuous readings are the not wholly surprising outcome of these emphases. Lynda Boose has suggested that
the opening scene of *Lear* enacts a warped variant of a wedding
ceremony, where the father is meant to give the daughter away
(Boose, 1982: 325–47). Lear wants to cling to his daughters, ex-
pecting Cordelia to nurse him in old age, and gives her away only
when he has wholly rejected her qualified version of love. Cordelia
seems to be troublingly aware of this in one speech which, attempting to articulate her relationship with her overbearing father,
both echoes and flinches from the vocabulary of the vows of a
traditional marriage ceremony:

> Good my Lord,
> You have begot me, bred me, lov'd me: I
> Return those duties back as are right fit;
> Obey you, love, and most honour you.
> Why have my sisters husbands, if they say
> They love you all? Happily when I shall wed,
> That lord whose hand must take my plight shall carry
> Half my love with him, half my care and duty.
> (1.1.94–101)

For Kahn, *Lear* is a 'tragedy of masculinity' (36), a play more
about the failure of absolute patriarchy than an endorsement of it.
Judging from her comments in print, this does not appear to be
Smiley's reading. Hers accords more with Kate McLuskie's deep
reservations about the play's potential for a recuperative feminist
interpretation: 'Feminism cannot simply "take the woman's part"
when that part has been so morally loaded and theatrically circumscribed' (1985: 102). McLuskie argues further that 'A feminist
reading of the text cannot simply assert the countervailing rights
of Goneril and Regan, for to do so would simply reverse the emotional structures of the play' (1985: 102). While Smiley might
share McLuskie's concerns about the co-opting of Shakespeare by
the feminist movement, and the suppressions and evasions this
might entail, the reversal of the emotional structures of *Lear* is
exactly what she effects in her 're-vision' of the text.

In the play, Lear constructs his madness as feminine, even
calling it 'mother', asserting the etymological link between hys-
teria and the *hysterus* or womb. The wombs of *A Thousand Acres*

prove as polluted and violated as the farmland that defines the
landscape. In this respect, Smiley's feminism can be viewed as a
product of a particular strand of late-twentieth-century feminist
thinking, influenced by environmental politics. Mother Earth as
much as literal mothers is a central topos of *A Thousand Acres*.

'Daddy's not much for untamed nature': an ecocritical perspective

A first acquaintance with the title and epigraph of *A Thousand
Acres* reveals that Smiley has interests which extend far beyond
appropriating the plotline of *Lear* and its major or minor characters. Land is at the heart of this novel; land, and human relationships to it. Larry Cook's thousand acres of prime Midwestern
farmland are what the family wars over, the cause of age-old
quarrels with neighbours whose plots and houses he has accumu-
lated, and the source of envies, worries and even illnesses, physical
and possibly psychological. It is the land which has been steadily
poisoned by expansionist farming activities. The epigraph, which
derives from Meridel le Sueur's *The Ancient People and the Newly
Come*, indicates this complicated interrelationship between land
and people: 'The body repeats the landscape. They are the source
of each other and create each other.'
   Our first view of this densely described novel's location in the
American Midwest is equally instructive; it is a vast landscape
viewed from a distance and, revealingly, from a car. The overriding feeling in this opening passage is one of alienation from the
natural world, a feeling which prefigures the novel's trajectory of
increasing severance from the land: 'At sixty miles per hour, you
could pass our farm in a minute' (3). There is an implicit irony in
this fact that the Cook farmstead is just a dot on the horizon of
the 'Zebulon County Scenic Highway', almost 'imperceptible', in
view of the deep and lasting traumas that will be acted out in this
locality; the reader will be afforded no such opportunity to speed
past the lives that conduct themselves in this place. Indeed, much
that was or seemed imperceptible in terms of the Cook family's
history and relationships will be exposed and anatomised in the
course of the narrative.

What looks like a tiny bump on the horizon to the uninvolved
car driver is in fact a vast farm, of deep familial significance to
Ginny. Embodied in this landscape are the lives and livelihoods of
Ginny and her kind: 'Acreage and financing were facts as basic as
name and gender in Zebulon County' (4). The landscape of the
novel is clearly established in its opening pages. The *Lear* subtext
remains below the level of the visible – like the all-important
Zebulon River, vital for the well-being and irrigation of the county
farmsteads, which flows 'below the level of the surrounding farm-
lands' (4) and which, of course, proves to be a site of pollution.

A Thousand Acres offers what can be described as an ecocritical
perspective on the world it surveys and portrays. People both act
upon and are acted upon by the land they inhabit: 'Landscapes are
created by people – through their experience and engagement with
the world around them. They may be close-grained, worked-upon,
lived-in places, or they may be distant and half-fantasised' (Bender,
1993: 1). The soils, rivers, pesticide-polluted watercourses – even
the farm machinery used to work the land – all prove crucial
players in the particular drama of *A Thousand Acres*. Ginny sums
this up towards the close of the narrative, when she looks at Rose's
daughters, Pam and Linda, whom she fosters following her sister's
demise from breast cancer:

> Looking at them forces me to know that although the farm and all its
> burdens and gifts are scattered, my inheritance is with me, sitting in
> my chair. Lodged in my every cell, along with the DNA, are molecules
> of topsoil and atrazine and paraquat and anhydrous ammonia and die-
> sel fuel and plant dust, and also molecules of memory... (369)

The ways in which Smiley's interpretation of *Lear* is strongly
influenced by feminist criticism of Shakespeare has already been
indicated. The topographical concerns of the novel are also a product of a personal politics shaped by the environmental movements
of the 1960s and 1970s, and their attendant texts.[7] Rachel Carson's
Silent Spring (1962), an account of the USA's potential destruction
of the natural world via widespread and advancing use of chemicals
and pesticides in farming and agriculture, is frequently described
as the seminal text of the North American environmental tradition.[8]
It is also an important text for feminism; Carson, as a female
scientist, was condemned by scientific circles for her emotive

response to the pesticide problem, and her self-conscious use of emotional terminology and descriptive techniques. An important strand of feminist philosophy, particularly the one that emerged from the French academic sphere, was the argument that women had distinctly different means of writing and speaking – different, that is, from the male of the species. Hélène Cixous promoted the cause of *écriture féminine* at length in her work in the 1970s. These theories were attacked – not least from within the feminist camp – partly because of the essentialist theories of nature and gender to which they ascribed, but they were extremely influential. In anthropological and ecological circles, a related understanding of women's particular relationship to the natural world emerged: *écoféminisme*, a term first coined by Françoise d'Eaubonne in 1974 (Rose, 1993: 150). Women, it was argued, had an intrinsic connection to the natural world by dint of their reproductive capacities (the widely used term 'Mother Earth' embodies those connections[9]), and the domination of womanhood by patriarchy was related to the domination of nature by the patriarchal system.[10] The relevance of this for *A Thousand Acres* is clear: Mathieson has shown how the agricultural rape of the land is directly compared to the abuse of women's bodies: 'The novel repeatedly parallels the technological invasion of the landscape with the mastery and abuse of the female characters' (1999: 135).

But Smiley's novel parallels Carson's environmental treatise in more direct ways than merely echoing its ecofeminist discourse. The opening section of *Silent Spring*, entitled 'A Fable for Tomorrow', strikes a remarkably familiar note to readers of *A Thousand Acres*:

> There was once a town in the heart of America where all life seemed to live in harmony with its surroundings. The town lay in the midst of a checkerboard of prosperous farms, with fields of grain and hillsides of orchards where in spring, white clouds of bloom drifted above the green fields. In autumn, oak and maple and birch set up a blaze of colour that flamed and flickered across a backdrop of pines. Then foxes barked in the hills and deer silently crossed the fields, half hidden in the mists of autumn mornings ... The countryside was ... famous for the abundance and variety of its bird life ... So it had been from the day many years ago when the first settlers raised their houses, sank their wells, and built their barns ... Then a strange blight crept over the area and everything began to change. Some evil spell had settled on

the community: mysterious maladies swept the flocks of chickens ...
Everywhere was a shadow of death. The farmers spoke of much illness
among their families. (Carson, 1991: 21)

This passage could almost be a blueprint for Smiley's novel, where
a family that appears thriving on the surface starts to succumb to
illness and collapse in remarkably rapid succession. Certainly it
provides a template for one specific passage:

> My walk along the riverbank carried me to where the river spread out
> into a little marsh ... where the surface of the earth dipped below the
> surface of the sea within it, and blue water sparkled in the still limpid
> sunlight of mid-spring. And there was a flock of pelicans, maybe twenty-
> five birds, cloud white against the shine of the water. Ninety years ago,
> when my great-grandparents settled in Zebulon County and the whole
> county was wet, marshy, glistening like this, hundreds of thousands of
> pelicans nestled in the cattails, but I hadn't seen even one since the
> early sixties. I watched them. The view along the Scenic, I thought,
> taught me a lesson about what is below the level of the visible. (9)

This passage is instructive in that it indicates, in one compacted
moment of observation, the destruction of the pelicans' wetland
habitat (caused when drainage of the Zebulon County marshlands
occurred in order to increase the available farmland) and, in a
wider sense, the loss of water – and, more importantly, pure water
– that will prove so crucial to the events of the novel. Like Carson,
the novel looks back almost nostalgically to the moment of original
white settlement, but it also indicates that below the surface American society is deeply poisoned, not least by that 'originating' act of
colonialism.[11]

The holistic approach to society for which Carson argued
provides important parallels with Smiley's stress on the inter-
connectedness of things: 'The history of life on earth has been a
history of interaction between living things and their surroundings' (Carson, 1991: 23). Like Smiley, Carson directly related the
pesticide problem to expansionist agricultural policies:

> We are told that the enormous and expanding use of pesticides is
> necessary to maintain farm production. Yet is our real problem not one
> of *over-production*? Our farms, despite measures to remove acreages
> from production and to pay farmers *not* to produce, have yielded ... a
> staggering excess of crops... (1991: 26)

Once again, the fate of the Cook family farmstead is imaged in these words. The first response of Ty, Ginny, Pete and Rose when Larry signs over the management of the farm to them is to expand – to increase, by means of considerable bank loans, on which they eventually default, the hog operation, and to build the huge slurry-store. The latter building, when its construction is halted at mid-point by Caroline's legal action, becomes symbolic of the dangers of aggrandising dreams: its concrete floor is cracked and damaged after lying so long exposed to the elements. By the time the roof can be constructed, the project is already fatally flawed.[12]

Contrasted to these expansionist dreams are other – so-called non-conventional – farming practices: from those of the Ericsons in the half-remembered past to Jess's advocacy of organic farming. But the novel is scarcely optimistic about the fate of this method, either. Jess's commitment to it proves as short-lived as his sexual liaisons with Ginny and Rose, and the Ericson farm fails at much the same time that Ginny's mother dies (Larry appropriates their plots).[13] Ginny describes these events in terms of things draining away from her (136); her deployment of that metaphor reminds us that Larry's farming practice is all about draining the land, and the emotional strength of those around him. As with the location of sympathy in this novel, what seems simple, almost binary, on the surface of the text is deeply confused once we dig beneath.

Farming issues and concerns permeate this realist novel. We know what Ginny is growing in her vegetable garden, we learn about Harold's (tragically significant) purchase of a brand-new trac-tor, and we know what chemicals are used to spray the crops from that tractor.[14] These issues are also the reason for the novel's self-consciously historicised setting in 1979.[15] That year was some two years into the one-term presidency of Jimmy Carter (1977–81), who was himself from a peanut farming background in the South-ern state of Georgia. He was in office during a period of major crisis for American farming. His presidency is dubiously credited with the death of the small family farm – a demise hinted at in *A Thousand Acres* not only with the impossible expansion and even-tual sale of the Cook family farmstead, but in the recurring theme of debts, repossessions and suicides on neighbouring estates. In the book's third section, Ginny is quick to stress that Iowa has not yet succumbed to the farming by huge corporation that is the way of

other States such as Dakota or Nebraska (131). Carter had entered
the White House on a campaign ticket of 'competence and com-
passion', but instead found himself governing during an oil crisis
(hinted at in the novel with concerns over how Harold's new tractor will be fuelled), and during the Iranian hostage crisis. His
presidency was deemed a failed one – by contemporaries if not
necessarily by political history.[16] Jess and Ty discuss Carter as
vacillating and unproductive in *A Thousand Acres*, stressing that a
realist in the White House is an undesirable thing (71). What
Smiley does not make explicit, but surely expects readers in the
1990s to realise, is that Carter's era of retrenchment, and the
recognition of limits to US power, was followed by the two-term
presidency of Ronald Reagan, a leader who promoted US
supremacy at all costs, and encouraged the American people to buy
into the capitalist dream wholesale. The Reaganite era of multi-
nationals and global control is hinted at darkly at the end of the
novel in the anonymous, and cynically named, Heartland Corporation's assumption of control over the Cook farmstead. Ty ends up
heading for Texas to seek work with a comparable group. The
individual farmer is as near extinction as the marshlands such
farmers themselves had drained for acreage.

Critics are surely correct to identify the land as an extra
character in Smiley's densely populated novel. Mathieson suggests
that Smiley has displaced traditional sympathy for Lear away from
the sketchily drawn Larry (sketchy by Smiley's own admission[17])
towards the land he acts upon:

> The 'thousand acres' of land and all that it represents in terms of
> power, status, place and spirit is arguably the site of tragedy and loss in
> the modern novel and the true claimant for our compassionate pity
> and respect ... The early modern tragedy of a great individual thus
> gives way in the late twentieth century to a tragedy of the natural
> world and of the interconnected lives that Nature supports. (1999: 128)

While the displacement of that central focus is clear, Mathieson's
distinction between the early modern concerns of the play and the
twentieth-century concerns of the novel may be too limiting.
Smiley's evocations of the ruin of Nature and Nature's potential
revenge (in the form of the poisoned well-water) offer clear links
to a play in which that theme has frequently been identified. As

early as 1949, John Danby observed that '*Lear* can be regarded as a play dramatizing the meanings of the single word "Nature"' (1949: 15). He noted that the play contained over forty occurrences of the term and its cognates, as contrasted with twenty-five in *Timon of Athens* and twenty-eight in *Macbeth*. Smiley is not embroidering land-related themes on to the play: she is recognising intrinsic elements of the drama. 'Nature' in *Lear* refers to both human nature and the natural world. When Regan counsels her father: 'O, Sir! you are old;/ Nature in you stands on the very verge/ Of her confine' (1.4.143–5), she invokes both senses. Only moments later, Lear will be pitted literally against Nature, both his own and that of the storm. In the fourth act, at Dover Cliff, Gloucester reflects on Lear as a 'ruin'd piece of Nature!' (4.6.132). In *Lear*, Nature is a polysemic concept. Carolyn Merchant has observed: '*Nature* in ancient and early modern times had a number of interrelated meanings. With respect to individuals, it referred to the properties, inherent characters, and vital powers of persons, animals, or things, or more generally to human nature' (1983: xxiii). *A Thousand Acres* echoes this complexity of reference, making manifest the way in which our relationship to, and with, the natural world shapes our physical and psychological make-up.

The fact that *A Thousand Acres*'s reflections on land and the natural world, however contemporary or contextualised, are also deeply embedded within an understanding of the source-play can be demonstrated by returning to a passage we identified earlier as pivotal: that section of the novel where Ginny sees the pelicans flying over the former wetland area. Pelicans were native to the American Midwest and have been particular victims of agricultural policies of drainage, but they also have an emblematic significance within *Lear* that serves to remind us that land and family are two sides of the same coin in Smiley's narrative. When, in Act 3, Lear shelters from the storm in the hovel where he encounters Edgar as Poor Tom, in his emotional distress he assumes that Poor Tom's daughters must have brought him to such a state: 'Didst thou give all to thy daughters?/ And art come to this?' (3.4.48–9). Reflecting on his own condition, he observes: 'Judicious punishment! 'twas this flesh begot/ Those pelican daughters' (3.4.73–4). In widely read early modern emblem books such as Geoffrey Whitney's 1586 *Choice of Emblemes*, the pelican embodied the moral of loving one's children too much. The pelican mother sacrificed herself for her brood: 'The Pelican, for to reuiue her younge,/ Doth pierce her breast, and geue them of her blood' (Whitney, 1969: 87). Lear may be remembering a further emblematic association between pelicans and kings who sacrificed themselves for their subjects, but it seems more significant that once again here he appropriates the maternal role when thinking of his relationship to his daughters.

An intrinsic part of Smiley's meticulous appropriation of *Lear* is her appropriation of the play's guiding metaphors. Those to do with the natural and animal worlds have already been mentioned, but the sight and blindness themes so beloved of A-level students' essays also have a major function in *A Thousand Acres*, most obviously in the central blinding of Harold Clark. Out in the fields, side-dressing his corn with chemical pesticides in an overt attempt to annoy Jess following the church supper confrontation, Harold tries to fix a fault on his new tractor, only to find himself sprayed in the face with anhydrous ammonia. This chemical is fast-acting on the corneas and his only hope would have been the immediate application of water. But the water tank is empty. Harold is blinded amid the corn, alone in this terrifying reality: 'There wasn't any water anywhere out there … Jess was out running. Pete was in Pike buying cement. Rose was helping Linda … Daddy was sitting in the glider on Harold's porch … Ty was working' (232). This image of isolated and separated individuals is a devastating one. It ricochets across the rest of the novel. The sense of distance between these people, like that registered in the novel's opening view, is palpable.

Water and poison prove all-pervasive metaphors in *A Thousand Acres*. One of the central tragedies of Zebulon County is that these two entities prove to be inextricably linked. Jess causes Ginny to see her habitat afresh when she informs him of the several miscarriages she has suffered: 'Didn't your doctor tell you not to drink the well water? … People have known for ten years or more that nitrates in well water cause miscarriages and death of infants. Don't *you* know that the fertilizer runoff drains into the aquifer?' (164–5). As the work of cultural geographers and anthropologists has shown, water is traditionally, in both religious and secular societies, an emblem of life. In practical terms, too, farming communities rely on water sources for crop irrigation:

The geography of human settlement has always been and remains today shaped in large measure by the distribution of available sources of
fresh water. But as with all brute facts of our existence, humans culturally appropriate water, and invest it with meanings ... It becomes a
metaphor mapped onto other dimensions of human existence, individual and social, material and spiritual. It is through the meanings
that we give to water and to its geographical manifestations – in rivers,
streams, and lakes – that we come to understand it and to exert forms
of human control over its inherent nature. (Cosgrove, 1990: 2)

In *A Thousand Acres*, this fact of life has been cruelly reversed: the
life-giving properties of water, like the marshlands of Zebulon
County, have been drained away, polluted by decades of agricultural
run-off, and in a parallel action the breaking waters of giving birth
are reduced in Ginny to the shameful fluids of miscarriage on her
nightgown, which she buries in the dairy-barn floor (this, like so
much else in the novel, will eventually be exposed and uncovered
when Ty is digging up the floor for the purposes of expansion).

For Mathieson, water imagery in *A Thousand Acres* 'offers a
crucial index of loss in nature and in the characters' consciousness' (1999: 136). The metaphorical as well as material operations
of this signifier are embodied in the swimming-hole Ginny recalls
from her youth:

When we were children, Rose and I used to swim in the farm pond
down toward Mel's corner. The pond, an ancient pothole that predated
the farm, was impressively large to us, with a tire swing hanging over
the deep end. Not long before the death of our mother, Daddy drained
the pond and took out the trees and stumps around it so he could work
that field more efficiently. (85)

Loss is signified as the loss of the maternal. The only swimming
site that remains is the Pike municipal pool, a sterile concrete
affair that leaves Ginny, Pammy and Linda oddly out of sorts after
a day in its hostile environment (94–5). Ginny heads to another
old swimming site, the local quarry, after the body-blow of being
served legal papers on behalf of Larry and Caroline, who are trying
to reclaim the farmland he has signed over (246). But when she
reaches the quarry, it is clearly unsafe to swim in, full as it is of
'hubcaps, tin cans, bashed-in oil drums ... Now I saw the place
with a new darkened vision. No telling what was in there' (247).
This moment introduces to the reader the ever-darkening vision

of the novel. Ginny's encounter with Rose's disaffected husband at the polluted quarry is sexually charged. Tellingly, a snake crosses their path. Ginny's earlier conversation about snakes – and Larry's extermination of those on the farmland – was with Jess. The snake comes to embody the age-old referent to sexuality and danger, but Smiley builds in the material relevance of species extinction. As with the pelicans, the images of this novel are doubly weighted, fraught with early modern and modern significances.[18]

Silent Spring devotes a chapter to 'Surface Waters and Underground Seas' in which Carson, like Smiley, considers the death of wetland bird species and the wider consequences of poisoned food chains. Water pollution, she stresses, is for the most part 'unseen and invisible' (clearly Smiley's central point), and toxicity wreaks particular havoc on the bodies of women and children. Water is essentially another absent presence in *A Thousand Acres*. Noticeably absent when Harold is blinded, water, when it is available, causes death and demise rather than well-being: Ginny's infertility, potentially Rose's cancer, and Pete's drowning.

For all her claims that Jess Clark helped her to see more clearly (370), Ginny seems to have learned little by the end. Returning when she learns that Rose is dying, Ginny destroys the poisoned sausages she made at the height of her sexual jealousy (ironically, Rose turned vegetarian during what she describes as her 'Jess Clark phase'). She does so by flushing the poisoned sausages down the waste-disposal system, simply washing the poison out into the wider unseen sea: 'I washed them away with fifteen minutes of water, full blast. I relied as I always did now that I lived in the city, on the sewage treatment plant that I had never seen' (366–7).

The poisoned sausages are often an uncomfortable presence in the novel. A semi-comic, semi-melodramatic subplot, they force those readers who have accepted Ginny's narrative version of events in an unqualified fashion to think again. Despite her claims to be vindicating Goneril and Regan in the writing of Ginny and Rose, by retaining this element of the play, Goneril's poisoning of her sister, Smiley does not allow an entirely unambiguous response to Ginny.

As Ginny herself is fully aware by the close of the novel: 'A farm abounds with poisons' (310). Those poisons are both emotional and material. Marv Carson's hyperanxiety about his diet has suggested as much early on (29). In truth, Rose does not die as a result of Ginny's warped cookery lesson but because of a recurrence of her breast cancer which, it is suggested, may be linked to the ongoing poisoning the Cook and Clark women have endured throughout their lives. It provides a physical parallel to the emotional poisoning caused by the memories of incest. Chedgzoy has described Smiley's novel as a 'precise translation of Shakespeare's plot and characters into contemporary terms' (1995: 56), and this is, for the most part, an accurate assessment, but – as I suggested at the very beginning of this chapter – unlike the five-act play of *King Lear*, *A Thousand Acres* has six books. It extends beyond the reaches of the play – structurally, at least. In the sixth section, and the particularly equivocal epilogue, Smiley deliberately undermines some of the assumed certainties of Ginny's earlier narrative. Book six is distinctly urban in setting. Ginny finds herself in the unnatural surroundings of a 'garden apartment' (the irony is palpable) on Interstate 35, where she can hear the cars passing and the hum of the air conditioner at all hours of the day and night. Even her job finds her working in the transient surroundings of a diner:

> There was nothing time-bound, and little that was seasonal about the highway or the restaurant. Even in Minnesota, where the winter was a big topic of conversation and a permanent occasion for people's heroic self-regard, it was only winter on the highway a few hours out of the year. The rest of the time, traffic kept moving. (333)

Rachel Carson's emphasis on the importance of the seasonal cycle at the beginning of *Silent Spring* surely echoes around the sterile world described here. Unlike the Goneril of the play, Ginny survives, but it is a questionable triumph, despite Smiley's claims of rehabilitation: 'I saw this as my afterlife, and for a long time it didn't occur to me that it contained a future' (334). When that future comes, it is tinged with sadness: Ginny agrees to foster Rose's daughters, having dreamed of such a moment from the beginning. Her dreams of motherhood, however, are never fully realised. The description of her relationship with Pam and Linda is distinctly cool. Again genes prove inescapable:

> I have inherited Pam and Linda. Pam looks like a heftier Rose ... Linda looks like a more skeptical, less passionate Pete ... They are also

cautious ... I recognize that they don't have a great deal of faith in my guardianship, though they like me, and we get along smoothly. (369)

In *The Death of Nature*, Carolyn Merchant describes an agrarian history in Western culture that witnesses a gradual movement away from a natural relationship with Mother Earth to one of mastery via machinery and technology (1983: 2). The death of Nature appears to be charted by the closing sections of *A Thousand Acres*. The Cook farmstead, crippled by debts, is sold to the anonymous multinational Heartland Corporation, and all signs of human habitation on the land – Rose's bungalow, Ginny's house (the former Ericson farm) – are taken down to make room for a further expansion of the hog operation. The distanced viewpoint of the novel's opening pages is repeated, yet altered: 'When you stand at the intersection of County 686 and Cabot Street Road now, you see that the fields make no room for houses or barnyards or people. No lives are lived any more within the horizon of your gaze' (368). Equally chilling is the knowledge we are given that Linda is now keen to work for multinational food conglomerates (369). Her commitment to food production remains, but in Reaganite America it is held in thrall to global capitalism.

Discussing the end of the novel, Smiley has suggested that the outcome is positive for Ginny, and to a certain extent for Rose's daughters, free from the burden of inheriting the farm at their mother's deathbed insistence (1998: 71). While the lifting of a burden seems an inevitable interpretation of Ginny's sale of the farm, Smiley's analysis seems an otherwise oddly optimistic gloss on the rather more reserved claims of the text. In many respects the overriding claim of the epilogue is that the farm, like family memories, will never really be escaped. It is in the psyche and consciousness of all who experienced it, and, in terms of pesticides, quite literally present in their bloodstreams. As Ginny concedes, nothing is really forgotten:

> Remorse reminds me of Daddy, who had none, at least none for me. My body reminds me of Daddy, too, of what it feels like to resist without seeming to resist, to absent yourself while seeming respectful and attentive. Waking in the dark reminds me of Daddy, cooking reminds me of Daddy, the whole wide expanse of the mid-continental sky, which is where we look for signs of trouble – that, too, reminds me of Daddy. (370)

In many ways the tone echoes the melancholic resignation of Edgar at the end of *Lear*:

> The weight of this sad time we must obey;
> Speak what we feel, not what we ought to say.
> The oldest hath borne most; we that are young
> Shall never see so much, nor live so long.
>
> (5.3.322–5)

The real clue may lie in the expression or declaration 'Speak what we feel, not what we ought to say'. That would have seemed to be the novel's message: one about the danger of keeping up appearances, of suppressing past hurts and abuse; and yet, in the epilogue, what we witness is Pam and Linda exercising caution, and Ginny accepting that she might never tell Caroline the whole truth. The strength of Smiley's appropriation is that it remains equivocal to the end, darker and more ambiguous in its vision, penetrating further below the surface of the visible, than even its author's printed claims suggest.

Notes

1 J. Todd (1998: 71) charges the novel with sentimentality and too great a love of detail.
2 The game and playing pieces chosen are symbolic in a rather heavy-handed way. *Monopoly*, as its name suggests, is about expansionism and the individual acquisition of property. Jess plays as the racing car – scarcely the environmentally friendly choice of an organic farmer but suggestive of his persistent departure from the scene: be it that of the Vietnam War or his relationship with Rose. Loyal Ty is a dog. Rose – subject of abuse by both father and husband – is a shoe, and the passive, domesticated Ginny is the thimble. J. Todd (1998) suggests it is symbolic that Rose aborts the Monopoly game, just as she will put a stop to the generational farming of land by refusing to bequeath the farm to her daughters (71).
3 This doubling is not unique. Edward Bond achieved as much in his character of the Boy, adviser to Lear, in his savage rewriting of the play, *Lear* (1972).
4 A suggestion made on 'Book Club', BBC Radio 4, January 1999.
5 Cordelia has less than 4 per cent, but sympathy for her could be said to be won via Lear's and others' references to her, and her earlier relationship with the audience via asides, which provide us with a sense of her point of view.

6 In *Lear*, Goneril is 'Lady Brach', a bitch, in the Fool's terminology, but this may be an instance of where obsolete terms lose their impact in the context of modern performance (1.5.109).

7 Smiley has acknowledged the input of ecological texts into her thinking, while not naming Carson in any explicit fashion. She names three books which moulded her novel: Dickens's *David Copperfield* (a clearly influential quasi-realist narrative); O.E. Rölvaag's *Giants of the Earth* (the story of Per Hensa and his family's immigration to Minnesota farmland); and a book on ecology, *The Web of Life* (Smiley, 1999). As further evidence of these books as shaping texts for the construction of *A Thousand Acres*, the former two are Linda's prescribed reading at school (349).

In addition, in the same essay Smiley discusses reading Barry Commoner's *The Closing Circle* on first moving to Iowa – a text which raises the issue of well-water contamination and its effect on unborn children, something she clearly applies to Ginny's narrative (1999: 170).

8 Andrew Dobson suggests that many people date the rise of the modern environmental movement from 1962, when *Silent Spring* was published in the USA: it was published in Great Britain the following year (1991: 25).

9 For a long time in the UK the slogan of the Women's Environmental Network punned on this connection: 'Love Your Mother'.

10 Seminal texts of ecofeminism include Merchant (1983) and Plumwood (1993). A helpful summary of the claims and inherent problems of ecofeminist theory is offered by Dobson (1990: 192–203). I am grateful to Andy for discussions on this and other ecological themes.

11 In a thought-provoking essay that reads Sylvia Plath's poetry in the light of Carson's theories on pollutants and toxicity, Tracy Brain emphasises the influence of *Silent Spring* on the North American feminist community (1998: 146–64).

Alter has demonstrated the significance of Smiley's naming strategies in the novel, which evoke the period of white 'discovery' and settlement – Ericson, Cabot, Drake, Smith, Stanley, Livingston, and so on. Ginny's full name, Virginia, is also evocative of the deliberate feminisation of the land that was 'settled' and 'mastered' by the early modern colonisers of America (1999: 155). For a more general discussion of the sexualising impulses of land settlement, see Olwig (1993: 307–43).

12 Interestingly, flaws of this nature in the concrete floor would ensure the continuing problem of polluted watercourses for future generations of farmers on the land; the cycle of abuse, Smiley implies, continues.

13 In an uncomfortable image of appropriation, Ginny and Ty now live in what was the Ericson homestead.

14 It is significant that this event, which provides a central moment of

fragmentation and emotional isolation in the novel, is cut from the 1997 film version (dir. J. Moorhouse). The film, one hour and forty-one minutes in length, understandably felt the need to compact and condense a novel of nearly four hundred pages, but in doing so it omits almost entirely the farming themes and concerns, focusing only on the family's emotional struggles. This fails to recognise how the latter are in part produced, and indeed nourished, by the former. Jess's organic farming interests are mentioned only in a passing aside, the part of Loren is lost entirely, and pivotal moments in the narrative to do with the central metaphors of water and poison, such as encounters at the swimming-pool and the polluted quarry, are not represented in the film.

15 In another move away from the book's careful contextualisation, the film version updates events to a contemporary moment. Jess's political cal stance on Vietnam and the relevance of the Carter Administration's dealings with small farms are lost in favour of Caroline's use of a lap-top computer and mobile phone.

16 For useful reassessments of the Carter Administration, see Dumbrell (1995); Abernathy, Hill and Williams (1984); and K. W. Thompson (1990).

17 In response to an audience question about the shadowy portrayal of Larry Cook, in the January 1999 edition of Radio 4's 'Book Club' series, Smiley confessed that she spent less time on those characters she felt little sympathy for – such as Larry and, by extension, Caroline. In print Smiley has made her limited sympathy for their source-characters explicit: Lear, she says, struck her as 'selfish, demanding, humourless, self-pitying'; Cordelia 'seemed ungenerous and cold, a stickler for truth ... a stickler for form' (1999: 161).

18 Snakes also form part of the patterning language of the play: Edmund confesses to the audience that he has courted both sisters' affections:

> To both these sisters have I sworn my love;
> Each jealous of the other, as the stung
> Are of the adder. Which of them shall I take?
> Both? one? neither?
>
> (5.1.55–8)

TEN

'Out of Shakespeare': Other *Lears*

If Jane Smiley marginalises Cordelia by sidelining the character of Caroline in *A Thousand Acres*, other women writers, as this chapter will show, have taken *King Lear*'s stubborn heroine as their central focus. Valerie Miner is a US academic who has written several novels. *A Walking Fire* (1994) was her contribution to the State University of New York Press series 'The Margins of Literature'. Its title is a direct quotation from *King Lear*: these are the words used by the Fool to describe the approach of a torch-carrying Gloucester across the storm-tossed heath: 'Look, here comes a walking fire' (3.4.104–5). In Jacobean terminology, a 'walking fire' was a will-o'-the-wisp or spirit of the wilderness, but in Miner's 1980s-located novel it stands for a series of metaphors and literal fires – from the arson attack on a Vietnam draft board office in which the protagonist, Cora, assists as a radical undergraduate, through the Napalm burnings of the Southeast Asian conflict carried out by US soldiers, to a general state of mind:

> They parked two blocks away and walked briskly to the draft board office. She conjured other flames. Girl Scout camp-outs with ghost stories. The destruction of Chicago after Mrs O'Leary's cow kicked over the lantern. The fires in Washington, D.C., after Martin Luther King was assassinated. (Miner, 1994: 67)

The innocent, the apocryphal and the political merge in this matrix of images.

Miner's novel is a re-vision of *Lear* as a political allegory, in which family affairs are played out on a national and international

217

scale. Cora (the novel's Cordelia analogue) has spent much of her life in Canada in hiding from the FBI following her student activism (her fellow arsonist, Ralph, died in the fire, apparently of his own volition). Her trenchant opposition to the Vietnam War has estranged her from both her father, Roy Casey (Roy functioning as a pun on *roi* or King), and her two brothers, George and Ron (the gender-transposed Goneril and Regan of this text).

Cora returns to her home town in Oregon only when she learns that her father is dying of emphysema. It is not a return without risk, as the tense border-crossing scene indicates. She travels with her adult daughter, Fran, a dancer. Fran's name is another conscious pun on a character from the play: following Lear's banishment of Cordelia, she marries the King of France. As a result, Fran, or Françoise, in many respects represents in a wider sense the French-Canadian province of Quebec and its own fight for political and linguistic autonomy (Brydon, 1993: 165–84).

Once back in Oregon, Cora finds herself again in conflict with her brothers, who are, it seems, trying to push Roy into a convalescent hospital against his will. Property is their motive: the real-estate value of the family home. As Cora learns more about her siblings, it emerges that George has been siphoning off money for the purposes of funding a right-wing political organisation, the AFN (Americans for Freedom in Nicaragua – there were numerous such groups that helped, frequently with US government complicity or knowledge, to bring down the left-wing Sandanista government in Nicaragua in the 1980s), and for illegal arms-running operations. Roy dies before this is fully revealed to him: his death scene mirrors the one in the play, except that in this instance Cordelia survives:

> 'There, look.'
> She raised her head, assuming Follie [the family dog] had found her way back into the house.
> 'Look, there.'
> Cora looked all around her father's bedroom, but saw nothing. When she turned back to him he was absolutely still. (235)

Compare 'Do you see this? Look on her, look, her lips,/ Look there, look there!.' (5.3.308–9).

The resonance of the word 'nothing' in the passage quoted above sends readers back into the language of the source-play.

'Nothing' and 'silence' are terms that remain indelibly linked to Cordelia following her first-scene refusal to speak publicly of her love for her father: 'What shall Cordelia speak? Love, and be silent.' (1.1.60):

LEAR: what can you say to draw
                A third more opulent than your sisters? Speak.
CORDELIA: Nothing, my lord.
LEAR: Nothing?
CORDELIA: Nothing.
LEAR: Nothing will come of nothing, speak again.

(1.1.84–9)

Other aspects of the play are embedded in the images and events of her life that Cora recalls in flashback form within the narrative (the structure of the book is anti-linear, shifting geography and time-frame throughout, moving in and out of different 'pasts' and the present tense). The map that provides the central prop of the explosive opening scene is here unfolded on the dashboard of Cora's car as she and Fran travel south. Territory in this text is as fought over as in *Lear* – be it in the personal terms of Roy's house, or the international implications of border wars.

The absent mother of *Lear* on whom Smiley reflected in *A Thousand Acres* is part of Cora's experience too. The theme of madness that ebbs in and out of the play in the form of the king's psychological breakdown, but also Edgar's assumption of the guise of Poor Tom, is linked to Cora's mother's breakdown and eventual sectioning. Ultimately, her mother commits suicide, hanging herself in an action that recalls one of Lear's lines: 'And my poor fool is hanged!' (5.3.304). In this respect, Cora's mother becomes the absent wife of Lear but also the 'fool' who shadows him throughout the play, trying to temper his worst excesses.

While this novel is certainly ranged against George and Ron in terms of their politics (the book is dedicated to all 'those Canadians who offered American women and men refuge and friendship during a period of turmoil, anger, fear, and loss'), it is not without sympathy for the brutality which their father visited on them. Gender issues are at stake in this, as Cora reflects, attempting to be understanding even when George has informed on her to the military authorities, wrongly accusing her of murdering Ralph in

the 1960s arson attack: 'In some ways I think the boys were in-
jured more. In some ways I think I got away with … a lot' (253).
Like Smiley's provision of motives for Ginny and Rose in *A Thousand Acres*, Miner offers the tyranny of domestic patriarchy as a
partial reason for George's and Ron's cruelties and selfishness in
later life.

The novel ends with Cora in prison. Readers are reminded of
Cordelia's arrest along with Lear, and his touching – if naive –
version of how their incarceration will pass:

> Come, let's away to prison.
> We two alone will sing like birds i'the cage.
> When thou dost ask me blessing, I'll kneel down,
> And ask of thee forgiveness. So we'll live,
> And pray, and sing and tell old tales, and laugh
> At gilded butterflies
>
> (5.3.8–13)

The people around Cora are hopeful of bail, but there is a note of
genuine pessimism in George's swift release (he has been informed
on in turn for his gun-running activities): a system portrayed as
oppressive throughout, be it in terms of military conscription or
controlling social workers, is still fully functioning at the end.

Cora is a freelance journalist: in this way she is given a 'voice'
like so many of the reclaimed Shakespearean heroines we have
considered here. But she ends up in a prison cell, in a state of
confinement rather than release. In this respect there is no simple
retrieval of Cordelia's tragic fate. Yet Cordelia was hanged; Cora,
in her survival, also represents the endurance of Edgar at the end
of the play: her comments on understanding what the 'boys'
suffered possibly echoes Edgar's 'The oldest hath borne most'
(5.3.324). Her daughter Fran is a marker of the future, although
radical feminists might choose to take note, as Cora herself does,
of the apolitical choice of career she has made:

> After a childhood as the daughter of a single mother, after years in
> progressive schools and weekends at antiwar marches, teach-ins and
> feminist rallies, her daughter had decided to become a dancer. A hoofer.
> Not your radical Isadora Duncan political art, not even your classical
> ballet, but show dancing … The only 'political' thing about Fran was
> her lesbianism. (8)

Of course, Fran's future will therefore be 'without men', and therein lies perhaps the most radical sense of optimism: '"You're going to be O.K." Cora said, believing her fatherless daughter would be fine' (254).

If Smiley re-visions *Lear* in terms of family politics and a 'green' awareness, Miner has read and rewritten the play as a political allegory. A text with comparable objectives is Sarah Murphy's *The Measure of Miranda* (1987), which reworks *The Tempest*. That text, which also has a Canadian angle on its Shakespearean source-text, is narrated by a lawyer, Susan, who is attempting, as the title suggests, to get the measure of her dead friend, Miranda, who was, like Miner's Cora, a political activist. Shown pictures of Central American torture victims, Miranda had decided to act by assassinating a Central American major. In the process she killed both herself and her father (an unusual take on the Prospero–Miranda dynamic of the play).[1]

What both Smiley's and Miner's versions of *Lear* offer are novels that depend quite heavily on the original plot of the play which forms their foundation or provenance. Other novels deploy *Lear* in a more diffuse or allusive (even elusive) manner. Like *A Walking Fire*, Lucy Ellmann's *Sweet Desserts* (1998; first published 1988) deals – at least in part – with a daughter who is watching her father die from a terminal disease. The narrator, Suzy Schwarz, is, like Ellmann herself, a transatlantic hybrid, brought – against her will, it seems – to England from the USA as a young girl. Sibling rivalry – in this instance with her high-achieving older sister, Fran – is a recurring theme in this text, too, occasioning self-conscious references to Goneril and Regan: 'Each jealous of the other, as the stung/ Are of the adder' (5.1.55–6; Ellmann, 1998: 93). The *Lear* references gain weight as we enter the latter stages of this novel, as Suzy's father wastes away before her: 'things that love night/ Love not such nights as these' (3.2.41–2; Ellmann, 1998: 134).

The overwhelming – but also confusing – nature of a daughter's love for a father is clearly invoked: 'Why have my sisters husbands, if they say/ They love you all?' (1.1.98; Ellmann, 1998: 123). The eventual loss is devastating:

He revived enough to take my face once more in his hand. I revived enough to finally try to fight his death … I held my father in my arms, for the first time in years, for the last time, my dear father who was

> still warm, still hot from life, and urged him to fight like an American, and he died. He died. (139)

That image is, of course, a direct reversal of the iconic stage tableau from *Lear* of the dead king holding the limp but still warm corpse of his youngest daughter. The point of the appropriation in *Sweet Desserts* is more piecemeal, more allusive, than the sustained template the play provides for Smiley and Miner. This is in keeping with the innovative narrative style of Ellmann's novel. The protagonist is an artist who specialises in collage, and the narrative is an unusual collage of different kinds of text and textual discourse, so that in any given chapter we might find plumbing instructions, a recipe, or a marketing survey questionnaire with boxes to tick, juxtaposed with more conventional narrative. Seventeenth-century literature provides material for this collage – not just in the form of Shakespearean quotation, but also Donne (whose mocking version of colonial adventure in a sexual encounter, Elegy 19 'On His Mistress Going to Bed', provides the chapter-title 'My New Found Land', referring in this new context to Suzy's uprooting from the USA to the UK) and Marvell. One of the innovative ploys of Ellmann's novel in print is to provide an Index that proves both inaccurate and unreliable and, at times, downright misleading. Shakespeare is entirely absent.

In Margaret Atwood's *Cat's Eye* (1990), Shakespeare is not exactly absent, but he is diffuse, debunked and subverted at numerous turns. There may be a case for seeing this in terms of the deviant or dissident forms of nostalgia Susan Bennett has written so lucidly about in *Performing Nostalgia* (1999) but the fact that Shakespeare is a presence at all calls into question the extent to which that dissidence is fully realised or performed. In a useful formulation, Bennett describes nostalgia as 'the inflicted territory where claims for authenticity ... are staged' (1996: 19). Nostalgia is not quite the approach of *Cat's Eye*'s narrator, Elaine, towards her past; her memories are a painful process of unearthing and recognition, but they undoubtedly raise questions of authenticity: of self, of subjective versions of the past, and even of national identities. Like Ellmann's narrator, Elaine is an artist; like Miner's protagonist, she is returning home after a long period 'in exile' for the purposes of a retrospective exhibition of her work. The return to Toronto initiates an encounter with her past, and in particular the childhood bullying she experienced at the hands of three 'schoolfriends': Cordelia, Grace and Carol. That encounter is only ever performed in flashback and memory; the feared and yet longed-for encounter with Cordelia, prime focus of the haunting Elaine still seems to endure, never occurs in the present tense. The reader, like Elaine, is worked up into a frenzy of expectation that is never satisfied or quenched: 'I've been prepared for almost anything; except absence, except silence' (Atwood, 1990: 413).

Cordelia is an unusual enough name for readers to suspect Shakespearean associations, and the narrative confirms this, although not until some pages in, at Chapter 14. Interestingly, this is also the chapter in which we first learn our narrator's name. The indissoluble link which Elaine sees between herself and Cordelia even at the close – 'We are like the twins in old fables, each of whom has been given half a key' (411) – is confirmed by this narrative gesture;[2] although the significance of Cordelia's name is hinted at earlier, when Elaine professes to giving her daughters, Sarah and Anne, 'sensible' names: 'These are sensible choices. I am a believer in sensible choices, so different from many of my own. Also in sensible names for children, because look what happened to Cordelia' (15). There is a pressure to live up to names, in life as in narrative, particularly those of Shakespearean derivation:

> Why did they name her that? Hang that weight around her neck. Heart of the moon, jewel of the sea, depending on which foreign language you're using. The third sister, the only honest one. The stubborn one, the rejected one, the one who was not heard. If she'd been called Jane, would things have been different? (263)

Cordelia's sisters also have Shakespearean monikers, although they resist their full implications: 'Cordelia's two older sisters are Perdita and Miranda, but nobody calls them that. They're called Perdie and Mirrie' (72). Only Cordelia opts for her name in full:

> Cordelia ought to be Cordie, but she's not. She insists, always, on being called by her full name: Cordelia. All three of these names are peculiar; none of the girls at school have names like that. Cordelia says they're out of Shakespeare. She seems proud of this, as though it's something we should all recognise. 'It was Mummie's idea,' she says. (72–3)

There is an irony that, as Shakespearean critics, the referential nomenclature is one of the first things we register in Atwood's dense and brilliant text; just as there is irony in the mention of Shakespeare only in order to decentre him.[3]

This Cordelia may recognise a significance in her nomenclature but it is not one she is able to live up to at all times. She is not the heroine of this narrative; frequently, with Grace and Carol, she forms a brutal group akin to Goneril and Regan in *Lear*, or even a triad like the witches in *Macbeth*. It is no coincidence that references to the Scottish play also resonate throughout *Cat's Eye*; tartan and plaid, signifiers of bloody cruelties and clan warfare, become troubling presences in the schoolgirl uniform of Elaine's associates, and one of Elaine's paintings, *Three Witches*, of three sofas, is clearly an abstract vision of the demonic power they wielded over her as a child. That tragic potential is, however, converted into comedy by Atwood when Cordelia causes the audience to laugh in a production of *Macbeth* after swapping the requisite mouldy cabbage used to represent the Thane of Glamis's decapitated head onstage with an uncontrollably bouncy fresh one.

Cordelia is drawn to the theatre and to Shakespeare, and this can be associated with the expectations of her naming. She is, however, always marginalised in this context, a position that is in stark contrast to the power she wields over the young Elaine. She is a spear-carrier in the sense that she is always cast in minor roles. When Elaine meets her later in life, performing at the Shakespeare Festival in Stratford, Ontario, her list of parts is almost laughable: one of Prospero's attendant spirits in *The Tempest*, a court lady in *Richard III*, and chief nun in *Measure for Measure*. This last role is her only speaking part, and her few quoted lines confirm this idea of effacement and erasure: 'Then if you speak, you must not show your face;/ Or if you show your face, you must not speak' (1.4.12–13). When Elaine goes to watch Cordelia in *The Tempest*, she cannot even identify her onstage (303). As Suzanne Raitt has observed: 'There is no place for Cordelia in Shakespeare: the dramas are indifferent to her, erasing her individuality and rendering her, at times, ridiculous' (1999: 184). The comic rewriting of tragedy is important here, but it is also telling that the last time Elaine sees Cordelia is in a psychiatric ward following a suicide attempt. Maybe in these ways her name does constrain her. In the final stages of the novel, as in the fifth act of the play, Cordelia is an absent presence only.

The comic-cabbage episode is certainly a factor in rendering ridiculous Cordelia's personal efforts to engage with Shakespeare, yet decapitation is a recurring trope in the novel. *Macbeth* and *Cymbeline* both feature decapitated bodies, and Elaine's dreams are haunted by the image of a head in a towel that at times manifests itself as Cordelia's. Elaine is made to play the headless Mary, Queen of Scots – the three girls barricade her into a hole in Cordelia's garden – and the colonial image of the Queen's Head on Canadian currency is referred to at various points in the narrative. In the 1980s, when this book was written, Canada was casting off the monarchy in a bloodless revolution which, unlike the English one of 1642–49, did not involve the execution of the monarch. In 1982 the Canada Act gave the nation control over its own constitution, severing all links with Britain in legal terms (Raitt, 1999). So it is telling that throughout the novel, images of royalty seem curiously disembodied in Elaine's thoughts and recollections: 'The car with the glove is moving away' (160).

Raitt has ingeniously indicated that *Lear* is about contested territory between England and France; after all, Cordelia returns on to the stage at the head of the French army. This, she suggests, can be seen in *Cat's Eye* as a figure for Canada's colonial history, another kind of haunting or spectral presence in the text: 'Haunting *Cat's Eye* is the ghost of a colonial power that has a bicultural history albeit in the long distant past' (1999: 185). In the time-scale of the novel we watch Canada change before Elaine's eyes: biased pro-imperial teachers such as Miss Lumley become a thing of the past, and Elaine is able to read the national flag differently after 1982. As Raitt notes: 'Recontextualizing Shakespeare in Canada is also a way of thinking about Canada's relation to Englishness and its own colonial past' (1999: 184). For Raitt, the images of decapitation are part of a deeper theme of cultural division that marks Canadian identities and literatures.[4]

What Elaine gleans from Miss Lumley's History lessons at Queen Mary's School is highly subjective:

In countries that are not the British Empire, they cut out children's tongues, especially those of boys. Before the British Empire there were no railroads or postal services in India, and Africa was full of tribal warfare, with spears, and had no proper clothing. The Indians in Canada did not have the wheel or telephones, and ate the hearts of their enemies in the heathenish belief that it would give them courage. The British Empire changed all that. It brought in electric lights. (79)

Like many of the narrative appropriations considered here, *Cat's Eye* is concerned with what constitutes History as a discipline and with using Shakespeare, among other things, to pluralise and multiply versions of the past. As she is recounting the local details of her brother's arbitrary killing in an aeroplane hijack, Elaine stops the narrative short: 'Here I stop inventing' (391). She also acknowledges that her memories can only ever be one perspective on what happened between her and Cordelia: 'She will have her own version. I am not the centre of her story, because she herself is that' (411). Elaine is too honest to be an archetypal unreliable narrator, but the bias of first-person narration and the tricks of memory are nevertheless acknowledged. At various points in the narrative, Elaine wonders which Cordelia she is conjuring up: 'There is never only one, of anyone' (6). Even when she is considering how she will react if she does meet Cordelia again, self-fashioning plays its part: 'If I were to meet Cordelia again, what would I tell her about myself? The truth, or whatever would make me look good? Probably the latter. I still have that need' (6).

Part of the honesty comes in the representation of the shift in power that occurs between her and Cordelia in their teenage years – years in which Elaine undoubtedly becomes the aggressor, the one with the 'mean mouth' (235). This is after the 'endless time', as Elaine describes it, when she was in the subject and subjected position of victim (113). The central terrifying moment in this time-period is the episode at the ravine, when the three other girls force her into icy water to retrieve her hat, only to desert her: a potentially life-threatening action. The ravine, its rickety wooden bridge, and the attendant notion of falling become recurring emblems in Elaine's aesthetics and narrative: Atwood shows beautifully here, through both Shakespearean allusion and Elaine's artworks, how we use art to interpret and define moments in our lives and experiences. There may be links to Shakespeare in the ravine episode if we consider the centrality of the Dover Cliff imaginings of Edgar and Gloucester in *Lear*. In the play, Dover Cliff becomes emblematic of whether we choose to live or die in the face of great trauma: Gloucester and Elaine choose life. That life has, until this point, been dictated for Elaine by others. Her powerlessness manifests itself in the self-harm she inflicts on her feet and fingers (114). In later life, art will provide a different kind of focus and compensation.

Elaine's brother Stephen is the mouthpiece for much of the novel's ruminations on time and matter (he is a scientist). These themes open the novel's sequence of recollections: 'Time is not a line but a dimension, like the dimensions of space. If you can bend space you can bend time also, and if you knew enough and could move faster than light you could travel backwards in time and exist in two places at once' (3). For Elaine, time has a precise shape: 'I began then to think of time as having a shape ... Nothing goes away' (3).

That use of 'Nothing' is, as in *A Walking Fire*, a deliberate use of one of *Lear*'s central terms. Other allusive metaphors and tropes thread in and out of the narrative of *Cat's Eye*. For example, we have absent mothers – absent at least in terms of the politics of the household, despite Elaine's claim that 'in the daily life of houses, fathers are largely invisible' (98). Towards the end of her life Elaine's mother seems to confess a knowledge of her daughter's bullying, and her own failure to act. The violent fathers of Smiley's and Miner's novels are reworked here as Carol's and Cordelia's oppressive patriarchs. Psychological reasons for their actions are therefore offered: what Shakespeare leaves open, the twentieth century feels compelled to answer.

If 'nothing' and 'silence' make reverberations in this novel, then so, too, do *Lear*'s themes of sight and blindness. Early on we learn of Elaine's need for bifocals, her difficulty in seeing clearly. Coming to terms with Cordelia and the past, an event prompted in part by the return to Toronto, is part of her seeing clearly: 'Cordelia I want to see' (411). This can be aligned with the self-knowledge Kent urges on Lear at the start of the play – 'See better, Lear' (1.1.158) – which is learned in gruesomely tangible ways by the blinded Gloucester: 'I stumbled when I saw' (4.1.20).

The Old Testament idea of revenge as just, 'An eye for an eye, a tooth for a tooth', which might have been used by Elaine as personal justification for the cruelty she wrought on Cordelia, is rejected towards the close of the novel in a paraphrase of Gandhi's claim that 'An eye for an eye makes the whole world blind': 'An eye for an eye leads only to more blindness' (405). The cat's-eye marble that provides a kind of talisman of strength for Elaine, and gives the novel its title, can finally be absorbed into her painting: the need for it relinquished. The novel closes on a poignant image of flight and sight, as Elaine, replacing her lost brother, finds herself in the window-seat of an aeroplane, looking out into 'old light' and describing it as 'enough to see by' (421).

There are, as we have registered elsewhere in this book, different methods and means of appropriating Shakespeare. Where Smiley and Miner find a way of asserting their own politics by both adhering to and diverging from the familiar plotline of *Lear*, other versions of that play emerge in the more diffuse and scattered allusions to families, nothing and silence, madness and blindness, of Ellmann, Atwood and others. In none of these texts is Shakespeare rejected outright, but he is not abjectly venerated either. These books, like Cordelia's name in *Cat's Eye*, come 'out of Shakespeare', but that very fact both promotes and thwarts the expectations of their readers.

Notes

1 Brydon (1993) has shown how the costume Miranda wears for the purpose of the assassination (white Oaxacan cotton) provides a grotesque rewriting of *The Tempest*'s 'Eurocentric' wedding masque (1993: 171). On the same novel, see Howells (1989: 39).

Another political novel which deploys Shakespeare is Vlady Kociancich's *The Last Days of William Shakespeare* (1990). In that text, by an Argentinian writer, *Hamlet* has been endlessly restaged for the past fifty years at the decaying National Theatre of an unnamed South American country. Part of the country's political maturation involves the discovery of this fact, and the substitution of an indigenous dramatist's work. As a result, however, the regime goes so far as to ban Shakespeare – an act of totalitarianism which results in an underground press producing annotated copies of *Hamlet*, and eventual street violence. This satiric novel has much to say about the bloody process of extracting emergent nations from postcolonial cultural strangleholds, but it also provides some touching emblems of Shakespeare's cross-cultural, transhistorical resonance and endurance. Recent efforts to ban *Hamlet* from the South African teaching curriculum provide a striking contemporary counterpoint.

2 Suzanne Raitt has written of Atwood's enduring interest in twins and twinning (1999: 193).

3 I should record that a recent BBC Radio 4 'Book Club' (April 1999) discussion of the novel, which involved Atwood herself, did not touch on Shakespeare once. See also Novy (1998: 157).

4 See also Hutcheon (1988a).

Expanding the canon
and casting ripples on the water

I had begun with Shakespeare ...

Erica Jong, *Serenissima*

Any reading of this book will indicate that certain Shakespearean texts have proved of especial interest to contemporary female appropriators. We have considered several versions of *Lear*, from Smiley to Atwood; several *Tempests*, from Warner to Naylor. The dominant themes in those plays of family and oppression lend themselves in particular ways to late-twentieth-century appropriations interested in addressing questions of power, voice and history, as all the novels studied here are. A particular predilection for the comedies and the late plays which deal with related themes, including those of gender and identity, as mapped out in cross-dressing trajectories and metatheatrical role-play, has been identified among a number of women novelists. Patricia Duncker's *James Miranda Barry* (1999), a recent fictional account of a real-life cross-dresser, is studded with references to the transvestite heroines of Shakespearean theatre.[1]

This might lead us to ask whether certain texts – and, indeed, their critical histories – lend themselves more readily to this form of adaptation into narrative, or whether certain genres are more predisposed to feminist readings and re-visions. For example, do the comedies' outspoken heroines provide particularly pertinent and positive templates, as opposed to the silenced women of tragedy? Are the only appropriations of tragedies likely to be counter-subversive ones, such as Smiley's pro-Goneril and Regan rewriting of *Lear*; and anyway, is *Lear* a special case? Jeanne Ray's comic rewrite of Shakespeare's youthful story of star-crossed lovers, *Romeo and Juliet*, as *Julie and Romeo* (2000), a tale of two rival florists, is self-consciously aimed at older readers, proving that the target population of Shakespearean appropriations is as fluid as the generic nature of their adaptations. Angela Carter found comic potential in the tragedies in *Wise Children*, and Iris Murdoch invoked both *Hamlet* and *Othello* extensively in two of her novels. Of course, we may have to bear in mind the exception made of *Hamlet* by Christina Angeletti in her Cambridge essay in Trapido's *Juggling*, where that play is rendered an honorary comedy on account of its feminine empathy. Certainly, Carter hints at something comparable in the virile (or otherwise) Melchior Hazard's conscious avoidance of the Prince's part, which had been previously performed by his pregnant mother. *Macbeth* appears in both Carter's and Atwood's work, but in a marginalised and debunked version. Perhaps there is some space yet to reclaim the voice of Lady Macbeth, now a troubling journalistic shorthand for ambitious political wives from Raisa Gorbachev and Hillary Clinton to Cherie Blair.

If we are thinking about gaps and absences in the female appropriators' canon, then the history plays might seem an obvious case. The limited potential of their female cast of widows and prostitutes has, however, been effectively challenged of late by critics (Howard and Rackin, 1997) and, in truth, the histories, too, make their mark on appropriations. Valerie Miner's politicised re-vision of *Lear* has already been explored, but her example is perhaps a notable exception in its choice of canonical tragedy as source-text. When women do turn to the subject of war and politics in Shakespeare, it is telling that they more often revert to texts regarded as marginal within the Shakespearean canon, as well as to marginalised figures such as Cordelia: *Titus Andronicus*, *Coriolanus*, and *Troilus and Cressida* are all relevant plays in this context.

In Margaret Drabble's trilogy which includes *The Radiant Way*, *A Natural Curiosity*, and *The Gates of Ivory*, these more marginal dramas ebb and flow within the narrative alongside the late plays and the ever-present *Hamlet*. In *A Natural Curiosity* (first published in 1989), a serial killer has been decapitating his victims, and allusions to *Titus Andronicus* provide an intellectual framework for

the arbitrary violence. For Drabble, Shakespeare is always the first
point of reference: a fictional analogue and, in this case, a chilling
marker of sameness:

> That month, in England, a tramp had been burned to death 'for a
> laugh' by two youths as he sheltered in his cardboard hut ...
> A man was killed when his mates playfully thrust him into the back
> of a refuse truck: the Vulture beak got him ...
> A woman was raped in a field, then had her throat cut by a gang of
> five. They slit her throat so that she would not be able to tell on them.
> Lavinia, speechless, gushes blood, from mouth and stumps of arms.
> Spot the one invented story, if you can. No prize offered. (1990
> (1989): 207–8)

It is in the third book of Drabble's trilogy, however, that, as Novy
has argued, the Shakespearean tragic frame of reference becomes
clearest (1998: 181–5). *The Gates of Ivory* (1991) contains allusions
to *Macbeth*, *Antony and Cleopatra*, *Hamlet*, and *Coriolanus*. This is
yet another novel obsessed by time, but in this instance by the
'Good Time' and 'Bad Time' represented by different political
moments in Southeast Asian history. Cambodia in the 1970s, under
the tyrannous regime of Pol Pot and the Khmer Rouge, is the
definitive 'Bad Time'. It is into this time-frame that Stephen Cox
– friend of Liz Headland, one of the main protagonists of
Drabble's triad of novels – crosses when he travels to Cambodia.
The novel opens with Liz's receipt from Cambodia of a package of
items that belonged to Stephen, who is now presumed dead. It
closes, after a series of flashbacks and acts of recall, with his funeral. Stephen's notebook, contained within the package, is studded with Shakespearean references, as if it was in those texts that
he found a possible analogue to the horrors of the killing fields:

> Liz Headland ran her eye down all this stuff and much more. She
> recognised Pol Pot and Sihanouk, the principal protagonists of the
> Cambodian tragedy, and correctly surmised that the Khieu sisters were
> the two Paris-educated Khmer women who had so intrigued Stephen.
> Had he not told her that one of them had studied English Literature?
> Was that his excuse for all his Shakespearian references? (Drabble, 1992
> (1991): 20)

In the London time of the novel, Drabble's more familiar middle-
class social ground, Liz's stepson, Aaron Headland, is staging a
production of *Coriolanus*, retitled *The Beast with Many Heads* (thus

continuing the decapitation trope identified in *A Natural Curiosity*). In Cambodia, Stephen reads *Macbeth*. It is as if Shakespeare enables a link between London and this nightmare of genocide in a world elsewhere. Aaron's production is 'all about crowds and power' (147):

> It is a rendering which mirrors forth the dark gullible complicity of man, his conniving murderous stupidity, his mass cowardice, his mass obedience. *This* is how people are governed and engineered to kill and to die – not by reason, not by self-interest, not even by threats, but by a craving for the safety of the horde. (180)

Cambodia, like Rwanda, has provided a case study for the psychology of mass killings. The piled-up skulls that remain for many an emblem of the massacres of the middle class (that linking social group across the novel's geography) become here resonant of Hamlet in the graveyard: 'Piles of skulls, emaciated living corpses, images of our time. Dirk Bogarde, the movie-actor-turned-novelist, was there at the liberation of Belsen. It did him no good. Alas, poor Yorick. It is hot' (164). In Cambodia, Stephen is given a poem by a Vietnamese writer, Ché Lan Viên, entitled 'Hamlet in Vietnam' and is told 'it is also about Cambodia' (215–16). Shakespeare's ability to reach across time, but also across language and geographical boundary, is physically enacted in this novel.[2] But the claim is not to some bland universality but – as I have argued throughout this book – for the relevance of the rewriting of Shakespeare in specific contexts and specific times. Shakespeare is also about Cambodia, Jamaica, St Kitts Warner, and sw10.[3]

Olivia Manning represents the multivalency of the Shakespearean text in another wartime situation in her 1960s *Balkan Trilogy* (1990). In the first volume, *The Great Fortune*, Guy Pringle, an English academic working for the British Council in Bucharest, stages an amateur production of *Troilus and Cressida*. There is the usual in-joke for the reader of recognising how apt parts prove for their players – such as the Marxist Dubedat cast as Thersites, or the louche Yakimov as Pandarus – but the play's theme of warfare and disintegration, already seen manipulated in the Introduction to this book by the dexterous hands of Virginia Woolf, becomes here an analogue to the Second World War as its events and implications cross Europe. Paris falls, quite literally, to Nazi occupation as the players enact the fall of Troy as depicted by Shakespeare.[4]

Elsewhere, the sonnets provide a version of Shakespearean cultural crossings in novels by Australian writer Kate Grenville and South African author Nadine Gordimer. In Grenville's *Lillian's Story* (1986), Lillian Singer lives on the streets, trading her knowledge of Shakespeare. For a shilling, she recites the sonnets, travelling around by taxi on the proceeds. In Gordimer's *My Son's Story* (1991), the occasional narrator, Will, is named for his father's obsession with the Bard: 'He was named for Shakespeare, whose works, in a cheap complete edition bound in fake leather, stood in the glass-fronted bookcase in the small sitting-room and were no mere ornamental pretensions to culture. Sonny read and re-read them with devotion' (Gordimer, 1991: 5). Sonny (the father), a township schoolteacher, is a figure of middle-class aspirations – a fact with which his son wrestles throughout, not least when his father becomes a political activist and takes a white mistress ('What a family he made of us. Poor Tom's a-cold' (1991: 62)). Yet, for all his surface rejection of his father's values, it is Shakespeare (and the canonical text of *Hamlet*) to which Will has recourse at the novel's close, even when he is defining what his own writing does *not* represent: 'I have that within that passeth show … It's not Shakespeare; well, anyway' (1991: 276). There is an echo of Gloria Naylor's Stanley from *Bailey's Cafe* in Gordimer's Will, struggling here with the patriarchal inheritance as symbolised both by the talismanic copy of Shakespeare's *Complete Works* and by his father. Thomas Cartelli has usefully described Gordimer's Shakespeare as 'decolonised or decommissioned … freed from his service to imperial interest' (1999: 167). He asserts that 'what Gordimer is doing throughout *My Son's Story* is at once putting Shakespeare in his place and opening up a space for Shakespeare to inhabit' (1999: 177).[5] Cartelli identifies a comparable decentring of Shakespeare in Michelle Cliff's experimental Jamaican novel *No Telephone to Heaven* (first published in 1987) (Cartelli, 1999: 105–19). In that text, Clare Savage, abandoned in New York by her mother, along with her father, can be seen as another postcolonial interpretation of *The Tempest*'s Miranda. Yet elsewhere it is to Caliban (and to Jean Rhys's figure of postcolonial appropriation, Bertha Rochester; *Jane Eyre*'s madwoman in the attic rewritten as central character of *Wide Sargasso Sea*) that she looks for a cultural reference point:

Comforted for a time, she came to. Then, with a sharpness, repri-
manded herself. No, she told herself. No, she could not be Jane. Small
and pale, English. No, she paused. No, my girl, try Bertha. Wild-maned
Bertha. Clare thought of her father. Forever after her to train her hair
... Yes, Bertha was closer the mark. Captive. Ragoût. Mixture. Confused. Jamaican. Caliban. Carib. Cannibal. Cimarron. All Bertha. All
Clare. (Cliff, 1996: 116)

This doubleness of treatment – rejecting yet reconfirming the
'English', male analogue – does seem to characterise both postcolonial and feminist engagements with Shakespeare.

But the Shakespeare starting to take shape in this Conclusion is
a more dispersed figure, a more diffuse cultural and literary inheritance than appears in those texts we considered in previous
chapters. In the process of identifying patterns and tying down
kinships among the authors and texts studied, I am aware that I
have cast a pebble into a vast body of water. The ripples stretch as
far as the eye can see; the pebble casts up endless 'limber sentences', 'mere sparks and clandestine glories'. This Conclusion
must, as a result, serve as a beginning rather than a summation.
The cultural phenomenon of 'Shakespeare' shows no signs of
waning and, as I write, new appropriations, new re-visions of
Shakespeare by women writers, are no doubt emerging. What you
are reading here, then, is – to paraphrase Barbara Trapido – a
moment of balance and 'precarious symmetry'. Elsewhere, in other
times and places, the story continues and the show goes on.

Notes

1 The novel's colonial sections also explain the epigraph from *The Tempest*.
2 See Gillies and Vaughan (1999).
3 In Drabble's recent novel, *The Witch of Exmoor* (1996), *Timon of Athens* provides a central image of the ungratefully received feast.
4 This was beautifully rendered in the BBC TV adaptation, starring Kenneth Branagh and Emma Thompson, via skilful editing which intercut real movie footage of the invasion of Paris with the perform-ance of the play. See also Healy (1994).
5 See also Novy (1998: 172–8); Newman (1995).

Bibliography

All quotations from Shakespeare are taken from S. Greenblatt (gen. ed.) (1997) *The Norton Shakespeare*, London and New York, Norton.

Abernathy, M. G., D. M. Hill and P. Williams (eds) (1984) *The Carter Years: The president and policy making*, London, Pinter.

Adelman, J. (1994) *Suffocating Mothers: Fantasies of maternal origin in Shakespeare's plays, 'Hamlet' to 'The Tempest'*, London, Routledge.

Alexander, M. (1990) *Flights from Realism: Themes and strategies in post-modernist British and American fiction*, London, Arnold.

Allen, G. (2000) *Intertextuality*, London, Routledge.

Allison, D. B. and M. S. Roberts (1998) *Disordered Mother or Disordered Diagnosis: Münchhausen by proxy syndrome*, London, Analytic Press.

Alter, I. (1999) 'King Lear and A Thousand Acres: Gender, genre and the revisionary impulse', in M. Novy (ed.), *Transforming Shakespeare: Contemporary women's re-visions in literature and performance*, London, Macmillan, 145–58.

Amigoni, D. (2000) *The English Novel and Prose Narrative*, Edinburgh, Edinburgh University Press.

Andreas Sr, J. R. (1999) 'Signifyin' on *The Tempest*: Gloria Naylor's *Mama Day*', in C. Desmet and R. Sawyer (eds), *Shakespeare and Appropriation*, London, Routledge, 103–18.

Apfelbaum, R. (1998) '"Welcome to Dreamland": Performance theory, postcolonial discourse and the filming of *A Midsummer Night's Dream* in Angela Carter's *Wise Children*', in J. Bate, J. Levenson and D. Mehl (eds), *Shakespeare in the Twentieth Century: The selected proceedings of the International Shakespeare Association World Congress, Los Angeles 1996*, Newark, University of Delaware Press, 183–93.

Ashley, M. (ed.) (1997) *Shakespearean Whodunnits*, London, Robinson.

Atkinson, K. (1995) *Behind the Scenes at the Museum*, London, Black Swan.

——— (1997) *Human Croquet*, London, Doubleday.

——— (2000) *Emotionally Weird*, London, Doubleday.

Atwood, M. (1990) *Cat's Eye*, London, Virago.
———— (1993a) 'Gertrude talks back', in *Good Bones*, London, Virago.
———— (1993b) 'There was once', in *Good Bones*, London, Virago.
Auden, W. H. (1938) *The Sea and the Mirror*, in *Selected Poems*, London, Faber.
Bachelard, G. (1985 (1942)) *L'eau et les rêves: essais sur l'imagination de la matière*, Paris, José Corti.
Baker, S. (1995) 'Shakespearean authority in the classic detective story', *Shakespeare Quarterly* 46: 424–48.
Bakhtin, M. (1984 (1965)) *Rabelais and His World*, Bloomington, Indiana University Press.
Barber, C. L. (1972 (1959)) *Shakespeare's Festive Comedy: A study of dramatic form and its relation to social order*, Princeton, NJ, Princeton University Press.
Barroll, L. (1991) *Politics, Plague and Shakespeare's Theater*, Ithaca, NY, Cornell University Press.
Barthes, R. (1981) 'Theory of the text', in R. Young (ed.), *Untying the Text: A post-structuralist reader*, Boston, MA, Routledge & Kegan Paul.
Barton, A. (1994) '*As You Like It* and *Twelfth Night*: Shakespeare's sense of an ending (1972)', in *Essays, Mainly Shakespearean*, Cambridge, Cambridge University Press, 91–112.
Bate, J. (1993) *Shakespeare and Ovid*, Oxford, Clarendon Press.
———— (1996) 'The Elizabethans in Italy', in J-P. Maquerlot and M. Willems (eds), *Travel and Drama in the Age of Shakespeare*, Cambridge, Cambridge University Press, 55–74.
———— (1997) *The Genius of Shakespeare*, London, Picador.
Bayley, J.(1981) *Shakespeare and Tragedy*, London, Routledge.
———— (1998) *Iris*, London, Duckworth.
Beard, J. (1998) *Romance of the Rose*, New York, Berkeley Books.
Belsey, C. (1995) 'Love in Venice', in D. Barker and I. Kamps (eds), *Shakespeare and Gender: A history*, London, Verso, 196–213.
Bender, B. (ed.) (1993) *Landscape, Politics and Perspectives*, Oxford, Berg.
Bennett, S. (1996) *Performing Nostalgia: Sifting Shakespeare and the contemporary past*, London, Routledge.
Berg, C. G. (1997) '"Giving sound to the bruised places in their heart": Gloria Naylor and Walt Whitman', in S. Felton and M. C. Loris (eds), *The Critical Response to Gloria Naylor*, London, Greenwood Press, 98–111.
Bevington, D. (1996) '"But we are spirits of another sort": The dark side of love and magic in *A Midsummer Night's Dream*', in R. Dutton (ed.), *A Midsummer Night's Dream*, London, Macmillan, 24–37.
Bond, E. (1972) *Lear*, London, Methuen.
———— (1974) *Bingo: Scenes of Money and Death*, London, Methuen.
Boose, L. (1982) 'The father of the Bride in Shakespeare', *PMLA* 97: 325–47.
———— (1987) 'The family in Shakespeare studies; or, Studies in the family

of Shakespeareans; or, The politics of politics', *Renaissance Quarterly* 40: 707–42.

Botting, F. (1999) *Sex, Machines and Navels: Fiction, fantasy and history in the future present*, Manchester, Manchester University Press.

Bown, N. (1996) '"There are fairies at the bottom of our garden": fairies, fantasy, and photography', *Textual Practice*, 10: 57–82.

Bradbury, M. (1993) *The Modern British Novel*, Harmondsworth, Penguin.

Brahms, C. and S. J. Simon (1999 (1941)) *No Bed for Bacon: The story of Shakespeare and Lady Viola in Love*, London, Black Swan.

Brain, T. (1998) '"Or shall I bring you the sound of poisons?": *Silent Spring* and Sylvia Plath', in R. Kerridge and N. Sammells (eds), *Writing the Environment: Ecocriticism and literature*, London, Zed Books, 146–64.

Brannigan, J. (1998) *New Historicism and Cultural Materialism*, London, Macmillan.

Bristol, M. (1985) *Carnival and Theater: Plebeian culture and the structure of authority in Renaissance England*, London, Methuen.

——— (1996) *Big-time Shakespeare*, London, Routledge.

Brotton, J. (1998) '"This Tunis, sir, was Carthage": Contesting colonialism in *The Tempest*', in A. Loomba and M. Orkin (eds), *Postcolonial Shakespeares*, London, Routledge, 23–42.

Brown, P. (1985) '"This thing of darkness I acknowledge mine": *The Tempest* and the discourse of colonialism', in J. Dollimore and A. Sinfield (eds), *Political Shakespeare: New essays in cultural materialism*, Manchester, Manchester University Press, 48–71.

Brydon, D. (1993) 'Sister letters: Miranda's *Tempest* in Canada', in M. Novy (ed.), *Cross-Cultural Performances: Differences in women's re-visions of Shakespeare*, Urbana and Chicago, University of Illinois Press, 165–84.

Buechner, F. (1998) *The Storm*, London, HarperCollins.

Burden, M. (ed.) (1998) *A Woman Scorned: Responses to the Dido myth*, London, Faber.

Burnett, M. T. (2000) 'Impressions of fantasy: Adrian Noble's *A Midsummer Night's Dream*', in M. T. Burnett and R. Wray (eds), *Shakespeare, Film, Fin-de-siècle*, London, Macmillan, 89–101.

Burt, R. (2000) '*Shakespeare in Love* and the end of the Shakespearean academic and mass culture constructions of literary authorship', in M. T. Burnett and R. Wray (eds), *Shakespeare, Film, Fin-de-siècle*, London, Macmillan, 203–31.

Butler, J. (1990) *Gender Trouble*, New York, Routledge.

Byatt, A. S. (1976) *Iris Murdoch*, London, Longman.

Cakebread, C. (1999) 'Sycorax speaks: Marina Warner's *Indigo* and *The Tempest*', in M. Novy (ed.), *Transforming Shakespeare: Contemporary women's re-visions in literature and performance*, London, Macmillan, 217–35.

Campbell, M. C. (1988) *The Maroons of Jamaica, 1655–1796: A history of resistance, collaboration and betrayal*, Massachusetts, Bergin & Garvey.

Carroll, W. C. (1996) *Fat King, Lean Beggar: Representations of poverty in the age of Shakespeare*, Ithaca, NY, Cornell University Press.

✝ Carson, R. (1991 (1963)) *Silent Spring*, Harmondsworth, Penguin.

Cartelli, T. (1999) *Repositioning Shakespeare: National formations, postcolonial appropriations*, London, Routledge.

Carter, A. (1982 (1977)) *The Passion of New Eve*, London, Virago.

———— (1985 (1984)) *Nights at the Circus*, London, Picador.

———— (1985) *Black Venus*, London, Picador.

———— (1992) *Wise Children*, London, Vintage.

———— (1993) *American Ghosts and Old World Wonders*, London, Vintage.

Chedgzoy, K. (1994) 'The (pregnant) prince and the showgirl: Cultural legitimacy and the reproduction of *Hamlet*', in M. T. Burnett and J. Manning (eds), *New Essays on 'Hamlet'*, New York, AMS Press, 249–69.

———— (1995) *Shakespeare's Queer Children: Sexual politics and contemporary culture*, Manchester, Manchester University Press.

Chevalier, J.-L. (ed.) (1978) *Rencontres avec Iris Murdoch*, Caen, Centre de Recherches de Littérature et Linguistique, l'Université de Caen.

Christian, B. (1990) 'Gloria Naylor's geography: Community, class and patriarchy in *The Women of Brewster Place*', in H. L. Gates Jr (ed.), *Reading Black, Reading Feminist*, New York, Meridian, 348–73.

Christol, H. (1994) 'Reconstructing American history: Land and genealogy in Gloria Naylor's *Mama Day*', in W. Sollors and M. Diedrich (eds), *The Black Columbiad*, Cambridge, Cambridge University Press, 347–56.

Clark, S. (ed.) (1997) *Shakespeare Made Fit: Restoration adaptations of Shakespeare*, London, J. M. Dent.

Cliff, M. (1996 (1987)) *No Telephone to Heaven*, London, Plume/Penguin.

Cobley, P. (2001) *Narrative*, London, Routledge.

Connor, S. (1996) *The English Novel in History, 1950–1995*, London, Routledge.

Cooper, S. (1999) *King of Shadows*, London, Bodley Head.

✝ Cosgrove, D. (1990) 'An elemental division: Water control and engineered landscape', in D. Cosgrove and G. Petts (eds), *Water, Engineering and Landscape: Water control and landscape transformation in the modern period*, London and New York, Belhaven, 1–11.

Currie, M. (ed.) (1995) *Metafiction*, London, Longman.

Danby, J. (1949) *Shakespeare's Doctrine of Nature: A study of 'King Lear'*, London, Faber.

Davies, A. and S. Wells (eds) (1995) *Shakespeare and the Moving Image: The plays on film and television*, Cambridge, Cambridge University Press.

Dentith, S. (1995) *Bakhtinian Thought*, London, Routledge.

Desmet, C. and R. Sawyer (eds) (1999) *Shakespeare and Appropriation*, London, Routledge.

de Sousa, G. (1999) *Shakespeare's Cross-Cultural Encounters*, London, Macmillan.

Dipple, E. (1982) *Iris Murdoch: Work for the spirit*, London, Methuen.

Dobson, A. (1990) *Green Political Thought*, London, Routledge.

—— (ed.) (1991) *The Green Reader*, London, André Deutsch.

Dollimore, J. (1985) 'Transgression and surveillance in *Measure for Measure*', in J. Dollimore and A. Sinfield (eds), *Political Shakespeare*, Manchester, Manchester University Press, 72–87.

Drabble, M. (1988 (1987)) *The Radiant Way*, Harmondsworth, Penguin.

—— (1990 (1989)) *A Natural Curiosity*, Harmondsworth, Penguin.

—— (1992 (1991)) *The Gates of Ivory*, Harmondsworth, Penguin.

—— (1996) *The Witch of Exmoor*, Harmondsworth, Penguin.

Drakakis, J. (1997) 'Afterword', in J. Joughin (ed.), *Shakespeare and National Culture*, Manchester, Manchester University Press, 326–37.

Dumbrell, J. (1995) *The Carter Presidency: A re-evaluation* 2nd edn, Manchester, Manchester University Press.

Duncker, P. (1999) *James Miranda Barry*, London, Serpent's Tail.

Dundee, N. (1996) *Natterjack*, London, Faber.

Eliot, T. S. (1932) *Selected Essays*, London, Faber.

—— (1985) *The Complete Poems and Plays*, London, Faber.

Ellmann, L. (1998 (1988)) *Sweet Desserts*, London, Virago.

Erickson, P. (1991a) *Rewriting Shakespeare, Rewriting Ourselves*, Berkeley, University of California Press.

—— (1991b) 'Sexual politics and the social structure in *As You Like It*', in G. Waller (ed.), *Shakespeare's Comedies*, London, Longman, 156–67.

—— (1993a) 'Review of *Bailey's Cafe* (*Kenyon Review*)', in H. L. Gates Jr and K. A. Appiah (eds), *Gloria Naylor: Critical perspectives, past and present*, New York, Amistad, 32–4.

—— (1993b) 'Shakespeare's Black?: The role of Shakespeare in Naylor's novels', in H. L. Gates Jr and K. A. Appiah (eds), *Gloria Naylor: Critical perspectives, past and present*, New York, Amistad, 231–48.

—— (1996) 'Shakespeare's Naylor, Naylor's Shakespeare: Shakespearean allusion as appropriation in Gloria Naylor's quartet', in T. Mishkin (ed.), *Literary Influence and African-American Women Writers*, New York, Garland, 325–57.

Felton, S. and M. C. Loris (eds) (1997) *The Critical Response to Gloria Naylor*, London, Greenwood Press.

Findlay, A. (1994) *Illegitimate Power: Bastards in Renaissance drama*, Manchester, Manchester University Press.

Finkelstein, R. (1999) 'Disney cites Shakespeare: The limits of appropriation', in C. Desmet and R. Sawyer (eds), *Shakespeare and Appropriation*, London, Routledge, 179–96.

Fischlin, D. and M. Fortier (eds) (2000) *Adaptations of Shakespeare: A critical anthology of plays from the seventeenth century to the present*, London, Routledge.

Foakes, R. A. (1996) 'King Lear: Monarch or senior citizen?', in R. B. Parker and S. P. Zitner (eds), *Elizabethan Theater: Essays in honor of Samuel Schoenbaum*, London, Associated University Presses, 271–89.

Forbes, L. (1998) *Bombay Ice*, London, Phoenix.

—— (2000) *Fish, Blood and Bone*, London, Weidenfeld & Nicolson.

Fowler, V. (1996) *Gloria Naylor: In search of sanctuary*, Boston, MA, Twayne Publishers.

Fowles, J. (1977) *The Magus*, revised version, London, Vintage.

—— (1998 (1963)) *The Collector*, London, Vintage.

Fraser, C. (1993) 'Stealing b(l)ack voices: The myth of the black matriarchy and *The Women of Brewster Place*', in H. L. Gates Jr and K. A. Appiah (eds), *Gloria Naylor: Critical perspectives, past and present*, New York, Amistad, 90–105.

Freud, S. (1971 (1908)) 'Family romances', in J. Strachey (ed.), *The Standard Edition of the Complete Psychological Works of Sigmund Freud*, London, Hogarth Press, vol. 9: 235–41.

Friedman, S. (1989) '"Remembering Shakespeare differently": H. D.'s *By Avon River*', in M. Novy (ed.), *Women's Re-visions of Shakespeare*, Urbana, University of Illinois Press, 143–64.

Frye, N. (1965) *A Natural Perspective: The development of Shakespearean comedy and romance*, New York and London, Columbia University Press.

Gale, P. (1998) *Tree Surgery for Beginners*, London, Flamingo.

Gamble, S. (1997) *Angela Carter: Writing from the front line*, Edinburgh, Edinburgh University Press.

Garber, M. (1993) *Vested Interests: Cross-dressing and cultural anxiety*, Harmondsworth, Penguin.

Gates Jr, H. L. (1988) *The Signifyin' Monkey: A theory of Afro-American literary criticism*, Oxford, Oxford University Press.

—— and K. A. Appiah (eds) (1993) *Gloria Naylor: Critical perspectives, past and present*, New York, Amistad.

Gilbert, H. and J. Tompkins (1996) *Post-colonial Drama: Theory, practice, performance*, London, Routledge.

Gillies, J. and V. M. Vaughan (eds) (1999) *Playing the Globe: Genre and geography in English Renaissance drama*, London, Associated University Presses.

Goldberg, J. (1992) *Sodometries: Renaissance texts/modern sexualities*, Stanford, CA, Stanford University Press.

Gordimer, N. (1991) *My Son's Story*, Harmondsworth, Penguin.

Grady, H. (1991) *The Modernist Shakespeare: Critical texts in a material world*, Oxford, Clarendon.

Greenblatt, S. (1988) 'Martial law in the land of Cockaigne', in *Shakespearean Negotiations*, Oxford, Clarendon, 129–63.

—— (1990) '"Learning to curse": Aspects of linguistic colonialism in the sixteenth century', in *Learning to Curse: Essays in early modern culture*, London, Routledge, 16–39.

———— (1991) *Marvelous Possessions: The wonder of the New World*, Oxford, Clarendon.

———— (gen. ed.) (1997) *The Norton Shakespeare*, London and New York, Norton.

Grenville, K. (1986) *Lillian's Story*, Sydney, Unwin.

Gross, J. (1994) *Shylock: Four hundred years in the life of a legend*, London, Vintage.

Hackett, H. (1997) *William Shakespeare's 'A Midsummer Night's Dream'*, Plymouth, Northcote House.

———— (1999) '"Gracious be the issue": Maternity and narrative in Shakespeare's late plays', in J. Richards and J. Knowles (eds), *Shakespeare's Late Plays: New readings*, Edinburgh, Edinburgh University Press, 25–39.

Hanson, C. (1997) '"The red dawn breaking over Clapham": Carter and the limits of artifice', in J. Bristow and T. L. Broughton (eds), *The Infernal Desires of Angela Carter: Fiction, femininity, feminism*, London, Longman, 59–72.

Harley, J. B. (1988) 'Maps, knowledge and power', in D. Cosgrove and S. Daniels (eds), *The Iconography of Landscape: Essays on the symbolic representation of design and use of past environments*, Cambridge, Cambridge University Press, 277–312.

Hayes, E. T. (1997) 'Gloria Naylor's *Mama Day* as magic realism', in S. Felton and M. C. Loris (eds) (1997) *The Critical Response to Gloria Naylor*, London, Greenwood Press, 177–86.

Healy, T. (1994) 'Remembering with advantages: Nation and ideology in *Henry V*', in M. Hattaway (ed.), *Shakespeare in the New Europe*, Sheffield, Sheffield Academic Press, 174–93.

Hodgdon, B. (1996) 'Gaining a father: The role of Egeus in the quarto and folio', in R. Dutton (ed.), *A Midsummer Night's Dream*, London, Macmillan, 161–71.

Hokutani, Y. and R. Butler (eds) (1995) *The City in African-American Literature*, London, Associated University Presses.

Holderness, G. (1988) *The Shakespeare Myth*, Manchester, Manchester University Press.

———— and A. Murphy (1997) 'Shakespeare's England: Britain's Shakespeare', in J. Joughin (ed.), *Shakespeare and National Culture*, Manchester, Manchester University Press, 19–41.

Holland, P. (ed.) (1995) *A Midsummer Night's Dream*, Oxford, Oxford University Press.

———— (1997) *English Shakespeares: Shakespeare on the English stage in the 1990s*, Cambridge, Cambridge University Press.

Holloway, K. F. C. (1992) *Moorings and Metaphors: Figures of culture and gender in Black women's literature*, New Brunswick, NJ, Rutgers University Press.

Hoskins, R. (1972) 'Iris Murdoch's midsummer nightmare', *Twentieth-Century Literature* 18: 191–8.

Howard, J. (1988) 'Cross-dressing, the theatre and gender struggle in early modern England', *Shakespeare Quarterly* 39: 118–40.

────── and P. Rackin (1997) *Engendering a Nation: A feminist account of Shakespeare's English histories*, London, Routledge.

Howells, C. A. (1989) 'Free-dom, telling, dignidad: Margaret Lawrence, 'A Gourdful of Glory', Margaret Atwood, *The Handmaid's Tale*, Sarah Murphy, *The Measure of Miranda*', *Commonwealth* 12: 39.

Hughes, T. (1992) *Shakespeare and the Goddess of Complete Being*, London, Faber.

Hulme, P. (1986) *Colonial Encounters: Europe and the native Caribbean, 1492–1797*, London, Routledge.

────── and W. Sherman (eds) (2000) *'The Tempest' and its Travels*, London, Reaktion.

Hutcheon, L. (1988a) *The Canadian Postmodern: A study of contemporary English-Canadian Fiction*, Toronto, Oxford University Press.

────── (1988b) *A Poetics of Postmodernism: History, theory, fiction*, New York, Routledge.

────── (1989) *The Politics of Postmodernism*, London, Routledge.

────── (1995) 'Historiographic metafiction', in M. Currie (ed.), *Metafiction*, London, Longman, 72–91.

Isler, A. (1994) *The Prince of West End Avenue*, London, Vintage.

────── (1997a) *Kraven Images*, London, Vintage.

────── (1997b) *Op. Non Cit.*, London, Jonathan Cape (retitled *The Bacon Fancier* in paperback edition (London, Vintage, 1998)).

────── (2001) *Clerical Errors*, London, Scribner.

James, C. L. R. (1963) *Beyond a Boundary*, London, Stanley Paul.

Johnson, D. (1996) *Shakespeare in South Africa*, Oxford, Oxford University Press.

Jones, E. (1971) *Scenic Form in Shakespeare*, Oxford, Oxford University Press.

Jong, E. (1997 (1987)) *Serenissima*, London, Bloomsbury.

Joseph, A. (1998) *A Dark and Sinful Death*, London, Headline.

Joughin, J. J. (ed.) (1997) *Shakespeare and National Culture*, Manchester, Manchester University Press.

Jouve, N. W. (1994) 'Mother is a figure of speech', in L. Sage (ed.), *Flesh and the Mirror: Essays on the art of Angela Carter*, London, Virago, 136–70.

Kahn, C. (1986) 'The absent mother in *King Lear*', in M. W. Ferguson, M. Quilligan and N. J. Vickers (eds), *Rewriting the Renaissance: The discourses of sexual difference in early modern Europe*, Chicago, University of Chicago Press, 33–49.

Kerrigan, J. (ed.) (1995) *The Sonnets*, Harmondsworth, Penguin.

Kociancich, V. (1990) *The Last Days of William Shakespeare: A novel*, trans. Margaret Jull Costa, London, William Heinemann.

Kutzbach, G. (1987) 'Concepts of monsoon physics in historical perspective: The Indian monsoon (seventeenth to early twentieth century)', in

J. S. Fein and P. L. Stephens (eds), *Monsoons*, New York, John Wiley and Sons, 159–209.

Lamming, G. (1984 (1960)) *The Pleasures of Exile*, London, Allison & Busby.

Lanier, D. (1996) 'Drowning the book: *Prospero's Books* and the textual Shakespeare', in J. C. Bulman (ed.), *Shakespeare, Theory and Performance*, London, Routledge, 187–209.

Levin, A. V. and M. S. Sheridan (1995) *Münchhausen Syndrome by Proxy: Issues in diagnosis and treatment*, Lexington, University of Kentucky Press.

Lodge, D. (1992) *The Art of Fiction*, Harmondsworth, Penguin.

Loveday, S. (1985) *The Romances of John Fowles*, London, Macmillan.

Lynch, M. F. (1995) 'The wall and the mirror in the promised land: The city in the novels of Gloria Naylor', in Y. Hokutani and R. Butler (eds), *The City in African-American Literature*, London, Associated University Presses, 181–95.

McGuire, P. (1996) 'Hippolyta's silence and the poet's pen', in R. Dutton (ed.), *A Midsummer Night's Dream*, London, Macmillan, 139–60.

McHale, B. (1990) *Postmodernist Fiction*, London, Routledge.

McLuskie, K. (1985) 'The patriarchal bard: Feminist criticism and Shakespeare: *King Lear* and *Measure for Measure*', in J. Dollimore and A. Sinfield (eds), *Political Shakespeare*, Manchester, Manchester University Press, 88–108.

Manning, O. (1990) *The Balkan Trilogy*, Harmondsworth, Penguin.

Marrapodi, M. *et al.* (eds) (1993) *Shakespeare's Italy: Functions of Italian locations in Renaissance drama*, Manchester, Manchester University Press.

Marsden, J. I. (ed.) (1991) *The Appropriation of Shakespeare: Post-Renaissance reconstructions of the works and the myth*, Hemel Hempstead, Harvester.

Mathieson, B. (1999) 'The polluted quarry: Nature and body in *A Thousand Acres*', in M. Novy (ed.), *Transforming Shakespeare: Contemporary women's re-visions in literature and performance*, London, Macmillan, 127–44.

Matus, J. L. (1993) 'Dream, deferral and closure in *The Women of Brewster Place*', in H. L. Gates Jr and K. A. Appiah (eds), *Gloria Naylor: Critical perspectives, past and present*, New York, Amistad, 126–39.

Meisenhelder, S. (1997) '"The whole picture" in Gloria Naylor's *Mama Day*', in S. Felton and M. C. Loris (eds), *The Critical Response to Gloria Naylor*, London, Greenwood Press, 113–38.

Merchant, C. (1983) *The Death of Nature: Women, ecology, and the scientific revolution*, New York, Harper & Row.

Mignolo, W. (1995) *The Darker Side of the Renaissance: Literacy, territoriality, and colonization*, Ann Arbor, University of Michigan Press.

Miller, J. H. (1995) *Topographies*, Stanford, CA, Stanford University Press.

Miner, V. (1994) *A Walking Fire*, Albany, SUNY Press.

Montrose, L. A. (1986) '*A Midsummer Night's Dream* and the shaping fantasies of Elizabethan culture: Gender, power, form', in M. W. Ferguson, M. Quilligan and N. J. Vickers (eds), *Rewriting the Renaissance: The discourses of sexual difference in early modern Europe*, Chicago, University of Chicago Press, 65–87.

Morris, C. D. (1997) 'The direction of *North By Northwest*', *Cinema Journal*, 36: 43–56.

Morrison, T. (1997 (1981)) *Tar Baby*, London, Vintage.

Mortimer, J. (1977) *Will Shakespeare*, London, Hodder & Stoughton.

Mullaney, S. (1988) *The Place of the Stage: License, play and power in Renaissance England*, Chicago, University of Chicago Press.

Mulvey, L. (1994) 'Cinema Magic and the Old Monsters: Angela Carter's Cinema' in L. Sage (ed.), *Flesh and the Mirror: Essays on the art of Angela Carter*, London, Virago.

Murdoch, I. (1954) *Under the Net*, London, Chatto & Windus.

———— (1969 (1968)) *The Nice and the Good*, Harmondsworth, Penguin.

———— (1970) *A Fairly Honourable Defeat*, Harmondsworth, Penguin.

———— (1973) *The Black Prince*, Harmondsworth, Penguin.

———— (1978) *The Sea, The Sea*, Harmondsworth, Penguin.

———— (1985 (1958)) *The Bell*, Harmondsworth, Penguin.

———— (2001 (1969)) *Bruno's Dream*, London, Chatto & Windus.

Murphy, S. (1987) *The Measure of Miranda*, Edmonton, Newest.

Nakadate, N. (1999) *Understanding Jane Smiley*, Columbia, SC, University of South Carolina Press.

Nanda, S. (1990) *Neither Man nor Woman: The Hijras of India*, Belmont, Wadsworth.

Naylor, G. (1983) *The Women of Brewster Place*, New York, Penguin.

———— (1986) *Linden Hills*, New York, Penguin.

———— (1992) *Bailey's Cafe*, New York, Vintage.

———— (1993 (1988)) *Mama Day*, New York, Vintage.

———— (1998) *The Men of Brewster Place*, New York, Hyperion.

Neely, C. T. (1999) '*The Winter's Tale*: Women and issue', in K. Ryan (ed.), *Shakespeare: The last plays*, London, Longman, 169–80.

Nesbit, E. (1947 (1908)) *The House of Arden*, London, Ernest Benn.

Newman, J. (1995) *The Ballistic Bard: Post-colonial fictions*, London, Arnold.

Nixon, R. (1987) 'Caribbean and African appropriations of *The Tempest*', *Critical Inquiry*, 13: 557–78.

Norbrook, D. (1992) '"What cares these roarers for the name of king?": Language and utopia in *The Tempest*', in G. McMullan and J. Hope (eds), *The Politics of Tragicomedy*, London, Routledge, 21–54.

Novy, M. (ed.) (1990) *Women's Re-Visions of Shakespeare: On responses of Dickinson, Woolf, Rich, H. D., George Eliot and others*, Urbana and Chicago, University of Illinois Press.

———— (ed) (1993) *Cross-Cultural Performances: Differences in women's re-visions of Shakespeare*, Urbana and Chicago, University of Illinois Press.

———— (1998) *Engaging with Shakespeare: Responses of George Eliot and other women novelists*, Iowa City, Iowa University Press.

———— (ed.) (1999)*Transforming Shakespeare: Contemporary women's re-visions in literature and performance*, London, Macmillan.

Nye, R. (1976) *Falstaff*, Harmondsworth, Penguin.

———— (1993) *Mrs Shakespeare*, London, Sceptre.

———— (2000) *The Late Mr Shakespeare*, Harmondsworth, Penguin.

O'Day, M. (1994) '"Mutability is having a field day": The sixties aura of Angela Carter's Bristol Trilogy', in L. Sage (ed.), *Flesh and the Mirror: Essays on the art of Angela Carter*, London, Virago, 24–59.

Olwig, K. R. (1993) 'Sexual cosmology: Nation and landscape at the conceptual interstices of nature and culture; or, what does landscape really mean?', in B. Bender (ed.), *Landscape, Politics and Perspective*, Oxford, Berg, 307–43.

Orgel, S. (1986) 'Prospero's wife', in M. W. Ferguson, M. Quilligan and N. J. Vickers (eds), *Rewriting the Renaissance: The discourses of sexual difference in early modern Europe*, Chicago, University of Chicago Press, 50–64.

———— (ed.) (1994) *William Shakespeare's 'The Tempest'*, Oxford, Oxford University Press.

Osborne, L. E. (1999) 'Romancing the bard', in C. Desmet and R. Sawyer (eds), *Shakespeare and Appropriation*, London, Routledge, 47–64.

Ovid (1986) *Metamorphoses*, trans. A. D. Melville, Oxford, Oxford University Press.

Peach, L. (1998) *Angela Carter*, London, Macmillan.

Phillips, C. (1997) *The Nature of Blood*, London, Faber.

Plumwood, V. (1993) *Feminism and the Mastery of Nature*, London, Routledge.

Pownall, D. (2000) *The Catalogue of Men*, London, Picador.

Price, R. (1975) *Saramaka Social Structure: Analysis of a Maroon society*, Rio Peidras, University of Puerto Rico.

Purkiss, D. (1996) 'The witch on the margins of "race": Sycorax and others', in *The Witch in History: Early modern and twentieth-century representations*, London: Routledge, 250–75.

Raitt, S. (1999) '"Out of Shakespeare?": Cordelia in *Cat's Eye*', in M. Novy (ed.), *Transforming Shakespeare: Contemporary women's re-visions in literature and performance*, London, Macmillan, 181–97.

Rankin, I. (1998) *A Good Hanging and Other Stories*, London, Orion.

Ray, J. (2000) *Julie and Romeo*, London, Harmony.

Retamar, R. F. (1989) *Caliban and Other Essays*, Minneapolis, University of Minnesota Press.

Rich, A. (1979) 'When We Dead Awaken: Writing as re-vision', in *On Lies, Secrets, and Silence*, New York, Norton.

Rifkind, D. (1993) 'Review of *Bailey's Cafe (The Washington Post)*', in H. L. Gates Jr and K. A. Appiah (eds), *Gloria Naylor: Critical perspectives, past and present*, New York, Amistad, 28–30.

Romberg, B. (1962) *Studies in the Narrative Technique of the First-Person Novel*, Stockholm, Almquist & Wiksell.

Rose, E. C. (1993) 'The good mother: From Gaia to Gilead', in C. J. Adams (ed.), *Ecofeminism and the Sacred*, New York, Continuum, 149–67.

Ross, C. L. (1999) 'The plague of *The Alchemist*', in R. Dutton (ed.), *Ben Jonson*, London, Longman, 149–66.

Roy, A. (1998) *The God of Small Things*, London, Flamingo.

Rowe, M. (1991) 'Shadow on blue', in *Sacred Space*, London, Serpent's Tail.

Rushdie, S. (1995) *The Moor's Last Sigh*, London, Vintage.

Sage, L. (1992) *Women in the House of Fiction: Post-war women novelists*, London, Macmillan.

———— (1994a) *Angela Carter*, Plymouth, Northcote House.

———— (ed.) (1994b) *Flesh and the Mirror: Essays on the art of Angela Carter*, London, Virago.

———— (ed.) (1999) *The Cambridge Guide to Women's Writing in English*, Cambridge, Cambridge University Press.

Sanders, J. (1999) 'Midwifery and the "New Science" in the seventeenth century: Language, print and theatre', in E. Fudge, R. Gilbert and S. Wiseman (eds), *At the Borders of the Human*, London, Macmillan, 74–90.

Sharpe, T. (1991) *T. S. Eliot: A literary life*, London, Macmillan.

Sherman, W. (1995) *John Dee: The politics of reading and writing in the English Renaissance*, Amherst, University of Massachusetts Press.

Showalter, E. (1991) 'Miranda's story', in *Sister's Choice: Tradition and change in American women's writing*, Oxford, Oxford University Press, 22–41.

———— (1992) 'Representing Ophelia: women, madness and the responsibilities of feminist criticism', in J. Drakakis (ed.), *Shakespearean Tragedy*, London, Longman, 280–95.

Sidney, Sir P. (1960) *A Defence of Poetry*, ed. J. A. Van Dorsten, Oxford, Oxford University Press.

Singh, K. (1987) 'The Indian monsoon in literature', in J. S. Fein and P. L. Stephens (eds), *Monsoons*, New York, John Wiley and Sons, 35–49.

Smiley, J. (1992) *A Thousand Acres*, London, Flamingo.

———— (1998) 'Interview', *The Mail on Sunday*, 1 March, 69–71.

———— (1999) 'Shakespeare in Iceland', in M. Novy (ed.), *Transforming Shakespeare: Contemporary women's re-visions in literature and performance*, London, Macmillan, 159–79.

Smith, B. (1991) *Homosexual Desire in Shakespeare's England: A cultural poetics*, Chicago, University of Chicago Press.

Smith, E. (2000) '"Either for tragedy or for comedy": Attitudes to *Hamlet* in Kenneth Branagh's *In the Bleak Midwinter* and *Hamlet*', in M. T. Burnett and R. Wray (eds), *Shakespeare, Film, Fin-de-siècle*, London, Macmillan, 137–46.

Smith, M. N. (2000) 'H. D.'s *The Tempest*', in P. Hulme and W. Sherman (eds), *'The Tempest' and its Travels*, London: Reaktion, 250–6.

Spear, H. (1995) *Iris Murdoch*, London, Macmillan.

Storhoff, G. (1997) '"The only voice is your own": Gloria Naylor's revision of *The Tempest*', in S. Felton and M. C. Loris (eds), *The Critical Response to Gloria Naylor*, London, Greenwood Press, 166–77.

Strong, R. (1984) *The Renaissance Garden in England*, London, Thames & Hudson.

Sullivan Jr, G. A. (1998) *The Drama of Landscape: Land, property, and social relations on the early modern stage*, Stanford, CA, Stanford University Press.

Taylor, G. (1990) *Reinventing Shakespeare: A cultural history from the Restoration to the present*, London, Hogarth.

Tennenhouse, L. (1986) *Power on Display: The politics of Shakespeare's genres*, New York, Methuen.

Thompson, A. (1995) '"Miranda, where's your sister?": Reading Shakespeare's *The Tempest*', in D. Barker and I. Kamps (eds), *Shakespeare and Gender: A history*, London, Verso, 168–77.

—— and N. Taylor (1996) *William Shakespeare's 'Hamlet'*, Plymouth, Northcote House.

Thompson, K. W. (ed.) (1990) *The Carter Presidency: Fourteen intimate perspectives of Jimmy Carter*, Lanham, NY, University Press of America.

Tindall, G. (1982) *City of Gold: The biography of Bombay*, London, Temple Smith.

Tobin, P. D. (1978) *Time and the Novel: The genealogical imperative*, Princeton, NJ, Princeton University Press.

Todd, J. (1998) 'A dysfunctional portrait', *The Mail on Sunday*, 1 March, 71.

Todd, R. (1979) *Iris Murdoch: The Shakespearian interest*, London, Vision.

Trapido, B. (1982) *Brother of the More Famous Jack*, London, Black Swan.

—— (1984) *Noah's Ark*, London, Black Swan.

—— (1990) *Temples of Delight*, Harmondsworth, Penguin.

—— (1995 (1994)) *Juggling*, Harmondsworth, Penguin.

—— (1998) *The Travelling Hornplayer*, Harmondsworth, Penguin.

Traub, V. (1992) *Desire and Anxiety: Circulations of sexuality in Shakespearean drama*, London, Routledge.

—— (1993) 'Rainbows of darkness: Deconstructing Shakespeare in the work of Gloria Naylor and Zora Neale Hurston', in M. Novy (ed.), *Cross-Cultural Performances: Differences in women's re-vision of Shakespeare*, Urbana and Chicago, University of Illinois, 150–64.

Tudeau-Clayton, M. (1998) *Jonson, Shakespeare and the Early Modern Virgil*, Cambridge, Cambridge University Press.

Updike, J. (2000) *Gertrude and Claudius*, New York, Knopf.

Valicha, K. (1988) *The Moving Image: A study of Indian cinema*, London, Orient Longman.

Veeser, H. A. (ed.) (1989) *The New Historicism*, London, Routledge.

—— (ed.) (1994) *The New Historicism Reader*, London, Routledge.

Wagner-Martin, L. (1988) 'Quilting in Gloria Naylor's *Mama Day*', *Notes on Contemporary Literature*, 18: 6–7.

Walther, M. L. (1993) 'Toni Morrison's *Tar Baby*: Re-figuring the colonizer's aesthetics', in M. Novy (ed.), *Cross-Cultural Performances: Differences in women's re-visions of Shakespeare*, Urbana and Chicago, University of Illinois Press, 137–49.

Warner, M. (1992) *Indigo; or, Mapping the Waters*, London, Chatto & Windus.

——— (1993) 'Between the colonist and the creole: Family bonds, family boundaries', in S. Crew and A. Rutherford (eds), *Unbecoming Daughters of the Empire*, Sydney, Dangaroo Press, 197–204.

——— (1994) 'Angela Carter: Bottle blonde, double drag', in L. Sage (ed.), *Flesh and the Mirror: Essays on the art of Angela Carter*, London, Virago, 243–56.

——— (1995) *From the Beast to the Blonde*, London, Vintage.

——— (2000) '"The foul witch" and her "freckled whelp": Circean mutations in the New World', in P. Hulme and W. Sherman (eds), *'The Tempest' and its Travels*, London: Reaktion, 97–113.

Webb, K. (1994) 'Seriously funny', in L. Sage (ed.), *Flesh and the Mirror: Essays on the art of Angela Carter*, London, Virago, 279–307.

White, H. (1973) *Metahistory: The historical imagination in nineteenth-century Europe*, Baltimore, MD, Johns Hopkins University Press.

——— (1987) *The Content of the Form: Narrative discourse in historical representation*, Baltimore, MD, Johns Hopkins University Press.

——— (1995) 'The question of narrative in contemporary historical theory', in M. Currie (ed.), *Metafiction*, London, Longman, 104–41.

Whitney, G. (1969 (1586)) *A Choice of Emblemes and Other Devises*, Amsterdam, Da Capo Press.

Wideman, J. E. (1995 (1990)) *Philadelphia Fire*, London, Picador.

Wilcox, H. (1994) 'Gender and genre in Shakespeare's tragicomedies', in A. J. Hoenselaars (ed.), *Reclamations of Shakespeare: DQR Studies in Literature 15*, Amsterdam, Rodopi Press, 129–38.

Williams, G. J. (1997) *Our Moonlight Revels: 'A Midsummer Night's Dream' in the Theatre*, Iowa City, University of Iowa Press.

Wilson, R. (1997) 'Voyage to Tunis: New history and the old world of *The Tempest*', *English Literary History*, 64: 333–57.

Wolfson, S. (1990) 'Explaining to her sisters: Mary Lamb's *Tales from Shakespeare*', in M. Novy (ed.), *Women's Re-visions of Shakespeare: On responses of Dickinson, Woolf, Rich, H. D., George Eliot and others*, Urbana and Chicago, University of Illinois Press, 16–40.

Wood, R. S. (1997) '"Two warring ideals in one dark body": Universalism and nationalism in Gloria Naylor's *Bailey's Café*', in S. Felton and M. C. Loris (eds), *The Critical Response to Gloria Naylor*, London, Greenwood Press, 240–52.

Woolf. V. (1992) *Between the Acts*, ed. G. Beer, Harmondsworth, Penguin.

——— (1993) *A Room of One's Own*, in *A Room of One's Own and Three Guineas*, ed. M. Barrett, Harmondsworth, Penguin.

Index

Note: 'n.' after a page reference indicates the number of a note on that page.